D0893675

PROPERTIES OF WRITING

ROBERT S. DOMBROSKI

PROPERTIES OF WRITING

IDEOLOGICAL DISCOURSE IN
MODERN ITALIAN FICTION

THE JOHNS HOPKINS UNIVERSITY PRESS

BALTIMORE AND LONDON

This book has been brought to publication with the generous
assistance of the Research Foundation of the University of Connecticut.

The Johns Hopkins University Press
2715 North Charles Street
Baltimore, Maryland 21218-4319
The Johns Hopkins Press Ltd., London

Library of Congress Cataloging-in-Publication Data will be
found at the end of this book.
A catalog record of this book is available from the British Library.

ISBN 0-8018-4919-5

CONTENTS

PREFACE

The studies collected in this volume take as their focus significant transitional moments in the development of modern Italian fiction. Each gives priority to the political interpretation of narrative by foregrounding ideological questions that address the historical foundation of literary form. I use the word *ideology* throughout this book descriptively, to refer to specific modes of consciousness and discursive strategies reflective of belief systems. At the same time, I have tried to incorporate into its meaning the sense of lived experience and the unconscious and symbolic dimensions that comprise such experience.[1] My general view is that a relatively neutral focus on the complex relations between literary ideology and social interests is a useful way of defining text and context in historical terms. My arguments rest on the premise that the sociohistorical context provides a kind of structural guarantee for the production of narrative form. Form is made possible by history, that is, by the material conditions of its possibility. To write means, among other things, to confront a norm of writing, inscribed in specific cultural institutions and rhetorical conventions.

As references throughout this book to contemporary Marxist thought attest, I believe not in any direct access to literary ideology but rather in numerous mediations. My discussions presuppose, therefore, much less a critical method than a field of vision. For although they are centered on the literary text, they adjust their focus continually to incorporate the sociohistorical perimeter into the picture, distinguishing between, but never separating, aesthetic production and its historical moment. The fictive realities produced by the texts under examination are considered as purposeful projects, designed to recompose "worlds" by means of writing, thus reclaiming through artifice things once felt to be possessed that history has expropriated. In other words, the literary work (of its very nature a cultural text) is a site on which social conflicts and contradictions are resolved aesthetically. All literary ideology is generated by and ultimately depends on what Frederic Jameson calls "utopian impulses" that reflect nothing less than the desire to achieve in, or by means of, the creation of fictions some measure of unalienated social existence.[2] This is another way of formulating the description of the modernist project Erich Auerbach provides in *Mimesis*.[3]

My emphasis, however, falls much less on the reunification of discontinuous fragments of experience into some cosmic view than on how such a procedure is part of distinct narrative processes designed to manage ideologies for the purpose of connecting historical subjects to some real or imagined social totality. Althusserian Marxism has made a convincing case for viewing ideology in this vein as a necessary human function. Jameson has extended this concept to narrative itself, arguing the ideological, and therefore historical, nature of all narrative paradigms.[4] Despite the diversity of ideological forms contained in the narratives interpreted here, they are united by one common purpose: they all engage in the construction of reality and claim (implicitly) to instruct the reader as to what reality is and how to think about it. The ideological questions they underline are understood best when placed against the background of their historical coming into being as texts set in motion by the human agents, their authors, responsible for their history. It goes without saying that books are meant to be read in light of the real predicaments of particular social groups whose members are, in one way or another, the protagonists of literary texts.

By way of summary, the ideological question dealt with in Alessandro Manzoni's *I promessi sposi* regards a kind of social compromise expressed in the accommodation of religious and secular interests. Such a conciliation can be viewed as a strategy employed to nurture the utopian longings of a social class that was, historically, bourgeois in its aspirations but still prebourgeois in its effective capacity to realize those aspirations. Rather than divert attention from the profoundly moral character of *I promessi sposi*, this discussion suggests that the ideology from which Manzoni's moral sense derives reflects a social unity linked inextricably to the socioeconomic uncertainty affecting a unique historical juncture: a "moment," as Antonio Gramsci puts it, when the old order was dead and the new had yet to be born.[5] The symbolic structuring of social and moral experience in the novel, I argue, derives from such a historically lived system of relations.

In the chapter on Giovanni Verga, the blueprint for defining fictional narrative by appealing to dispassionate neutrality is examined primarily as an allegory for the problematics of writing on the borders of capitalist secularization. Behind the world of *I Malavoglia*, described in all its primitive otherness and symbolic uniqueness, stand the controls that normalize the representational authority of positivist liberalism. Verga's anxiety of identity becomes apparent at the moment these different spaces intersect in the creation of an ethnographic fiction.

The kind of historical reading I propose in my approach to Gabriele D'Annunzio also centers on the invention of a primitive consciousness. Verga regarded primitiveness as an anthropological category whose components had to be juxtaposed to other cultural formations to be fully understood. In D'Annunzio, the primitive is an epistemological model, the illuminating perspective of a secular religion that lives on the mysteries of the sacred and, as such, is the only sensibility capable of defeating the fragmentation and alienation characteristic of the modern, bourgeois world. D'Annunzio's response to the collapse of liberalism and the rise of fascism consisted in the creation of a mythical dimension of life that, because it was an end rather than a means, resisted appropriation by politics.

In the works of Luigi Pirandello, epistemology itself promotes mythical thinking; it provides the agency through which the self is deconstucted to the point of negation, then reconstructed as perpetual life and authentic Being. Pirandello's most fundamental questions are: What does it mean to be a person in a world of degraded values? What happens to the power of individual initiative when we realize that its objectives are illusory? My discussion of *Uno, nessuno e centomila* attempts to decipher the paradox at the base of Pirandello's work: the schizoid fantasy that it is possible to be dead and alive at the same time. The ultimate rationality of Pirandello's desperate questioning, in which conventional logic is undermined, leads to the validation of intuition and paradox as antidote to the logic of capitalist development.

In historical terms, Pirandellian epistemology worked to subvert the logic of the machine era, the factory, and the rationalized city as a means of avenging nature and vitality, the forces modern industrial society sought to tame. The narrative art of Verga and D'Annunzio sprang from acknowledgment of the same objective conditions. Verga's response contested their dreaded material effects by representing the lost unity of social life, while D'Annunzio concentrated his vision on the immutable sensual correspondences and transcendental beauty the chaos of modernity had effaced.

Their contemporary, Italo Svevo, whose work offers the best ideological expression of capitalism, appears to swim with the tide of rationalization and fragmentation, accepting the bourgeois predicament of living a fortuitous existence as a natural consequence of life. *La coscienza di Zeno* is a unique text in this respect, for as it recounts the events of a closed, subjective world, its narrative subjects them to a process of dissolution, questioning the reliability of the events as well as the way they are seen. The task of my reading of Svevo's novel is not, as it is with Verga and D'Annunzio, to reinstate a sociopolitical subtext but rather to show how Svevo blends the rationalistic liberalism of his characters' social milieu with their quotidian actions and motivations, thus presenting a charged personalization of the gray, reified world of the capitalist marketplace.

The kinds of ideological readings described are meant to examine particular textual strategies aimed at defining worlds of cultural representation in which interpretive authority and the network of knowledge about the social reality it produces are solidly in place. The writers' representations thus appear as a privileged locus, indicating worlds to be transformed, as in Manzoni, Verga, and D'Annunzio, or the epistemological faultlines of consciousness, as in Pirandello and Svevo. Taken together, the works of these authors are all founded on the transformational power of the word. They all depend on literature as institution and convention; they all adopt the novel form, either as a means of affirming life in the face of a troubled reality or as a refuge for the fragmented self.

By contrast, the fictions of Carlo Emilio Gadda and the other writers examined in the latter part of this book abandon, albeit in different ways, the quest for certainty in representation and sustain a tolerance for incompleteness and fragmentation. The practical work of interpreting these more contemporary writers poses once again the question of ideological analysis. But now it does so in relation to texts that do not merely illustrate positions supportive or critical of some form of class or group consciousness. Economic liberalism has become a hegemonic force. The last vestiges of the social tensions created in the triumph of capitalist rationality have mostly been put to rest. Reification has been successfully counteracted, either through artificial, mythical totalities, as in Pirandello, or by means of a wholly psychologized world where the bourgeois individual learns to adapt to the prison of disease, as in Svevo. In both solutions, private life, the site of knowledge and power, is cut off from ideology and politics. Svevo's novel, in particular, is literally a medium of repair for a psyche embattled by historical contingency and the demands of scientific reason.

In the works of Gadda and Antonio Pizzuto, psychic fragmentation turns into schizophrenic texts that blot out the past and thus make it impossible for the subject to relate to the present, except in the form of a moment of performance or event. That is to say, the sphere of private life is retained, but not as a realistic context in which individuals try to grasp the reasons for their malaise. Rather, it becomes a scene—in Gadda, of some unfathomable and undecipherable crime, in Pizzuto, of the haunting permanence of a dead ideal. In both cases, the reified subject of the earlier works strikes back by subverting the very concept of itself as a definable object of representation. As a result, the primary object of ideological analysis, the text as the expression of a socially conditioned subjectivity, is displaced to the margin of critical inquiry. One of our tasks is to resituate ideologically what has become now a very elusive object: the subject, viewed from the standpoint not only of its fictional existence as a person but also of its consistency as a narrative structure.

Giuseppe Tomasi di Lampedusa's *Il Gattopardo* contains all the mechanisms characteristic of earlier forms of historical realism. Paradoxically, it also includes a metaliterary dimension that questions the traditional narrative categories and textual determinants that regulate its form. To demonstrate the complexity of the ideological question in Lampedusa—one which has been largely avoided by the author's supporters and trivialized by his detractors—I attempt to articulate the novel's historical text, that is, the failure of the risorgimento in Sicily, as interpreted by Lampedusa's narrative, using Luchino Visconti's film version of that narrative. My purpose is at once to examine Lampedusa's rhetorical strategy from the standpoint of Visconti's Marxist interpretation and to show how two politically very different texts are reciprocally illuminating as pragmatic forms of cultural discourse.

The last chapter of this book concerns the concept and practice of postmodernism as seen from the perspective of a preeminently postmodern text: Italo Calvino's *Le città invisibili*. It is, among other things, an inquiry into the deep-seated politics of Calvino's novel, which address both the need for and the possibility of constructing a new kind of human community on the ruins of epistemological doubt. This community speaks the language of postmodernism; it recognizes and has learned to live with the various "deaths" (of God, ideology, meaning, etc.) and is skeptical of universal codes and absolute truths. At the same time, it believes in the ultimate materiality and historicity of its world, even though it is at a loss to provide its rationale. Calvino urges us to reconstitute the human subject on the basis of variable relations and modes of signification, all couched, in the end, in the experience of need, labor, and production from which all cities, visible and invisible, derive.

I am much indebted to several friends and colleagues, who have read the manuscript of this book in whole or in part and have offered many useful criticisms and thoughtful suggestions. I am grateful also to the University of Connecticut Research Foundation for the generous support it has given this project, to those who have invited me to speak on subjects addressed in this book at conferences and public lectures, and to the editors of the journals and essays in which some of these studies have appeared previously, in a somewhat different form.

PROPERTIES OF WRITING

CHAPTER ONE

Alessandro Manzoni

The Cultural Transformation of Narrative

Alessandro Manzoni's introduction to *I promessi sposi* would not surprise readers of the seventeenth- and eighteenth-century English novel, which almost always began with some form of authorial disavowal—a convention according to which the story to be told, legitimate in its own right, comprised a series of real historical events.[1] In *I promessi sposi,* the author plays the part of a literary editor who has discovered an uplifting story that has to be recomposed, because it is unreadable in its original version. The *manuscript trouvé* was a device used to efface all arbitrary intentions on the author's part and to show how narrative authority derived from the fact that the truth of the text consists in its autonomy. But at the same time, it made clear that the setting of distance between invention and history— thereby the achieving of a more realistic narrative as the product of real events rather than fantasy—undermines the assurance that reality is discovered rather than invented. The convention of disavowal replaces literary artifice by a fictitious process of rewriting; verisimilitude, meaning, and reality come to the foreground to supplant allegory and myth.

Manzoni's parody of the anonymous author's style reveals two important features of the process whereby an allegorical romance becomes a novel. First, the general procedure of recomposition and transformation, requiring as it does the transcription of reality (i.e., the factuality of the original text) into language, underscores the centrality of language as repesentation. Second, the remaking of the narrative entails divesting the factual events of their mythical aura and ascribing to them values of historical and moral truth. Both aspects of this approach provide the novel with an overriding focus on human eperience and ordinary life. Yet instead of calling attention to what can only be described as a social practice, *I promessi sposi* seeks, much like the discovered manuscript, a meaning that transcends the events and experiences it recounts. The result is a story that finds its sense and message as a religious narrative and its form as a historical novel—two aspects of the work that are never quite the same.

Manzoni's novel may be seen as a bridge between the transcendental and the secular, in that it reinscribes history within religious norms and proposes a workable accommodation of secular and religious values. The restrictions Manzoni places on the experience of fictional characters through authorial intervention and commentary suggest the need to suppress and recode what may be potentially subversive in their outlook and behavior. This procedure may be seen to produce an overall ideological effect that cannot be accounted for within the novel's general thematics. What ostensibly occurs in almost all the novel's episodes is something quite different from what, under analysis, these events indicate. The elements of difference and opposition are aesthetically as important as the sense the narrator gives us of fixing and normative condensation. The stories of the Innominato and Gertrude, both of which have decisive and far-reaching consequences for the novel's thematic structure, illustrate this point. The structural principles described in the following readings can be duplicated in different ways and applied to almost all the book's main episodes, the result being the construction of a narative paradigm adaptable to the work as a whole.

In approaching the episode of the Innominato, the reader is initially struck by the emphasis Manzoni places on the historical verification of his character and his deeds, more crucial here than anywhere else in the novel because of the marvelous transformation of the Innominato's identity. Relying on Ripamonti's authority, Manzoni summarizes his hero's extraordinary past, thus preparing us for the momentous occasion of conversion, which will be no less extraordinary or legendary.[2] The narrative is reduced to a bare outline; the action is ritualized, in the mode typical of romance, to strengthen the aura of this unnamed tyrant and the spell created by his exceptional prowess. History tells us that his life was the subject of popular memory and that his name alone summoned an irresistible, almost magical, force. But Manzoni adjusts the vertical perspective adopted by Rivola and Ripamonti by enriching their examplaristic simplicity and moral pattern with a sense of logical and historical continuity.

He begins the episode on a projected note of anxiety and apprehension (Don Rodrigo's decision to enlist the help of a "terrible man" [1110]), immediately defining the contrast between a world of petty, practical acts of lawlessness and oppression and a mythological universe of symbolic acts. Tradition, too, strengthens the hold of this figure on our imagination by withholding his name, referring to him only as a rich and powerful lord of truly noble stock. The technique of the nameless hero lends a romantic air of mystery to his exploits, suggesting a supernatural revelation. The historical concreteness associated with named identity fosters the distinction between selfhood and otherness. Namelessness promotes the illusion of the capacity to go beyond particular conditions of environment and momentarily shed one's historical identity in behalf of some ideal, desire, or aspiration. As a result, Manzoni's Innominato inspires greatness and an urge to ascend to the heights of true nobility, to become independent of society, to seek liberation through the contrasting virtues of physical strength and humility. But however romanticized the historical account of the Unnamed may appear, Manzoni has skillfully removed himself one step from heroic portrayal, by ascribing the information to his sources—note again the importance of disavowal—and embellishing the factual text of his mentors with moral and psychological dimensions.

Ripamonti's account provides the factual evidence and the context for historical analysis, which the narrator then incorporates in delineating the emotional structure of his character. We learn that he had no care for laws of any kind and that, master as he was of the fate of others, his only enjoyment was the pleasure of commanding obedience. But we also learn that the tyranny of his times unsettled him and that he experienced both envy and contempt for the despotic and cruel acts that characterized life in his world. The story goes on to illustrate how the Innominato's misdirected power leads him to a life of exile and criminal compromise and how within his great tyrannical nature existed much fortitude, magnanimity, and justice. Manzoni chooses not to dwell on his specific criminal activity, referring back to Ripamonti's listing of specific instances. His aim is to depict a great but tyrannical feudal lord whose power and fame far exceed the limits of the commonplace tyranny of his times. He is likened to an eagle, who, from the heights of his blood-stained nest, surveys the land over which he rules.

As would be expected of epic characterization, the magnitude of the Innominato's deeds corresponds to his overwhelming physical stature and keenness of mind. Thus, according to the mode of epic romance, Manzoni formulates a vast distance of inequality between the Unnamed and others, radically separating him from the vulgarity of his criminal followers and from the cautious baseness of Don Rodrigo. He stands alone amid the general comedy of ordinary existence. The tragic singularity of this great figure will ultimately testify to the power of God. His perverted ambitions will, in the end, serve God's glory.

From the standpoint of the novel's Christian world, the Innominato carries out an exemplary function. His existence is a representation of human life in a universal perspective. His psychological transformation brings about a new social cohesion between the great and the humble, as expressed in the miraculous interpenetration of magnanimity that results from his conversion. As Bernard Groethuysen writes in his *Origines de l'esprit bourgeoise en France*, "Les grands, une fois qu'ils pèchent, y vont de tout coeur, ils donnent du relief à leurs péchés, ils pèchent bien, si j'ose m'exprimer ainsi. . . . Le grand fait figure dans un monde où Dieu, pour prouver sa toute-puissance, doit trouver des puissants qu'il puisse abattre." [The great, when they sin, sin wholeheartedly; they sin in style, sin well, so to speak. . . . The noble could cut a figure in a world where God, to demonstrate his omnipotence, must find powerful men to cast down.][3] It is in this sense that we can consider the Unnamed's actions as ritualized, for their purpose is to link humankind to God.

The specific formal problem of this episode consists in giving logical continuity to conversion: to show that the passage from evil to good is not a sudden magical leap, prompted by some fateful encounter or by direct supernatural intervention, but rather a slow process of acquisition in which the dialectic between providential necessity and free will is played out dramatically. The Innominato, in fact, acquires his new identity gradually, as the conatus of salvation develops along the track established by lineage, experience, and environment. Thus, Manzoni demonstrates that God is an integral part of history.

To give a realistic tone to the Innominato's conversion, Manzoni weaves a psychological dimension into the character's epic integrity. The Unnamed's singularity consists in his noble blood, wealth, courage, and strength and, by way of contrast with Don Rodrigo, in the absence of such comic characteristics as craft, guile, and deceit. From the very beginning of the story, the reader's attention is directed toward a fundamental discordance between the Innominato's being and his appearance, between the way he exists for himself and in the eyes of others, which, in the wake of his conversion, becomes a comic incongruity. The first trace of inner conflict appears in the mixed feelings of anger and envy he experienced as a boy when confronted with instances of tyranny. His physical description, for example, his deeply furrowed face, also makes us suspect the existence of internal pressures. With unrivaled omniscience, the narrator then recreates the psychological event in its entirety. From the Innominato's troubled mind a new and more complex human totality will emerge. The passage describing the psychological turmoil that leads the Innominato to convert displays what has been aptly called the "marbled" structure of a text that works to integrate dissimilar paradigms, each containing its own "specific and contradictory ideological meaning."[4]

Già da qualche tempo cominciava a provare, se non un rimorso, una cert'uggia delle sue scelleratezze. Quelle tante ch'erano ammontate, se non sulla sua coscienza, almeno nella sua memoria, si risvegliavano ogni volta che ne commettesse una di nuovo, e si presentavano all'animo brutte e troppe: era come il crescere e crescere di un peso già incomodo. Una ripugnanza provata ne' primi delitti, e vinta poi, e scomparsa quasi affatto, tornava ora a farsi sentire. Ma in quei primi tempi, l'immagine di un avvenire lungo, indeterminato, il sentimento d'una vitalità vigorosa, riempivano l'animo d'una fiducia spensierata: ora all'opposto, i pensieri dell'avvenire eran quelli che rendevano più noioso il passato. "Invecchiare! morire! e poi?" e, cosa notabile! l'immagine della morte, che in un periodo vicino, a fronte di un nemico, soleva raddoppiar gli spiriti di quell'animo e infondergli un'ira piena di coraggio, quella stessa immagine, apparendogli nel silenzio della notte, nella sicurezza del suo castello, gli metteva addosso una costernazione repentina. Non era la morte minacciata da un avversario mortale anche lui; non si poteva respingerla con armi migliori, e con un braccio più pronto; veniva sola, nasceva di dentro; era forse ancora lontana, ma faceva un passo ogni momento; e intanto che la mente combatteva dolorosamente per allontanarne il pensiero, quella s'avvicinava. Ne' primi tempi, gli esempi così frequenti, lo spettacolo, per dir così, continuo della violenza, della vendetta, dell'omicidio, ispirandogli un'emulazione feroce, gli avevano anche servito come una specie d'autorità contro la coscienza: ora, gli rinasceva ogni tanto nell'animo l'idea confusa, ma terribile, d'un giudizio individuale, d'una ragione indipendente dall'esempio; ora l'essere uscita dalla turba volgare de'malvagi, l'essere inanzi a tutti, gli dava talvolta il sentimento d'una solitudine tremenda. Quel Dio di cui aveva sentito parlare, ma che, da gran tempo, non si curava di negare né di riconoscere, occupato soltanto a vivere come se non ci fosse, ora, in certi momenti d'abbattimento senza motivo, di terrore senza pericolo, gli pareva sentire gridare dentro di sé: Io sono però.

[For some time now he had been feeling not remorse but a sort of disquiet at the thought of his own past crimes. The numerous offences which had piled up in his memory, if not on his conscience, seemed to come to life again whenever he committed a new one. They came before his mind's eye in too large and too ugly a throng; it was like a steady increase in the weight of an already uncomfortable burden. At the time of his first crimes, he had felt a certain repugnance, which he had later overcome and almost completely banished from his mind, but now the feeling was beginning to come back. In those early days he thought of a long future, a future of indefinite length, and the consciousness of great vigor and vitality, had filled his heart with happy confidence; but now thoughts of the future were the very thing that poisoned his memories of the past. "Old age! Death! And what then?" Strange to say, although in times of immediate danger, in the face of an enemy, the image of death always breathed new spirit into him in the silence of the night, in the safety of his own castle, afflicted him with sudden dismay. For this time it was not death at the hands of a mortal like himself that threatened him; not a death that could be driven off by better weapons or a quicker hand. It was a death that came all alone, from within; it might still be far away, but every moment brought it a stride nearer. Even as the mind painfully thrust the thought of it away, the reality came closer. In earlier times the constant examples, the non-stop spectacle of violence, revenge and murder had filled him with a ferocious competitive spirit and had also served as a sort of counterweight to conscience. But now a confused but terrifying idea revisited his mind every so often—the idea that the individual is responsible for his own judgement, and that rightness cannot be established by examples. The fact that he had outdistanced the ordinary crowd of evil-doers and left them far behind sometimes gave him a horrifying feeling of loneliness. The God of whom he had often heard—he had never troubled for many years either to acknowledge or to deny him, having been concerned only to live as if he did not exist; and yet now he had moments of inexplicable depression, of causeless terror, during which he seemed to hear a voice within his own heart crying: "AND YET I AM!"]⁵

Two psychological processes are at work in exhibiting the verisimilitude of this great character. The first is introspection. Guilt, the awareness of the conflicts between gratification and resentment, doubt and certainty, all contribute to creating a problematic human identity that provides the reader with an open perspective on possibility and creative action. The second psychology to account for, one that overdetermines the unrestricted horizon just described, evokes the Christian meaning of death. Death is stronger than life. Death, Jacques-Bénigne Bousset writes, "finit tout, détruit tout, nous réduit au néant, et, en même temps, nous fait voir que nous ne pouvons sortir de ce néant, et nous relever par conséquent, qu'en nous élevant vers Dieu, qu'en nous portant à Dieu, qu'en nous attachant à Dieu par un immortel amour" [puts an end to all, destroys everything, reduces us to nothingness and at the same time shows us that we cannot escape this nothingness save by reaching toward God, by cleaving to God through a deathless love].⁶ The seed of conversion having already been sown, the Innominato will never lose sight of his eternity; his thoughts of death will never let him forget that he is dying. He is already a Christian, for through introspection he has challenged his own identity: he is in that he belongs to God. The main line of Manzoni's psychological portrayal will now consist in the shaping of defensive measures to fortify the barriers of consciousness and the inner workings of his character's mind.⁷

The course leading to redemption and to the resolution of the story's principal conflict is familiar. There is little need to present an extensive theological decoding of the episode, which to the present has consumed the energies of a significant number of Manzoni's critics. Let it suffice to say that Manzoni's theological system lays emphasis on the relationship between divine Providence and free will: human beings are endowed with a basic moral sense, conditioned by experience, that enables them either to accept or to reject God. Such a position denotes unequivocally Manzoni's rejection of the Jansenist idea of miraculous salvation while indicating Manzoni's preoccupation, in the wake of Jansenism, with the questions of sin, free will, and grace.[8]

It is more useful at this point to link the process of conversion to the narrative structures that shape it. The episode's focus on the psychological transformation of the sinner underlines Manzoni's disposition to avoid a romantic polarization of meaning. Although the antithesis between good and evil obtains at the level of ethical choice, it does not determine the way the reader apprehends the experience contained in the story. The Innominato does not live in two separate worlds presented alternately to the reader, as is typical of romance. The picture Manzoni draws of his hero's conversion stresses assimilation rather than distinction. The romantic dichotomy between nature and art, between mind and passion, is bridged by a continuous flow of doubt and anxiety. Thus, the narrative prompts us to be conscious of unity in conflict. Rather than a reenactment of the age-old struggle between angelic and demonic forces, the author presents a profound and complex analysis.

With the story of the Innominato, the novel achieves dramatic coherence through the fusion of conflict and transformation. The representational completeness of the work is flawed, however, by an imbalance in the dialectic employed in furthering it. Although the principles of divine Providence and free will are equally present and operative throughout the narrative, the simple fact that Manzoni chooses to reveal the hand of Providence in allowing the Unnamed to convert to God suggests that Providence has acted with perfect necessity. In effect, the role of free will in the conversion process is more apparent than real. The scales are tilted in favor of the absolute of God's commands. The human values manifest in the deep process of self-knowledge are not sufficient as ends in themselves and must be validated by transcendental necessity. Hence, in the final analysis, the Innominato story is one of spiritual edification, belonging to a long and complex tradition of penitential literature, despite its realistic structure and its prevailing concern for historical verisimilitude. It is, so to speak, a modern legend of conversion: modern in that it centers on the soul's vacillation rather than on the swift passing from one state of mind to another; modern, furthermore, because it embodies a rational quest for freedom, emphasizing a realistic awareness of the limits of human action, at the very moment it exalts the power of the will.

From the standpoint of narrative structure, the episode is a good example of what Jameson has called the secular decoding of a romance paradigm ("the secularization of romance as a form"). In this sense, Manzoni's novel plays a significant role in forming the consciousness of selective human action and initiative crucial to the development of all bourgeois cultural revolutions, a transformational process that prepares the human psyche for a new way of perceiving reality in the new world of market capitalism.[9] But because of the Austrian control of Lombardy during the Restoration period, Manzoni's world, although largely bourgeois in its economic designs and sociopolitical aspirations, was in effect unable to develop a fully operative bourgeois social ideology.[10] These circumstances may account for the fact that the mechanism of human psychology in the novel, which undercuts the magical givens of angelic and demonic polarization, neither produces nor fosters a new subjectivity of the bourgeois individual. The textual determinant in the Innominato episode does not let the reader forget eternity; the dialectic of conversion will allow us neither to attribute importance to the things of this earth nor to forget death.

In fact, the Innominato story confirms the moral rule of pre-bourgeois Christianity: that the great and the poor must interact harmoniously for the glory of God. And so we witness power becoming humility and meekness the catalyst for human redemption. As ideological discourse, however, the episode's message is one of social and political moderation; it presents an ideology of compromise and accommodation with respect to the forces of tradition and sociopolitical reform. Like all the great, the Unnamed is a legendary character whose actions are symbolic. But everyday reality is not made up of symbolic acts; it is order, ordinary living, and common sense. The great and the humble do not have, strictly speaking, a "profession." They have their own rank, their own dignity, acquired by birth and consecrated by God. Whatever their practical or private deeds might be, nothing changes the part they are destined to play on earth. It is in this sense, as Groethuysen has pointed out, that the great and the poor resemble each other; each exists for the other's salvation (202).

But in *I promessi sposi*, it is exactly such an elective interaction, the Innominato's fateful encounter with Lucia and their reciprocal liberations, that make possible the eventful resolution of the novel's plot in a direction opposed to the prebourgeois Christian outlook just described. It brings about the relocation of the reader from a world of symbolic acts, populated by Fra Cristoforo, Cardinal Federigo, and the Unnamed, to a radically different sphere where people exist in relation to the work they do, where one talks mainly about the ordinary things of ordinary lives. It is in this new sphere of bourgeois living that the works of divine Providence have become apparent. Here, the Church imprints its morality, and the bourgeoisie (Renzo and Lucia, at the novel's conclusion) are made mindful of the limits of their condition. Although these limitations prevent them from understanding the complexity of divine justice and planning, they will serve God, nevertheless, by carrying out their civic and familial duties and responsibilities, thus creating for themselves an honest well-being.

But if we consider the episode from the standpoint of its ideological effects, we can discern what appears to be a contradictory process at work. Namely, the omniscient narrator, by fixing and arresting meaning, overdetermines the text's semantic heterogeneity. In other words, he represses what narrative language renders possible by virtue of its own strategies. The dimension of introspection offers results in freeing the human personality from the bonds of typological closure; it therefore gains in effectiveness by concentrating on verisimilar human emotions and states of mind. The ideological effect is one of highlighting the validity of individual initiative and will power in creating a life different from the one prescribed by fate and circumstance. The narrator, however, responds by formalizing the effect of that ideology, ascribing a course and completeness to it. The imaginary plenitude he endeavors to represent stands in opposition to the text's capacity for open-endedness, that is, the potential subversiveness of spontaneous emotion and dutiful moral action. The recasting of providential design in the guise of history validates the transition from the absolute objective closure of historical romance and the absolute subjective closure of romantic biography to a narrative in which deviance and closure are combined. The story within the novel that best illustrates such a combination is that of Gertrude, which focuses on the problem of self-discovery in a way even more crucial for the novel's form.

Gertrude's story is no doubt a tale of tyranny. Its burden of interest falls on the unfortunate victim of a domineering and unyielding father who through relentless coercion, forces his daughter into cloistered exile. As it has been argued often, Gertrude's story reveals much of the eighteenth century's obsession with forced religious vocations. The tale's charged atmosphere, monastic setting, stock characters, general themes of victimization and imprisonment, and the protagonist's moods of reverie and abandonment all recall Diderot's *La Religieuse*, a work from which Manzoni is said to have gained his inspiration, while the aura of mystery, melancholy, and ambiguity surrounding Gertrude suggests a nearness to certain Gothic modes of narration.[11]

Two basic plots coexist within the framework of the story: an outer one of victimization and suppressed revolt, which leads to vengeance and murder, and an inner one that focuses on the psychology of the protagonist. The outer plot narrates how a father-despot, proud of his lineage and desirous that his oldest son carry on the family name, forces his daughter to take the veil. Here, Manzoni paints a masterful picture of the tyranny practiced against a once innocent and sensitive child, whose future of confinement and alienation was fixed irrevocably from the time of her conception. He unmasks with ruthless disrespect for the institutionalized prerogatives of the family the atrocious mechanism of conspiracy and deceit that produces the signora, the psychological torture of obscure punishments that wear away Gertrude's resistance, forcing her to accept her father's demands. But no matter how much Manzoni's nun's story may suggest, in the wake of Diderot, the need for emancipation from oppressive parental, social, and religious structures, the author's principal interest lies neither in asserting the fundamentally social nature of man nor in exposing the unnatural life of the convent. Despite some oblique references to Gertrude's frustrated need for physical love, which leads to her encounter with Egidio and the crime that follows, Manzoni steers clear of turning his story into a pamphlet against claustration.

Instead, the forcible controls exercised on Gertrude's will, leading her to a life of isolation from society, are the conditions that make possible a drama of greater magnitude, played within the character's mind. Giovanni Getto once remarked that the "È qui" [She's in here] with which the good father introduces Lucia into the nun's parlor has a disquieting effect on the reader: "Esso fa pensare alla presenza, al di là di quell'uscio, di un corpo immobile, di un ammalato o di un cadavere."[12] [It gives us the impression that behind that door there is something present, a motionless body, a sick person, or a corpse.] The signora appears, in fact, standing behind a barred window, "con una mano appoggiata languidamente [alla grata] e le bianchissime dita intrecciate ne'voti" (164) [with one hand languidly resting on the iron and her white fingers entwined between the bars (171).] The image, with its iconic quality alludes to the contradictory but interrelated psychic and emotional impulses that characterize the nun's biography: on the one hand, the dread of immobility and confinement, as exhibited in the restlessness her figure elicits; on the other, a yearning for repose, as suggested by the listless activity of her hand. Her physiognomy manifests an obscure or undefined quality of being, which Manzoni displays by revealing the flaws and incongruities in her appearance:

> Le gote pallidissime scendevano con un contorno delicato e grazioso, ma alterato e reso mancante da una lenta estenuazione. Le labbra quantunque appena tinte d'un roseo sbiadito, pure, spiccavano in quel pallore: i loro moti erano, come quello degli occhi, subitanei, vivi pieni d'espressione e di mistero. La grandezza ben formata della persona scompariva in certe mosse repentine irregolari e troppo risolute per una donna, non che per una monaca. (1021)
> [The descending line of her pallid cheek followed a delicate and graceful curve, but its full beauty had begun to waste away. The color of her lips was the palest pink: and yet they stood out against the pallor of her skin. Their motions, like those of her eyes, were abrupt and lively, full of expression and mystery. Her figure was tall and shapely; but the effect was lost in a certain carelessness of posture, or spoilt by her movements, which were hasty, uneven and much too full of determination for a woman—let alone a nun.] (171)

At this point, it is useful to consider briefly the character of Gertrude's predecessor, Geltrude of *Fermo e Lucia*, for what is truly specific to *I promessi sposi* consists in the measure of difference that separates Manzoni's first writing of the story from its definitive version: the positioning of the character at an equal distance between two extremes. Neither good nor evil in herself, Gertrude develops her character beyond the influence of the corruption of her upbringing.

In both novels, the themes of paternal oppression, guile and subtle coercion are equally present and operative in determining the protagonist's fate. In *Fermo e Lucia*, however, Manzoni writes the nun's story in terms, notably more consistent with the mode of romance, of a radical polarization between the variables of evil and a potential good that ultimately succumbs to malevolent pressures and forces. The first sign that Gertrude was meant originally to be more a legendary than a historical figure is the reference to her as "Signora" (313); in *I Promessi sposi,* she is called simply "signora," indicating common respect for her position as an abbess. The character of Marquis Matteo, Geltrude's father, also determines the kind of moral representation typical of romance. The first of the two villains who will triumph over Geltrude, Matteo combines the negative qualities of pride, greed, and ignorance into a moral essence that influences directly all those around him: "Il Padre dell'infelice . . . era per sua sventura e di altri molti, un ricco signore, avaro, superbo e ignorante."[13] [The Father of the poor girl . . . was, unfortunately, for her misfortune and that of many others, a rich, greedy, prideful, and bad-mannered lord.] The capitalization of "Padre" and the emphasis given to his ethical character lends to his figure a mythical aura of dread that transforms his would-be historical person into a deviant, quasi-supernatural force. No matter how much Manzoni embellishes his account with realistic detail and no matter how many times he refers to the anonymous manuscript for verification, the Geltrude story cannot escape being a moral tale of aberration and victimization. The process of secularization Manzoni seeks to initiate is hampered by the imposition of universal, overarching essences.

By contrast, in *I promessi sposi* a very different narrative paradigm begins to emerge from the presentation of Gertrude's father. No longer "avaro," "superbo," and "ignorante," he is referred to simply as a "gran gentiluomo" from Milan and, although he carries out the same narrative functions as the Marquis Matteo, the emphasis falls not so much on his evil character as on his misguided deeds, conditioned largely by his upbringing and the social reality of his times. This modification in the figure of the father makes Gertrude appear much more a product of historical forces than a victim of evil. A historical perspective is thereby opened to enable us to view Gertrude's actions in terms of the consciousness she displays of her own predicament.

To illustrate further this process of secularization, consider the different ways the narrator comments on the nun's disposition after having taken her vows. In *Fermo e Lucia,* Manzoni writes: Geltrude . . . continuava ad opporre nel suo cuore un ostacolo ai rimedi e alle consolazioni che la religione avrebbe data alla sua sciagurata condizione: e questo ostacolo erano le consolazioni ch'ella andava cercando altrove, e particolarmente nelle cose che potevano lusingare il suo orgoglio (341). [In her heart, Geltrude . . . continued to place an obstacle in the way of the correctives and consolations that religion would have offered her woeful state; this obstacle was the comfort she was seeking elsewhere, particularly in the things that could cajole her pride.]

In *I promessi sposi*, however, Manzoni provides a detour from the ethical juxtaposition of religion (i.e., humility) and pride. Our attention is drawn instead to the recriminations of Gertrude's conscience and to her paradoxical choice of a life of moral suffering:

L'infelice si dibatteva . . . sotto il giogo, e così ne sentiva più forte il peso e le scosse. Un rammarico incessante della libertà perduta, l'abborrimento dello stato presente, un vagar faticoso dietro ai desideri che non sarebbero mai soddisfatti. Tali erano le principali occupazioni dell'animo suo. Rimasticava quell'amaro passato, ricomponeva nella memoria tutte le circostanze per le quali si trovava lì, e disfaceva mille volte inutilmente col pensiero ciò che aveva fatto con l'opera: accusava sé di dappocaggine, altri di tirannia e di perfidia; e si rodeva. Idolatrava insieme e piangeva la sua bellezza, deplorava una gioventù destinata a struggersi in un lento martirio, e indicava, in certi momenti, qualunque donna, in qualunque condizione, con qualunque coscienza, potesse liberamente godersi nel mondo quei doni. (1037)

[But the poor wretch struggled under the yoke, which made her feel its weight and its jolting all the more. The main occupations of her mind were an incessant regret for her lost freedom, a loathing for her present condition, and a painful dwelling on desires destined never to be satisfied. She ruminated over the bitter events of the past, went over all the circumstances which had led her to being where she was. Time and again her thoughts unavailing disavowed the words that her tongue had uttered. She accused herself of cowardice, and the others of tyranny and bad faith; she tortured herself unmercifully. She worshipped her own beauty, and wept over it; she mourned for her own youth, condemned to perish in a slow martyrdom. At times she envied any woman— any woman at all, whatever the conditions of her life or the state of her conscience—who could enjoy the fruits of her youth and beauty freely in the world.] (204)

Manzoni's rewriting of his story in terms of the nun's inner world or psychology is an attempt to offer his readers something more complex than romantic victimization. In the remade episode, the tyranny conditioning

Gertrude's life is only an ultimate frame of reference for her deeds. The substance and content of her actions reveal both the necessity of her history and her ability to change or alter its course. Gertrude is not a victim of fate or chance; rather, in a Vichian sense, she succumbs to the providential economy of her choices.

Critics have taken different stands on Gertrude's responsibility for her actions. Getto sees her as a person constantly besieged and subjected to the deceitful needs of others more resolute than she. Her will, incapable of remaining free, becomes the accomplice of its very own oppressor.[14] Leone De Castris underscores her inability to reject oppression. She is not, in his view, the unknowing victim of an obscure destiny but is, rather, lucidly aware of her own infirmity of purpose.[15] In spite of her conditioning, Gertrude undoubtedly is capable of making a moral or rational decision on her own and is, therefore, to be held accountable for her actions.

Manzoni writes her story in such a way that the emphasis falls less on one or the other of the terms in the dialectical movement of necessity and free will than on the dialectic itself: that is, on the permanent tension between restlessness and calm, between the desire for love and affection and the glory of social distinction. Gertrude's fear of confinement, the repugnance she feels toward the cloistered life, is linked inextricably to her yearning for rest and her voluntary taking of the veil.[16] Manzoni shows how the contradiction inherent in this process involves a vicious circle. The more Gertrude attempts to preserve her identity and independence by nullifying in fantasy the forceful individuality of her father, the more she will continue to do so, until the cloistered world of her daydreaming becomes the real fortress of the convent, where she seeks "un rifugio tranquillo e onorevole" (697) [peaceful and honorable refuge].

At the psychological core of the nun's life is the complex question of relatedness. Gertrude's indecision and, thus, her equivocal identity derive from her inability to experience separateness from her father in a way that would preserve her autonomy. The feudal context of her story, moreover, objectifies her ontological dependence. To reject her father, who embodies the social and moral forces of her history, is as unfeasible as rejecting her very own nature. Her attempt to contain both her father and her own self, to succumb to the other and remain autonomous at the same time, cannot but lead to the contradiction and ambiguity her figure expresses.

Yet however suggestive a psychological reading of Gertrude's story may be and no matter how extensive we may find the range of the author's descriptive options, the certain pieces of Gertrude's experience that are chosen and those that are ignored show that Manzoni's interests lie primarily in describing a dialectic of history in conformity with humankind's common experience. To this purpose, Gertrude's emotional states, like those of the Innominato, illustrate the realistic complexity of a historical process in which the principles of freedom and necessity are equally true and operative. It is, thus, in *I promessi sposi* that narrative and historical truth are brought together.

The ideological paradigm established in the Gertrude tale sanctions the prevailing dialectic between particular aims and universal ends, determining the action of all Manzoni's characters and, therefore, the sense of the novel in its totality. No matter how much Don Abbondio's cowardly refusal, Gertrude's fateful decisions, and other numerous acts of private utility contribute to the realization of Don Rodrigo's objective, they ultimately serve the ends of divine and human justice. In other words, Lucia's dreadful captivity becomes the occasion for redemption, resolution of conflict, and the transformation of what could appear as a human drama of ambition and perversity into a divine comedy of truth. The anonymous text has so ordained and disposed the characters' actions that they all contribute, in one way or another, to preserving Christian society. The deep irony motivating this process stems from the Vichian idea that in history humans do not know what they have willed, for what they have chosen freely has resulted in something different from what they intended.[17]

Like Vico's, Manzoni's theological perspective indicates that the means of Providence and salvation are in themselves connatural to the development of history. The dialectic of necessity and free will, as exemplified in the Gertrude story, determines thoroughly the novel's form, situating it midway between a literature based on the organizing principle of supernatural forces, magic, and the conflict between good and evil and one reflective of wholly secularized societies, marked by a fusion of character, environment, and historical age into an immanent psychological oneness. It is, therefore, important to distinguish Manzoni's understanding of history from that of his characters, who believe that the whole course of their lives is guided by Providence. Their prebourgeois faith in Providence inspires confidence in the eventual fulfillment of a benevolent and just design in which they play a significant role. No matter how much they may seem to be abandoned to the mercy of evil powers, they are ultimately in the hands of God, who ultimately will work out his purpose in their behalf.

Manzoni, however, is concerned with free will in the attainment of the ends of Providence. The distinction is important because, while the characters' view of life stresses the involuntary cooperation of human actions in the fulfillment of God's will, the narrator focuses on the natural human means of decision and on the circumstances by which the historical course unfolds in accordance with divine will. Manzoni's adoption of the Vichian idea of Providence enables him to organize his novel according to the principle of selective human action and thus leave to the historical milieu he has chosen to represent the fateful and miraculous operations of a transcendent God.

In Manzoni's narrative system, as in Vico's, history moves by virtue of God's Providence in ways often difficult to detect and to understand. A counterweight to human selfishness, Providence acts to preserve the divinely institutionalized orders of family and society. Its mode of operation is essentially ironic, for it uses human selfishness to realize its own objectives, working through secondary means that unwittingly carry out the divine plan. The actions of all Manzoni's narrative subjects contain, therefore, an innate potential for counterpoint. Providence's operations, juxtaposed to these actions, constitute a kind of demythicizing and delyricizing parallel text that ensures balance, control, and the stable positioning of the characters within the boundaries of Christian humility.

Manzoni's concept of Providence offers a means for conveying the sense of historicity generated by the social dynamics of capitalism. Yet because of the delay in Lombardy of an effective bourgeois revolution, Providence functions to safeguard society against the logic of secular individualism characteristic of economic liberalism, namely, against the idea that human existence is essentially a social phenomenon, governed by the laws of this world. So, in the last analysis, in spite of the novel's variegated complex of incident and movement, Manzoni's narrative strategy may be reduced to a single, oppositonal tension between private utility and collective good, between a world where personal ambition prevails and one in which individuals carry out their own particular duties as a way of preserving the social order and, therefore, advancing in Christian perfection. It is not by chance that *I promessi sposi* begins as it does, with the refusal of a pastor to fulfill his divinely sanctioned obligations in administering the sacrament of marriage. And it is no less accidental that in Don Abbondio we have the novel's most coherent model of ironic representation, as well as the one most charged with comic incongruity.

But to capture the oppositional tension in its most subtle manifestations we must return to Gertrude, for it is in her story that the novel's ideological substance becomes most explicit. Before doing so, it should be noted that the nun's tale, like the novel's several other "histories," is, as a biographical form of telling, a kind of "dogmatic biography."[18] It is produced in the service of a truth existing beyond the self, and, as such, it is opposed to the more modern forms of self-recognition, dependent on an immanent process of self-naming and discovery.

Of the characters essential to the development of the novel's plot, only Gertrude can be seen as a truly problematic individual. Her position in the novel's prebourgeois world is less definite than that of the other major characters. Her power is limited to her role within the confines of convent life. She, therefore, cannot be considered great in the sense of either the Innominato or Federico Borromeo. Unlike the Innominato before his conversion, she is not a bold and arrogant sinner, and, unlike the Cardinal, her high birth does not provide her with the noble and heroic sentiments demanded by the Catholic faith. Nor, unlike Fra Cristoforo, does her title of nobility lead to a fusion of greatness and humility, symbolic of a Christ-like existence. Being neither completely evil nor completely good, she is unable to act directly on the lives of Renzo and Lucia, the novel's main characters.

In spite of her position as abbess and prioress of the convent, Gertrude lives, internally, in a totally secular world. Her experience presupposes that nothing outside the self, no authority, either religious or paternal, is worthy of reverence or imitation. Forced to assume an identity not her own, her life becomes of necessity one of self-recognition. Although her heart contains the seeds of virtue and although she, by virtue of her noble breeding, is capable of rising above herself, Gertrude lives out an existence of ambiguous longing. She is not at home in the world of symbols and allegories that claustration affords her, nor can she raise her uncertainty and exile to the dignity of a religious symbol.

Yet, Gertrude's problematic isolation does not promote self-sufficiency. Having taken her vows, she does not conform to the ideal world of the convent. Such a permutation would entail converting her irresolution into decisiveness and her pride into humility. Instead, she attempts to attain a state of self-reliance, not by overcoming the dependencies of her past that led to her fateful decision but rather by simply blotting them out of her mind. Her tale, then, is not one of moral edification, along the lines provided by biographies of Fra Cristoforo, the Innominato, or the cardinal; nor does it offer a resolution to the question of identity in terms of self-invention. This latter possibility would certainly contradict the novel's closed form by establishing a narrative principle whereby all the selves in Manzoni's story become potentially open to doubt.

It could be objected that the Innominato is also a notably problematic individual who, before his conversion, lived a life of uncertainty and doubt. It cannot be denied that he, too, was seeking an identity. Manzoni, in fact, makes a point of dramatizing his predicament in the protrayal he gives of his hero's dreadful night, a scene unparalleled in the literature of the times. By concentrating memory, reflection, and introspection upon a specific moral action (the liberation of Lucia) and by describing the smallest details of movement in relation to the collision of the character's old and new selves, Manzoni achieves an intense and moving representation of the experience of willful choice. But, as noted above, Manzoni reveals the hand of Providence in allowing the Unnamed to convert and thus tilts the scales in favor of God's plan. Transcendental necessity prevails, resolving in one sweep the questions of identity and relatedness.

So, too, with Gertrude, we are faced with a necessity that undercuts the depth of psychological richness deriving from the synchronic interaction of states of mind. But because of the absence in her biography of a transcendental norm, Manzoni does not put forth another modern legend of conversion. What we have instead is the wisdom of a moral code, leading the reader to understand her life as an example of the weakness of the will, as opposed to the power of the will exhibited in the figures of the great. Nevertheless, it is precisely Gertrude's inability to discover herself that lends to her character the provisionality required of a problematic individual.

In terms of the narrative, Gertrude is a kind of traveler in time; and if her life offers no solution to the questions of identity and relatedness, it suggests that the narrative form it embodies is linked to the question of self-invention. Thus, it provides an openness unknown to the novel's other major biographies. In Gertrude's tale, the unity of character is not split into the two contrasting modes of narration that obtain with the Innominato: namely, romance, characterized by exemplary and overarching absolutes, and the novel, typified by its emphasis on limitedness and relatedness. With Gertrude, it is the latter mode that is dominant: dominant, yet controlled by authorial intervention. Although this procedure influences the form of the story, it does not prevent the reader from capturing the potential autonomy of the self. In other words, the figure of Gertrude as a problematic individual contradicts the form of writing that ultimately determines that figure.

If it is true that Gertrude's conscious acts define her character, it is also true that their ethic, or normative force, must be made subject to the process whereby her self is corrected according to authorial ideology. The dogmatic form of telling has but one purpose: to achieve the proper balance between the creative subjectivity that her deviation from the Christian norm elicits and the transcendental imperative that, although absent from Gertrude's life, justifies the narrator's intrusion into her story. The interaction of these two mutually independent narratives generates the irony that, in turn, achieves the end of ordering the reader's mind against any form of ethical self-sufficiency not sanctioned by an absolute norm. The point at issue here is that, although Manzoni's authorial viewpoint rejects Gertrude's individual choices and desires, it does not negate the narrative of self-discovery through which her story is conveyed but rather seeks to make it commensurate with the standpoint of final causes and metaphysical necessity. Without the metaphysical assumption contained in the authorial plot, Gertrude's approach to her self would provide the reader with a wholly secular outlook on existence.

From the standpoint of the social reality represented in *I promessi sposi*, Gertrude's problematic subjectivity can be seen as harboring aspirations that cannot be reconciled with Christian teaching. It reflects an idleness contrary to the useful industry that, according to religion, is the sustenance of the soul; as a result, it fails to recognize the divine laws governing the order of things. At the same time, it implies that effective human action can determine one's destiny. Mystical influences have been shut out of

Gertrude's perspective, so they must be restored by the narrator's system of logic, which illustrates that there is no situation, however insignificant, not ordered by God. When, at the story's end, Gertrude has her fatal encounter with Egidio, the reader has already understood the truth of her life.

The biographical form of the story may be seen as a model through which Manzoni conveys his position vis-à-vis the emerging bourgeois values of his time. The pride and vanity that nourish Gertrude's self-deception threaten the stability of the traditional Christian social structure in which the novel is set. But the Christian community that the narrator's intervention seeks to safeguard by revealing the methods of self-deception— this now undeceived community, strengthened by the rhetoric of irony— must absorb or, at least, reconcile with its own beliefs the negative term of the narrative dialectic. It must recognize that authority serves a truth beyond the existence of the self. But at the same time, it must also understand that the Christian perspective does not exist completely apart from the self. In other words, transcendence and immanence are not irreconcilable opposites. The secular process of self-discovery must be accommodated with religion, so that being an honest bourgeois does not exclude being a good Christian. This ideological compromise is extremely important in understanding the realism of *I promessi sposi*. For by reinscribing the workings of a transcendent God in the realm of personal pyschology, Manzoni combines within history individual experience, universal teaching, and fable, thereby blurring the distinction between history and poetry that, in his theoretical works, he sought to maintain.

From the standpoint of politics, the cultural transformation of narrative that generates the ideological compromise just described evolves into a powerful force within the revolutionary process aimed at transforming Italy into a modern capitalist country. Its ideal of accommodation becomes, in fact, a project designed and executed by the more advanced sectors of the Italian bourgeoisie of the time, in whose ranks Manzoni stood as a preeminently organic intellectual. In this sense, Manzoni's novel is a social text that produces a legitimizing strategy for Catholic moderatism. It is a truly hegemonic work, in that it does not impose its ideology on the reader but rather promotes ideological adherence by offering what Jameson calls "substantial incentives" in the form of utopian impulses.[19] It legimitizes a particular form of class consciousness by producing a lived system of meaning and values, which provides the logic underlying the benevolent impulses diffused by the text.[20]

In conclusion, it is important to note that ideological analyses of the kind undertaken above bracket, rather than overlook, the complex process by which Manzoni brought his novel to its final form. As I have stated elsewhere,[21] the making of *I promessi sposi* did not entail simply the transition from an original concept (realized in *Fermo e Lucia* and later deemed unsatisfactory) to the structurally definitive texts of 1827 and 1840. In fact, it called for a much slower operation, carried out over several intermediate drafts, which involved a careful redimensioning of characters and episodes. Recent philological inquiry has illuminated, better that ever before, the ongoing tension between Manzoni and his subject matter: how Manzoni plucked away at his text, refusing and unraveling previous narrative solutions and repressing certain provisional impulses until the story took on the shape dictated by his changing attitude toward his art and his commitment as a social novelist.[22] This difficult and problematic gestation can never be accounted for totally in the finished product.

Properties of Writing

CHAPTER TWO

Giovanni Verga

Science and Allegory in I Malavoglia

Foremost among the many innovations Giovanni Verga brought to the Italian novel was the concept and practice of impersonal narration. The Manzonian model of an enlightened, ironic commentary and authorial omniscience provided a particular means of control, interpretation, and judgment. The objective realities that Verga converts into literature through "dispassionate" and "scrupulous" observation were for Manzoni the dormant materials of literary art,[1] which, to become universally significant, had to be enlivened by moral truth. Verga was certainly no less a moral writer than his distinguished predecessor, but, unlike him, he held the materialist belief that human nature was determined by social existence and that morality was essentially a sociocultural phenomenon integrally connected to the life processes of particular social groups and societies.

The textual ideology separating Manzoni from Verga can also be viewed from the standpoint of the strategies they employ in defense of their literary authority. Manzoni's rediscovered manuscript underlined as fact that his story antedated its textualization, both in its original and rewritten forms. His task as author was only to make the story readable so that its moral truth could be made visibile. In claiming that *I promessi sposi* is at once a product of discovery and mediation, Manzoni performs a paradoxical epistemological maneuver: he exposes the text's reality as artifice and at the same time draws attention to its authenticity and universality. Hence, he removes himself one step from attempting a romantic search for immediate meaning in history. While he denounces the false artifice of rhetoric, he is not ready to eschew the writer's function as spontaneous creator. Rather, he retains the author as a thoughtful arbiter between meaning and its artful realization in fiction. In other words, the author for Manzoni still plays the role of a scribe transmitting a text, whose omniscience is, ironically, all too transparent. The rhetorical formula of disavowal serves to underline the essential naturalness of Manzoni's project of transcription, while setting the stage for the emergence of an individual style.

Verga's materialism prevents him from envisaging writing as a means of connecting text and context in the Manzonian sense, for there is no basis for such a linkage. The wholeness of social existence for Verga is not governed by a transcendental norm; there is no essence, deformed by artifice, demanding expression; no divine authority controlling the checks and balances of history. From Verga's point of view, the context or situation on which literature acts is a social variable that cannot be integrated into or appropriated by the literary text; it can only be juxtaposed to it. In this sense, it is an alien reality, regulated by its own particular logic, which the literary imagination must approach first and foremost as an object of scientific inquiry. In contrast to Manzoni, the literary text for Verga was a controlled fiction of a difference to be interpreted; not a specific identity and unity that, once purged of its impurities, could be transmitted as an uplifting account of human experience. Verga's work thus contains no deep, symbolic level of meaning; rather, like ethnographic narrative, it pays attention mainly to descriptive surface. Its meaning is of a more comparative and abstract nature, allegorical rather than symbolical or representational.[2]

Given the alien context, Verga's major concern was how to express the thoughts and feelings of people of a particular social stratum in a language appropriate to both characters and author, which could be conveyed to a large and diversified reading public without any apparent mediation. His project involved creating a narrative that was not a reconstruction, in the

Manzonian sense, or a documentary-like transcription (incomprehensible to a public unfamiliar with Sicilian dialects) but a replica or, as one critic aptly put it, a "mimicking" of specific mental and behavioral events.[3] His greatest achievement in writing *I Malavoglia* was to create a level of linguistic abstraction that united Sicilian and Italian with other local and literary idioms (mostly Florentine and Milanese). No less original is the complex narrative fabric resulting from Verga's artful combination of the points of view of an anonymous, popular narrative voice and chorus with the rich and subtle responses and interpretations that he as narrator—as omniscient as his Manzonian counterpart—provides.

Given the novel's highly elaborate creative dimension, criticism has viewed the principles of Verga's new form of realism as inherently contradictory: scientific precision in the creation of an autogenous art that is an objective, unbiased investigation of human life; the aesthetic priority of real, demonstrable human events, particularly of the mysterious and contradictory processes of human psychology; progress conceived, according to socioevolutionist thematics, as the struggle for survival, achieved at the expense of the weak and misfit—all these precepts appear to influence only minimally, if at all, Verga's art, either because they are never fully realized or because, if taken literally, the goal of studying human consciousness positivistically would amount to reducing literature to an exclusively material imperative. It has, then, been easy to discount Verga's "scientific" method on the grounds that it contradicts his ongoing absorption with aesthetic concerns. The position that Verga creates his masterpieces in spite of and in opposition to his inclination toward positive analysis has gained much currency over the years. *Il vero*, as Asor Rosa once remarked, is for Verga, and for verismo in general, primarily an aesthetic concept; the positivist and materialist foundations on which Verga's methodological premises rest do not affect in the least his creative process.[4]

Since my purpose is to explore the ethnographic dimension of *I Malavoglia*, it is useful to address in a preliminary way the issue of science-versus-art in the Verghian canon. The notion of positivism that is seen to be a hindrance to Verga's art derives largely from a neoidealist and irrationalist critique of scientific inquiry. Positive knowledge is thus equated with the accumulation, classification, and inductive rearrangement of facts into theories about nature and social life. Although Verga states that his stories will speak for themselves, the mere rearrangement of the plain facts of peasant life does not cast light on the general plight of humanity. In the tradition of Compte and Darwin, Verga maintains that facts and events, in order to yield knowledge, have to be guided and interpreted by some kind of theory. As is clear from his introduction to *I Malavoglia*, his "studio sincero e spassionato" [sincere and dispassionate study] presupposes hypotheses based in values; the inquiry itself is a strategy aimed at achieving knowledge about human social life in a large cross-section of society, extending from the lowest to the most privileged classes.

His guiding principle, deterministic and consistent with naturalism's valorization of cause-effect progression, holds that humanity, in its desire to move ahead, is engaged at various levels in a struggle exhibiting a complex range of human emotion: "le irrequietudini, le avidità, l'egoismo, tutte le passioni, tutti i vizi che si trasformano in virtù, tutte le debolezze che aiutano l'immane lavoro, tutte le contraddizioni" (6) [restlessness, greed, egotism, all the passions, all the vices transformed into virtues, all the weaknessess that assist (humankind's) immense labor, all the contradictions] This "scientific" hypothesis does not dispute the aesthetic constructs of fiction, nor is it summoned as a counterpoint to imaginative or symbolic representation. Rather, it enables him to produce a narrative whose truth value consists not in metaphysics or theology (as is the case with Manzoni) but in the material determinants of specific sociocultural systems. By means of "scrupulous" observation, literature can capture the characteristic aspects of mankind's efforts to progress amid the pressures generated by material self-interest.

The pictures that Verga draws are from life, but they are nonetheless pictures, highlighted and focused through the color, tone, and proportion that he supplies. They are meant to render the "physiognomy of modern Italy,"[5] to illustrate its ideal character and, therefore, foretell its destiny. Moreover, Verga's positivist and materialist orientation guide his adoption of such theoretical principles as the priority of economic constraints over mental superstructure—principles that find their justification in Verga's own experience of isolation and displacement—that enable him to criticize technical progress and the logic of capitalist enterprise and to take his stand on the side of the victims. Finally, there is no doubt that Verga's pessimism is linked to his quest for positive knowledge; like the science it espouses, it issues, paradoxically, from the belief in the ultimate perfectibility of social life. What was said of Herbert Spenser could easily be applied to Verga: "He was a man for whom the definition of tragedy was a beautiful theory killed by an ugly fact."[6] For Verga, the beautiful theory is the romantic idealism of the risorgimento, the ugly fact the subaltern reality of southern Italy's, particularly Sicily's, disinherited masses.

But although there can be no contradiction between Verga's concern for achieving a scientific understanding of particular sociocultural realities and the aesthetic forms he creates to represent them, his representations (like science) are not value free. Verga's "impersonal" narration finds its logic and powerful motive force in his experience of the culture of postunification Italy. His science, then, is his literary ideology, his literary forms are his social polemics. And the very fact that Verga seeks through fiction to make a different way of life comprehensible to a largely northern, middle class reading public makes it impossible to limit his stories to a project and rationale of scientific description.

Still, the principles of positivist inquiry operative throughout *I Malavoglia* remain highly significant. For they provide the basis for establishing Verga's authority as artist and historian-ethnographer of a subaltern people. In creating his authority as literary artist, he adopts scientific authority to enable him to apprehend (particularly in the case of *La vita dei campi* and *I Malavoglia*) forms of life in the process of becoming extinct. His authority, moreover, lends support to his thoroughly pessimistic view of humanity as victim of nature and history and his pervading sense of life as a desperate struggle toward death.

In a recent essay, Angelo Marchese, drawing extensively on two decades of Verga criticism, unwittingly sanctions the authority just described. He argues that Verga's novel charts the tragic decline of an "archaic-rural" way of life and, thus, marks the end of "idyllic man" (padron 'Ntoni), who cannot survive in the triumphant world of bourgeois progress.[7] At the same time, however, *I Malavoglia* looks back nostalgically at the great human powers embedded in that world, which, by virtue of their resistance to historical progress, become mythical archetypes, restored through the filter of authorial memory. The message that Marchese derives from his thorough exploration of the novel's thematic structure in relation to the narrative is a another variant of the absolute pessimism that generations of commentators have taken as Verga's conservative response to emergent capitalism's myths of socioeconomic progress: "Nei *Malavoglia* i 'mala mundi' sono irredimibili e insensati, tanto più crudeli quanto più le piccole formiche umane si disperdono abbandonando il nido, sotto i colpi di un'improvvida sventura: ché tale è il destino di tutte le creature" (189). [In *I Malavoglia* the *mala mundi* are irredeemable and senseless, all the more cruel the more the small human ants disperse, abandoning their nest under the blows of unforeseen misfortune. Such is the fate of all creatures.]

As the most recent in a long line of distinquished commentaries on *I Malavoglia*, Marchese's study employs considerable analytic skills in reconstructing the formal dimension of the text. He builds on the large body of criticism (Romano Luperini and Vitilio Masiello, in particular) to conclude that *I Malavoglia* reflects the crisis of liberal-bourgeois ideology in the wake of Italian unification.[8] But in Marchese's reading, Verga's thematics of dissolution and exile refer to something more universal than either the northern Liberals' incapacity to make capitalism work for the South or the failure of the land-reform projects proposed by *Meridionalisti* like Franchetti and Sonnino.[9] Verga's pessimism, in his view, expresses the impotence of all ideologies in the face of humanity's endless struggle for survival against the forces of nature and human intrigue and duplicity.

But *I Malavoglia* can be viewed from a different perspective, one that addresses, rather than the connection between text and context, the relation of mode of production to context. From this standpoint, it is possible to raise again the issue of Verga's ideology not as the endproduct of observation and analysis but as a "socially symbolic strategy," to use Jameson's well-known formulation,[10] identical to the writing process itself. It is within this perspective that I address the ethnographic dimension of *I Malavoglia*.

The novel's grand anthropological theme is that individual creeds and private conscience do not ensure the survival of a way of life in a society dominated by materialistic self-interest. Pressures exerted by the ruling classes on politically and economically subordinate groups or individuals, combined with the demands of social progress, will ultimately force changes in the underclass's behavior and cognitive orientations. But the adaptation to change summoned by the lure of material progress does not guarantee either the continuance of past subsistence or a change for the better. The logic of capitalist market economy justifies, for the sake of majority interest, sacrifice not only of the weak and unable to cope but also of the strong and resourceful. In society, the battle lines are drawn; from the conflict the vanquished will emerge, either to die in isolation or to begin once again the process of survival.

Without spending time to know the language and customs of the inhabitants of Aci Trezza directly and in intimate detail, Verga assembled selected data, most of which, it is known, he derived from Luigi Franchetti and Sydney Sonnino's *Inchiesta*.[11] In this way, he could get to the heart of Trezza quickly and draw a picture of the cultural whole. His aim was not to provide a description of habits and beliefs but to capture the essence of what he saw to be a process of living through one or more of its parts. One such part is padron 'Ntoni and his Malavoglias. Together, they function as an oppositional term within the larger cultural system. Padron 'Ntoni illustrates the plight of the small proprietor described by Sonnino. He owns a house and a boat with which he and his family make a modest living in fishing.

Verga begins the novel's action in 1863, a time when external pressures generated by the unification of Italy and the expansion of capitalist enterprise were beginning to take effect even in such remote and culturally backward communities as Trezza. The decline of the small, family-based fishing trade caused by the development of the fishing industry forced families like the Malavoglias to yield to the agrarian alternative championed by liberal politicians. In addition, the government's policy of universal conscription deprived the families of the strongest segment of their workforce and set the stage for the assimilation of different cultural attitudes. These two principal external factors, combined with the predatory tactics of the dominant groups within Trezza, make the extinction of the Malavoglias' way of life almost certain.

Thus, *I Malavoglia* recounts the end of a way of life, the disappearance, displacement, or rupture of an a priori good ("tutti buona e brava gente di mare" [all good and capable people of the sea]); origin and tradition ("da che il mondo era mondo . . . li avevano sempre avuto delle barche sull'acqua e delle tegole al sole . . ." [from time immemorial . . . they have had their boats on the water and their tiles in the sun]); and organic essence ("uomini fatti come le dita della mano" [men made like the fingers of one's hand]). The reader's attention is immediately drawn to the remains of a particular differential identity ("Adesso a Trezza non rimanevano che i Malavoglia di Padron 'Ntoni" [127] [Now in Trezza only the Malavoglias of padron 'Ntoni were left]) and to the beginning of the time of the narrative, which coincides thematically with the beginning of the process of rupture and disintegration. The disappearance of the Malavoglias could be seen, however, as only relatively complete; at the novel's end, Alessi marries Nunziata, refounding the economic base of the homestead and initiating what may appear as an attempt to restore tradition. But the past can be rescued only in the form of compromise and accommodation; the *casa del nespolo* with its survivors has relinguished its once organic operativeness; it remains more the symbol of a lost plenitude than a building block; its material substance emphasizes its presence as ruin, a disappearing structure that can be looked upon only with nostalgia.

The thematic components just summarized constitute the general structure of ethnographic narrative, as described by James Clifford in his essay on ethnographic allegory.[12] The beginning of the novel makes it clear, first, that its subject is a vanishing entity and, second, that the authority on which the narrative is based are the conditions of existence articulated by means of the peasants' own voices, whether directly, in dialogic form, or by means of an anonymous peasant narrator. The strategy of impersonal narration allows Verga to translate experience into text and thereby recover and temporarily revitalize a lost ideal. At the very moment the Malavoglias' dissolution begins, at the first symptoms of a loss of unity and authenticity, we begin the process of "salvage," "textual rescue," or "redemption."[13] The concept of cultural loss, in other words, preexists the writing; the textualization recovers those values perceived as distant and irretrievable.

An awareness of this fundamental allegorical dimension of *I Malavoglia* opens Verga's textual ideology to reconsideration and reevaluation.[14] For now, the absolute pessimism seen manifested in the predominant theme of "bisogna vivere come siamo nati" (215) [we must live the way we were born] can also be viewed as a rhetorical construct aimed at drawing attention less to universal metaphysical solutions than to the patterns of association and meaning within the historically bound context of writing. The allegory of recovery also demands that we focus more on the process of telling than on the resolution of conflict; the structure of meaning is itself the message.

Verga begins *I Malavoglia* twice: first, with a preface, in which he communicates to the reader the criteria for interpretating his presentation. The criteria he presents are relatively definitive:

> Questo racconto è lo studio sincero e spassionato del come probabilmente devono nascere e svilupparsi nelle più umili condizioni le prime irrequietudini pel benessere; e quale perturbazione debba arrecare in una famigliuola, vissuta sino allora relativamente felice, la vaga bramosia dell'ignoto, l'accorgersi che non si sta bene, o che si potrebbe star meglio (3).
>
> Perché la riproduzione artistica di cotesti quadri sia esatta, bisogna seguire scrupolosamente le norme di questa analisi; esser sinceri per dimostrare la verità, giacché la forma è così inerente al soggetto, quando ogni parte del soggetto stesso è necessaria alla spiegazione dell'argomento generale. (5)
>
> [This story is the sincere and dispassionate study of how probably, in the most humble of conditions, the first manifestations of dissatisfaction come into being and evolve; and of the distress that a vague desire for the unfamiliar and the realization that things are not going well and that life could be better is capable of causing in a family until then relatively content.
>
> In order that the artistic reproduction of these pictures be exact, it is necessary to observe scrupulously the norms of this analysis; to be sincere in demonstrating truth, for the story's form is as much an integral part of the subject as every part of the subject itself is crucial to the argument in general.]

These well-known passages are generally summoned to establish the operational principles of Verga's verismo; they constitute the poetics of narrative objectivity that Verga opposes to romantic fantasy and subjective involvement. The author claims to produce a text that is a translation from the real. There exists an objective reality to be explored and rendered meaningful to readers for whom that reality is unfamiliar. Verga's interpretation is at once hypothetical and definitive ("come probabilmente devono nascere"), while it is the presentation's aim to demonstrate a sociocultural truth.

In constructing his authority, Verga encounters a paradox endemic to ethnographic writing: his perspective is disinterested, objective, and sincere, but it is also a strategy of justification. By distancing himself from the reality he proposes to represent and at the same time claiming the totalistic nature of his description, Verga establishes a bond with a readership involved with the problems of evolutionary progress and natural selection that Darwinian "bourgeois" science made known.[15]

The appeal of his story is twofold. First, through the process of "scientific" distancing, it confronts the anxieties arising from the abandonment of absolute and supernatural agency in determining the evolution of human social existence. With Darwinian science, chance was introduced into nature, not as an element of chaos but as the mechanical action of time and circumstance. Progress, which leads nowhere in particular, provides no certitude. Instead, truth consists in the unifying power of an abstract good. This good is nothing else than the liberalist ideal of a rational plenitude achieved through the unity of contrasting interests. It presupposes the displacement of the struggle associated with concrete social life, for it is only thus that progress can be considered a desirable objective. From an epistemological standpoint, truth, then, is attainable only through scientific distancing. Verga places his readership before a constructed understanding; the Malavoglias and their environment are one and the same with their author's objectifying perspective. This is to say that they cannot be distinguished from his ("scientific") subjectivity.

Second, Verga constructs his text's appeal from a distinctively ethnographic perspective. His presentation carries the civilized reader back into the space of myth. The Malavoglias and their village society reveal an elementary or primitive form of cultural organization. Distant, authentic, childlike, they allow us to relive, at least imaginatively, an alternative experience. From the corrupt, inauthentic, alien world of the city, the "mondo-pesce-vorace" [the dog-eat-dog world] described in *Fantasticheria*,[16] we return to the psychological comforts of rural simplicity; from the displacement of hierarchy and value, to the patriarchal order where unity and honor reign supreme; from the religion of profit and material gain, to the *casa-nido* and the bonds of family life; from the disintegrative effects of linear time, to lived patterns of cyclic return.

The attraction of such a movement, however, does not consist in its potential as pastoral refuge. The edenic qualities of this world are celebrated not as viable alternatives but as ideals destined for extinction. In this sense, the appeal of Verga's Trezza is somewhat more complex. It consists in its being a fiction or, better, its being at once reality and fiction. The story, as an extended metaphor of loss, enables the reader to take solace in the redemptive power of textualization. The dystopia that results from the tragic demise of the good society is stabilized in representation. By slight of hand, Verga shows his readership the mythical model of pastoral good at the same time that he makes it disappear. If the good world of the Malavoglias is irretrievably lost, perhaps it never existed at all. The truly simple is like a mirage, the product of literary imagination. Verga enacts a movement typical of every ethnographic report: he transforms an essentially oral culture into a text.[17] The world of authenticity and essence is prey to history ("la fiumana del progresso"[3] [stream of progress]), and so it is destined to disappear ("il cammino fatale" [6] [the fatal journey]); in becoming a text, it is inscribed in the eternally present record of human struggle.

If the thematic content of pastoral is lost or portrayed as an unattainable ideal, the structure of pastoral, however, remains intact. The reader thus finds compensation in being once removed from the loss Verga describes. By sharing the authorial vantage point, we embrace his objectifying perspective; we share in his "scientific" understanding and recover, therefore, what has disappeared into history.

Verga's last and perhaps most important conceptual move in his preface is to persuade the reader that he considers the Malavoglias' experience as meaningful in itself and, therefore, not susceptible to his judgment:

> Chi osserva questo spettacolo non ha il diritto di giudicarlo, è già molto se riesce a trarsi un istante fuori del campo della lotta per studiarla senza passione, e rendere la scena nettamente, coi colori adatti, tale da dare la rappresentazione della realtà com'è stata, o come avrebbe dovuto essere. (7)
>
> [Whoever observes this spectacle has no right to judge it; it is already an achievement if he succeeds momentarily in standing outside the field of conflict to study it dispassionately and to depict the scene explicitly, with suitable colors, in order to represent that reality the way it was, or the way it should have been.]

Unlike his romantic predecessors and contemporaries, Verga does not involve himself with the passions of his characters nor allow himself to be influenced by moral and ethical prerogatives. Instead, he portrays the event's unmediated meaning: "this happened" or, given certain conditions of existence, "this ought to have happened."

But there is a notable ambivalence in the way Verga stakes his claim for neutrality. While stating his criteria for scientific detachment, he expresses negative judgment on the cultural dynamic he has chosen to study: "il congegno della passione" (5) [the movement of desire], prejudged as "perturbazione," "vaga bramosia," "vanità" (3), "ambizioni" (5). Verga's science fails because it cannot reconcile the competing demands of ideology. Every move to strengthen his objective imperative through distancing is reduced to an exercise of authority disguised as reason.

However, what if the position taken by Verga in his preface were viewed as the mirror image of the conditions of his existence as author? Then the rhetoric of detachment could be seen as a means to conceal his being a non-participant, an observer positioned on the margin of culture with the passionate remorse of one defeated in his own desire to progress. Science, then, becomes the means to regain control over history, to provoke a new aesthetic integration there, where the memory of exile persists. The everyday reality that gives rise to the contradiction in perspective produces a vision that frames the alienation, displacing it from its original context to a strange yet familiar land. Verga's search for unmediated meaning in representation becomes also a sign of the anxiety of identity. As he reenacts the loss-salvage structure of ethnographic narrative, he relives allegorically the conditions of his and his readership's existence under capitalism, the kind of "death in life" realized in transforming the life experiences of a small fishing village into a literary text.

From the narrative point of view, the story itself may be viewed as an allegorical construct. Such an approach allows us to bracket, for the moment, conventional assessments of Verga's pessimism and to focus on plot apparatus and style as rhetorical strategies that conflate the alien worlds of author and subject matter. In this way, it is possible to see how Verga, in portraying the cultural reality of Aci Trezza, creates a politically significant paradigm of his own experience as author.

At a crucial juncture in his essay on Joseph Conrad, Frederic Jameson, drawing heavily on Max Weber, addresses the problem of value in a way that is useful for our discussion. In traditional societies (the traditional village or tribal culture), the role played by the individual in the labor process is inherited. The value of this or that activity is an integral part of the activity itself, and therefore the question of the relative value of what one does is not posed. It is only with the secularization of life under capitalism that value becomes problematical, that is, it begins to exist in its own right as an object of study. People in middle-class cultures choose their profession; they weigh the benefits and liabilities of various activities as alternative life forms. To do so, they must seek a common denominator that unites the different forms of activity. They thus need to attain a certain level of abstraction and rationalization in order to make value visible. At the very moment value becomes a criterion for assessing competing activities, it ceases to exist: "The characteristic for rationalization is indeed the reorganization of operations in terms of the binary system of means and ends; indeed, the means/ends opposition, although it seems to retain the term and to make a specific place for value, has the objective result of abolishing value as such."[18]

As argued above, *I Malavoglia* is clearly a text that exhibits Verga's nostalgia for the wholeness of a primitive collective system in which each activity, as Jameson puts it, is "symbolically unique" (249). Its uniqueness consists in its being meaningful in itself as a way of life. It is, in fact, a world unto itself, sustained by proverbial knowledge, needing no expressive outlet other than that found in the realization of the activities through which it survives. The community of Aci Trezza becomes a problematic entity only at the moment of writing, when experience and essence are juxtaposed. Verga places this primitive community on the fringes of the capitalist social order; though it still exists, the storm that will render it inoperative is on the horizon, distant yet inevitable. The metaphorical prefiguration of the end of tradition and the beginning of capitalist secularization is the shipwreck, a true moment of epic significance in which the terms of value and activity become synthesized. The integral connection between activity and life is destroyed precisely at the point when the material source of the Malavoglias' livelihood, *La Provvidenza*, ceases to exist. Now value comes onto the scene in the form of loss and becomes one with the characters' lives. They, like their author, will think back to a time when the Malavoglias were all linked together in their life's activity, "like the fingers of one's hand."

Verga's life as a writer, like the social community he creates, is experienced on the borders of capitalist secularization. It is contained within a zone of possible exploitation while being excluded from the imagined wholeness resulting from the spread of the market system. Verga wrote *I Malavoglia* in Milan at a time of notable industrial expansion and optimism in the course of economic progress. "Era iniziata," Giulio Cattaneo writes in his biography of Verga,

> la grande ascesa industriale della Lombardia che presto sarebbe stata ulteriormente potenziata dall'ingresso in un moderno sistema di comunicazioni con l'Europa centrale attraverso la ferrovia del Gottardo e dalla realizzazione del trasporto a distanza della energia idroelettrica. . . . L'industria delle costruzioni meccaniche si avviava a posizioni di primato mentre si registrava una notevole ripresa cotoniera e si trasformava l'industria siderurgica.[19]
>
> [The great industrial rise of Lombardy had begun, and soon it would be even more strengthened by its entry into a modern system of communication with central Europe, by means of the Gottard railway and by the conveyance of hydroelectric power. . . . The machine industry was moving into positions of supremacy, while there was evidence of a notable renewal in the cotton, and iron, and steel industries.]

Verga's nostalgia for a form of total meaning, therefore, opposes the perceived wholeness of the market system; it is a means of counteracting his degraded inner experience as an artist who, to succeed, must abide by the logic of the culture from which he feels excluded. Criticism has shown that Verga identifies with the excluded figures of his novel, with 'Ntoni, in particular, but also with the entire Malavoglia family, which he portrays as isolated from its surrounding social context. According to Luperini, Verga's biography explains the attitude he takes toward his characters: particularly, his and their fear of being uprooted and living without a homeland. Also, his affiliation with a social class (the southern Italian rural bourgeoisie and petty nobility) cut off from capitalist industrial development contributed in large part to his belief that it was impossibile to change one's status in life. Since human existence follows the immutable laws of natural selection and people respond only to the demands of individual needs and interests, a genuine social revolution can never come about. The strong will always defeat the weak, the governed will always be at the mercy of those who govern.[20]

Verga's disbelief in human progress may also be viewed from the standpoint of the novel's style. In *I Malavoglia*, we see the crisis of the authorial self at a point of heightened conflict. In attempting to picture the life of a Sicilian fishing village in the most complete way possible, Verga invents a world of literally too many voices, indicative of the numerous roles played within the social community. If represented entirely with direct quotation (of which Verga makes ample use), the sheer discursive complexity of the whole would not permit him to coherently center his perspective. His free, indirect style allows him to assert his control over the composite interplay of voices embodied by his subject matter. By inhabiting the minds of his characters, he uses their thoughts and feelings as a vehicle for transcribing the anxieties of an uprooted and isolated author forced to compete in a world of material determinants.[21]

In chapter 2, for example, Verga concludes the creative dialogue between Piedipapera and padron Cipolla on a note of impending danger ("Lo sapete il proverbio 'Mare crespo, vento fresco.' Stasera le stelle sono lucenti, e a mezzanotte cambierà il vento; sentite la buffata?" [31]. [Are you familiar with the proverb "Crisp sea, cool wind." Tonight the stars are shining, and at midnight the wind will change, don't you hear it gusting?]), after which he inserts his own melancholic response in the place of padron 'Ntoni's apprehension about the fate of La Provvidenza: "Sulla strada si udivano passare lentamente dei carri." [You could hear the wagons passing by slowly on the streets.] This is followed by *compare* Cipolla's observation that "Notte e giorno c'è sempre gente che va attorno per il mondo" [Night and day, there are always people moving about the world], which leads to the authorial gloss: "E adesso che non si vedeva più né mare né campagna, sembrava che non ci fosse al mondo altro che Trezza, e ognuno pensava dove potevano andare quei carri a quell'ora". [And now you could see neither sea nor fields, and it seemed that only Trezza existed, and everybody was wondering where those wagons could be going at that hour].

The lyrical allusion following padron Cipolla's prediction is meant to evoke a sober musing on the loneliness of the solitary traveler; at the same time, it is a premonition of the loss of Bastianazzo. Juxtaposed are the sense of mystery emerging from the night and the senseless chatter of those characters who, unlike padron 'Ntoni, think only about the outcome of their practical investments. Accordingly, Verga's lyrical commentary is meant to mirror padron 'Ntoni's state of mind. Its poetic effect, as Luigi Russo once argued, consists in showing that "ogni dolore vero non è mai generico, ma individualmente determinato e conchiuso; e ciascuno piange in un dolore comune la propria sorte"[22] [all real grief is never generic but individually determined and circumscribed; every individual suffers his own fate in common grief]. The Malavoglias, like Homer's Achilles, are always alone in the sorrows they share with the whole of mankind: "Gli uomini sono sempre soli con sé stessi nelle loro sofferenze, e il fortuito accomunamento con gli altri dà una tenerezza tragica per questo ritrovarsi in comune in una sorte diversa, ma vicina. . . . Questa appunto la liricità di Verga" (157). [People are always alone in their sufferings, and the fortuitous sharing with others gives a tragic tenderness to this experiencing together different but similar lots. . . . Verga's lyricism consists precisely in this.]

There is, however, another side to Verga's lyricism, more relevant to our discussion, which brings us back to the question of value. If it is true that the Malavoglias are made to stand apart from the rest of Trezza's community by virtue of their moral spirit, it is equally true that their author's starkly pessimistic vision of human reality derives from his understanding of the organizational logic on which the economic well-being of Trezza is based. This logic, which systematically excludes the Malavoglias because it excludes value per se, is the logic of capitalist social organization, transferred to a primitive scene. The Malavoglias' tragedy is possible only because by being themselves they unwittingly resist; in resisting, they occupy a space somewhere between the optimism of the market system, which puts an end to their old way of life, and their narrator's cosmic pessimism. The Malavoglias are linked religiously to tradition; they believe in a religion of values that their community has been forced to abandon. Their faith, like Verga's faith in the wholeness of existence, is no longer possible. But, unlike Verga, they are unaware that their fate has been sealed by forces they cannot control, hence the tragic quality of their story. It is also in this perspective that we can discuss the meaning of Verga's lyricism.

The sentence "Sulla strada si udivano passare / lentamente i carri" (31), composed as it is of a hendecasyllablic and a septenarius, is deliberately poetic; its tonality is thoroughly musical, designed with soft, open vowels and the alliteration of dental consonants to evoke melancholy.[23] And at the chapter's end, we find another notably rhythmic passage, plentifully supplied with alliteration, which is meant to echo the collective feelings of the Malavoglias, if not the entire community:

Il mare russava in fondo alla stradicciola, adagio adagio, e a lunghi intervalli si udiva il rumore di qualche carro che passava nel buio, sobbalzando sui sassi, e andava pel mondo il quale è tanto grande che se uno potesse camminare e camminare sempre, giorno e notte, non arriverebbe mai, e c'era pure della gente che andava pel mondo a quell'ora, e non sapeva nulla di compar Alfio, né della *Provvidenza* che era in mare, né della festa dei Morti;—così pensava Mena sul ballatoio aspettando il nonno. (47)

[The sea was growling softly down at the end of the street, and at long intervals you could hear a wagon passing in the dark, bouncing over the stones; it was moving through the world so big that if one could walk and walk without stopping, day and night, he would never reach the end of his journey, but there really were people moving through the world at that hour of the night who knew nothing of *compar* Alfio, nor of *La Provvidenza* out at sea, nor of the holy day of the Dead; these were Mena's thoughts as she waited for her grandfather.]

But Verga's lyricism, which still for many readers appears to contradict his positivist literary principles, becomes more intelligible when if viewed as a rhetoric, designed as a sign of a wholeness no longer possible. Poetic thinking, in other words, is all that is left of a society and mode of productive activity on the verge of extinction. In this sense, the Malavoglias too, like the community of separate, inherited activities that has been destroyed by the market system, are symbolically unique. They have survived not only by virtue of their moral compactness but also because they are made to display a rounded form of life that has a center of its own (the *casa del nespolo*). In the real social world of Verga's primitives, there is no place for the sense of bewilderment expressed in Mena's thoughts. Thus, the reader must think her thoughts from the outside; with Verga, we must promote her inner, not directly expressible voice to the status of an aesthetic or sacred object, to be admired from a position removed from its possible origin.[24]

The human essence at the center of Verga's poetic musings is what the early Georg Lukàcs would describe idealistically as the postepic, solitary soul, alone in a menacing, incomprehensible world. Its mythical, primeval identity, total and complete, has been irrevocably lost: "No light radiates any longer from within into the world of events, into its vast complexity to which the soul is a stranger."[25] Verga's lyricism can be seen as a restorative act, a way of giving form to a lost essence and, ultimately, of preserving epic unity. His solitary traveler, who allegedly has departed from a meaningful, organic world, will never return home. He mirrors his author's utopian longing for fullness yet will never be reconciled to it, save in the form of a (lyrical) trace.

His realistic counterpart in the novel is 'Ntoni, a character who variedly embodies and illustrates Verga's predicament as a writer. In terms of the symbolic cohesiveness of the Malavoglias, 'Ntoni represents a dissonance that is crucial to the novel's inner form as well as to its thematics. While the other Malavoglias exhibit a fundamental coherence of being and action, emblematic of a preindustrial age, 'Ntoni's character unites contrasting traits. On the one hand, he is childlike, good-hearted, and trustful of the family ethic; on the other, he is not resigned to the completeness of padron 'Ntoni's outlook. In his rebellious desire for new experiences, 'Ntoni, in effect, experiences his family's world as imperfect. His departure violates the mythical space and the immanence of meaning on which the concrete existence of the rural archaic society depends. The outside world he has visited causes him to forcefully question the ideal, as, in chapter 13, when he denounces the absurdity of his grandfather's work ethic:

Ma voi altri ve la passate meglio di me a lavorare, e ad affannarvi per nulla? E la nostra mala sorta infame! ecco cos'è! Vedete come siete ridotto, che sembrate un arco di violino, e sino a vecchio avete fatto sempre la stessa vita! Ora che ne avete? Voi altri non conoscete il mondo, e siete come i gattini cogli occhi chiusi. E il pesce che pescate ve lo mangiate voi? Sapete per chi lavorate, dal lunedì al sabato, e vi siete ridotto a quel modo che non vi vorrebbero neanche all'ospedale? per quelli che non fanno nulla, e che hanno denari a palate lavorate! (257–58)

[But do people like you think that by working and agonizing for nothing that your life is better than mine? It's our damned bad luck, that's what it is! Look at yourself, crooked like the bow of a violin, and you've always lived the same life! Now what do you have to show for it? People like you don't know what the world's like, you're like kittens with your eyes closed. And do you eat the fish that you catch? Do you know for whose benefit you are working from Monday through Saturday, and you're in such bad condition that they don't even want you at the hospital? You're working for people who do nothing, who have tons of money!]

Here 'Ntoni questions the objective conditions of his family's real existence and identifies its illusion of well-being. At the same time, he opposes padron 'Ntoni's sense of inherited value with the concept of life as interested activity. The Malavoglias can only succumb to the economic logic of their subaltern existence or persist in their fantasy of wholeness. A resolution of their situation is both impossibile and unimaginable. On the other hand, 'Ntoni's primitive awareness of a secularized world and of the objective exploitation of human existence provides no compensation whatsoever for the loss of the center. As an outcast, he will never again experience the comforts of home and of life as it was always lived. At the end of the novel, he has undergone a crucial transformation, one that carries the burden of Verga's perspective. Unlike Manzoni's Renzo, who after an adventurous exile learned the rules of peaceful living, Ntoni's fate is sealed in his transgression. He can only revisit nostalgically the wholeness of family life.

> Ti rammenti le belle chiacchierate che si facevano la sera, mentre si salavano le acciughe? e la Nunziata che spiegava gli indovinelli? e la mamma, e la Lia, tutti lì, al chiaro di luna, che si sentiva chiacchierare per tutto il paese, come fossimo tutti una famiglia? *Anch'io allora non sapevo nulla, e qui non volevo starci, ma ora che so ogni cosa devo andarmene* (321; italics mine).
> [Do you remember how we used to chat in the evening while salting the anchovies? and Nunziata would explain the riddles to us? and mama, Lia, everybody together in the moonlight, and we could hear the village chatter, as if we were all one big family? *At the time I didn't know anything, either, and had no desire to stay here, but now that I understand everything, I am forced to go away.*]

Like Verga, 'Ntoni knows that the life he now yearns for is a romantic myth; the integrated unity, the transcendental binding of souls, the crystallization of value in common acts and deeds are the substance of a dream, necessary as compensation for the harsh realities of competition and survival in the market system.[26]

Lukàcs' concept of the novel's "inner form" (70–83) is relevant to 'Ntoni's function as a character and to the novel's structure as a whole. According to it, we could view 'Ntoni as having undergone a process of self-recognition. The reality he flees is organic and timeless and, as such, is impervious to history and an obstacle to individual development. The world he leaves can survive only because it is essentially timeless; only because its laws are meaningful to itself alone; only because it has no purpose other than to repeat itself. Within its ideal structure, there is no movement; its characters have no specific purpose other than to occupy a place within a system. The continuity of its eternal rhythms is broken when this world deviates from convention, as when padron 'Ntoni agrees to use his boat to transport the *lupini* to market or, as in the case of 'Ntoni, when an individual embarks on a destiny of his own. The structure of the narrative, its plot and characterization hinges on this crucial moment of deviance. It is then, at the moment in which an individual subject appears to challenge the timelessness and the monotony of a problem-free reality, that we pass from myth into history, from epic wholeness into the problematic world of the novel.

The action of the novel is constructed out of the "history" inscribed in padron 'Ntoni's decision to accept Campana di Legno's business offer, the socially relevant factor being usury which, as Luperini has remarked, was one of the prime causes of the downfall of small property holders such as padron 'Ntoni.[27] Thus, Verga brings into conflict two socially recognizable entities: the *piccolo proprietario* forced by circumstance to diverge from his inherited activity and the rapacious moneylender whose business, although not a direct product of capitalist enterprise, was certainly enhanced by it. The central event of the *lupini* deal is determined, furthermore, by two equally compelling historical circumstances that contribute to the destruction of Padron 'Ntoni's tradition-oriented system: compulsory military service ("Nel dicembre del 1863, 'Ntoni, il maggiore dei nipoti, era stato chiamato per la leva di mare" (15) [In December of 1863, 'Ntoni, the oldest of Padron 'Ntoni's nephews, was conscripted into the Navy]) and taxation. This objective grounding of the narrative in historical and social facts undermines the timeless world interiorized by the Malavoglias. It is at once the basis for the novel's conflict and the generating force of its irony. The objectification of social reality and the foregrounding of historical necessity prevent Verga from romanticizing the lives of his primitives. Yet he does not abolish the reality of their world as a meaningful, harmonious unity. Rather, he simply abandons it, sealing it off as an unattainable utopia. 'Ntoni's homecoming is paradigmatic in the sense that it directs us away from transcendence while retaining the balance between what is time-given and problematic and the ultimate security of illusion.

'Ntoni's story, however simple it might appear, describes a search for knowledge beyond the borders of Trezza. His travel, adventures, and misdeeds, while enlarging his sense of life, also make him "different" in the eyes of both his family and his village. His plight and dilemma consist, in the final analysis, in his inability to reconcile and unite two divergent perspectives and practices: life as subjectively felt and life as objectively understood. The explicit lessons the reader draws from 'Ntoni's experience can be translated into the known variants of Verga's pessimism and of his inability, as most commentators have underscored, to convert the optic of his subaltern characters, 'Ntoni in particular, into a sociopolitical alternative.[28]

To limit ourselves to this kind of mimetic reading, although obviously wellfounded in Verga's conservative politics, serves only to confirm what we already know about the author's "scientific" procedure—ultimately, to preserve the illusion of his positivist science. A different way of interpretating the novel's ending has been suggested recently by Luperini. 'Ntoni's farewell to his native Trezza, he argues, is a historical decision on Verga's part, which entails the acceptance of alienation and "progress" as a way of life: "Attraverso 'Ntoni, l'autore canta simbolicamente il distacco dalla propria formazione romantica che lo aveva indotto a cercare un momento di 'fresco e sereno raccoglimento' nel mondo arcaico-rurale e a rintracciarvi un'alternativa di valori."[29] [By means of 'Ntoni, the author celebrates symbolically his detachment from his romantic literary past, which had led him to seek out a 'moment of soothing and unperturbed refuge' with the archaic-rural world and to find there alternative values.] So, according to Luperini, the end of the novel symbolizes the end of Verga's romantic anticapitalism and sets the stage for the truly modern, secular, and profane representation of *Mastro don Gesualdo*.

But if it is true that the Malavoglias as a disappearing type are, from the beginning, a rhetorical construct and that their legitimacy is gained through textualization, then we have to account for 'Ntoni, too, as a rhetoric, that is to say, as another allegorical register of the text: the introduction of a problematic individual into a coherently conceived cultural subject. Once the world was a happier place; to dramatize its loss, Verga fabricates a consciousness that can be appropriated by his reading public. As a primitive who has experienced the "mondo-pesce-vorace" as it really is, 'Ntoni teaches us to read literature in a certain way. He teaches as that his author's fiction is scientific fact. He thus reaffirms the author's authority as historian-ethnographer, and prepares us for the truth of *Mastro don Gesualdo*, a story even more powerful than his.

CHAPTER THREE

Gabriele D'Annunzio

Mythical Narratives

If there is a single feature that sets Gabriele D'Annunzio's prose fiction completely apart from Verga, verismo, and all other varieties of realism, it is the belief that reality in all its manifestations is ultimately inaccessible and, therefore, incommunicable. Behind the textual artifice exist what Furio Jesi calls "idee senza parole," ideas that cannot be expressed in words.[1] "La parola è un segno imperfetto" (1:664) [The word is an imperfect sign], exclaims Giorgio Aurispa at the outset of *Il trionfo della morte* and the human spirit (in this case, the anima of Aurispa's beloved Ippolita), the stuff out of which in the previous traditions literary characters were made, is "intrasmissibile."[2] In D'Annunzio's canon, the literary artist is neither creator nor scribe. Rather, he operates as a kind of frequency that transmits Beauty and the hidden mysteries of Race and Tradition. Stelio Effrena, protagonist of *Il fuoco* and D'Annunzian poet par excellence, re-produces in the rhythm of the word the language of Tradition, manifest in the sacred artifacts through which the artificers of old had inscribed the hopes and ambitions of their race. ("Egli non faceva se non tradurre nei ritmi della parola il linguaggio visibile con cui già in quel luogo gli antichi artefici avevano significato l'aspirazione e l'implorazione della stirpe" [2:612].) [He did not but translate into the rhythm of the word the visible language with which, in that very place, the ancient artificers had expressed the aspirations and desires of their race.]

Nothing is more characteristic of D'Annunzio's style than its essentially oratorical and lyrical properties. His sentence production aims at creating a homogeneous amalgam of codes that give value to transcendental communion, poetic inspiration, and the organic primacy of the beautiful in opposition to the common referential activity of naturalist prose. D'Annunzio's protagonists bear the full weight of an overpowering aesthetic impulse to go beyond the degraded, valueless, disparate, and contingent world of industrial capitalism in search of a new vitality in old hierarchies. The D'Annunzian sentence is a unit of melody, referring to an arcane and mysterious reality; it employs words mythically, as utterances that at once exhibit and conceal. As an aesthetic gesture, it operates like a kind of mythological machine, not with common signs or unprivileged sublanguages but ritualistically, with command words such as "voluttà," "raro," or "profumo," and in the creation of cosmic mysteries like the sea in *Il piacere*, where the symbols evoked have no specific referent save that of obscurity:

> Il mare aveva sempre per [Andrea] una parola profonda, piena di rivelazioni subitanee, d'illuminazioni improvvise, di significazioni inaspettate. Gli scopriva nella segreta anima un'ulcera ancor viva sebben nascosta e gliela faceva sanguinare; ma il balsamo poi era più soave. Gli scoteva nel cuore una chimera dormente. (1:140)
> [The sea always spoke to Andrea in an overpowering way. It was full of instant revelations, sudden illuminations, and unexpected meanings. It uncovered in the recesses of his spirit a sore still open, although hidden, and it made it bleed; but the balm was sweeter. It awakened the chimera asleep in his heart.]

D'Annunzio's sea is a myth of an obscure potency. While awakening in the protagonist a sense of death, of things irremediably lost in the darkness of Being, it speaks the language of regeneration. Its function is to make us believe in an energizing force that inspires action; it contains unlimited concrete possibilities, has the power to cure, and thus generates optimism and hope.

D'Annunzio's faith in the regenerative power of myth translates itself as the creation of a style out of the evocative force of the written word. His description, in the introduction to *Il trionfo della morte*, of an ideal book of modern prose reads, in fact, like a description of myth itself. The book will endeavour to harmonize "tutte le varietà del conoscimento e tutte le varietà del mistero" [all the varieties of knowledge and all the varieties of mystery]; it will alternate "le precisioni della scienza alle seduzioni del sogno" [scientific precision with the seductive power of dreams]; and rather than imitating Nature or presenting itself as a replica of the real, it will extend Nature's course and recreate "la particolar vita—sensuale sentimentale intellettuale—di un essere umano collocato nel centro della vita universa" (1:653) [the sensual, emotional, and intellectual life of one human being positioned in the center of the life of the universe]. The narrative impulse is one of assimilation and reconciliation. The function of the imaginary is to resolve antinomies and contradictions, to speak in a language common to all of humanity, and to address and resolve the most crucial problems of the individualistic world by reforming through fiction a preindividualistic consciousness. The primary objective of D'Annunzio's ideal book, like all mythical narrative, is to attest and confirm the social unity of the race, whose poetry—D'Annunzio tells Francesco Paolo Michetti—he has captured in its pages:

> Qui sono le imagini della gioia e del dolore di nostra gente sotto il cielo pregato con selvaggia fede, su la terra lavorata con pazienza secolare. Sente talvolta il morituro passar nell'aria il soffio della primavera sacra; e, aspirando alla Forza, invocando un Intercessore per la Vita, ripensa la colonia votiva composta di fresca gioventù guerriera che un toro prodigioso, di singolar bellezza, condusse all'Adriatico lontano. (1:657)
>
> [Here are the images of joy and grief of our people beneath the heavens they implored with untamed faith and on the land they patiently toiled for centuries. At times, the dying hear the breath of the holy Spring in the air; and, yearning for Strength, invoking a Mediator for Life, they think back to the votive colony comprised of energetic young warriors who led a prodigious bull of unparalleled beauty to the distant Adriatic.]

It is much less useful to dismiss the inflated syntax and symbolic allusions of this passage as just one more instance of D'Annunzian rhetoric than to view its fundamental mechanism of mystification as an attempt to reinvent a primitive consciousness and to transfer its epistemological model to an exactly opposite social formation shared by author and reader. Faith, the sacredness of perpetual rejuvenation through religion, and the power to withstand dissolution by expanding the social body are all elements of ritualistic practice designed to further survival. Through a new art that refers to nothing except its own organic structure, to poetic inspiration itself—an estimation which reflects Vico's view of a genuinely primitive sensibility—D'Annunzio attempts to forge a collective language of regeneration.

However, the rhetoric of humanity's rebirth and the prospects of a nonalienated existence in the utopia of art, here and throughout D'Annunzio's fiction and dramas, is a disguise for the reality of his exclusion from history, just as "death's triumph" in the *Il trionfo della morte* can be read as a kind of wish fulfillment, the ultimate triumph of a displaced class through rejuvenation in the pure matrix of race. Myth, in other words, is the means by which D'Annunzio's hypothetical fallen aristocracy can redefine the channels of command by wrenching its own existence from historical time, thereby preserving it until the moment is right for retaliative action:

Se fossero distrutte da un altro diluvio deucalionico tutte le razze terrestri e sorgessero nuove generazioni dalle pietre, come nell'antica favola, gli uomini si batterebbero tra loro appena espressi dalla Terra generatrice, finché uno, il più valido, non riuscisse ad imperar su gli altri. Aspettate dunque e preparate l'evento. (2:421)
[If all earthly races were destroyed by an earthly deluge, and new generations came forth from the stones as in the ancient fable, mankind, scarcely out of the earth generator, would beat each other until one, the most powerful, succeeded in commanding the others. Wait then and prepare yourselves for the event.][3]

We move, hence, from a vanquished past to its recreation, by means of a new cosmic cycle. The upward journey toward man's recovery of the past begins, paradoxically, with the acceptance of its irremediable loss. Its history cannot be summoned to wage battle against the rising tide of middle-class mediocrity; nor can it serve as a model for the future. The elegant upper social class in which D'Annunzio's heroes find their roots and sustenance, its conventions and moral virtues, and its inestimable value belong to humankind's prehistory, to that previous cycle, which functions as a kind of archetype or collective unconscious. It becomes, thus, for the D'Annunzian present a social mythology or symbolic structure, devoid of pragmatic impulses and objectives. The irretrievable past is a world of arcane value, of value per se, the same kind of value D'Annunzio attributes to objects, places, and the unfathomable passions of his characters as a response to the utilization of value in a world of new middle-class dominance.

Objects in D'Annunzio's fiction are there to be seen, not used; they are to be visited and appreciated for their hidden, symbolic meanings. The protagonists of his novels are pilgrims for whom reality is a shrine before which they stand as voyeuristic devotees.[4] Amid the brutality of the masses, they pay homage to the sacred and venerable things over which they have lost their control. What, for example, Giorgio Aurispa sees when he visits the house of his aunt are not objects that can be evaluated according to some common standard or measure but rather the spiritual substance of mysterious essences, things divested of their menacing materiality and restored to value. D'Annunzio's sentence then becomes truly a symbolic act, as it captures a diversity of illuminations and raptures in the form of words:

> Le tende ondeggiavano come gonfiate in misure da un respiro, con mollezza, lasciando intravedere un paesaggio nobile e calmo. I lievi romori dei legni, delle carte, delle pareti, continuavano. Nella terza stanza, severa e semplice, le memorie erano musicali, venivano da muti istrumenti. Sopra un lungo cembalo levigato, di palissandro, ove le cose si riflettevano come in una spera, riposava un violino nella sua custodia. Sopra un leggio, una pagina di musica si sollevava e si abbassava ai soffii dell'aria, quasi in ritmo con le tende. (1:786)
> [The curtains, which a rhythmic breath seemed to swell, undulated softly, giving glimpses of a noble and calm landscape. The slight noises made by the wainscoting, the papers, and the partitions continued. In the third room, severe and simple, the recollections were musical, and came from mute instruments. On a long, rosewood piano, whose varnished surface reflected things like a mirror, a violin was resting in its case. On a music stand, a page of music rose and fell with the wind, almost in time with the curtains.][5]

The innumerable precious objects we find in D'Annunzio's fictions all belong to the Tradition of esoteric truth that is assumed to be lost forever. It is, however, on behalf of the Tradition that they are called forth. In themselves, these objects are useless relics, but they are useful as supports in the building of the new race that will emerge from the ashes of history to initiate a new cosmic cycle. Giorgio Aurispa is a survivor of a mythical, lost race. From the differentiated and fragmented materiality of the city from which he has been displaced, he returns to the locus of plenitude, where he savors the fertility of the land and the virility of his ancestors through objects that, like relics in a sanctuary, have the power to generate a new-lived experience of the arcane:

> Le cose suggerivano al superstite le memorie. Una moltitudine leggera e mormorante si levava dalle cose, veniva a circondarlo. Le emanazioni del passato sorgevano da ogni punto. Le cose parevano rendere qualche parte d'una sostanza spirituale onde fossero impregnate. "Mi esalto?" egli si domandò, guardando entro di sé le imagini che si succedevano con una straordinaria rapidità, evidentissime, non offuscate da ombra di morte ma viventi d'una vita superiore. "Questa rappresentazione che la mia anima fa a sé stessa è libera d'ogni elemento soprannaturale? Queste imagini si formano in me per la medesima operazione per cui si formano i sogni? Della medesima essenza?" (1:785)
>
> [The things suggested to the survivor a crowd of recollections. From these things arose a light and murmuring chorus which enveloped him. From every side arose the emanations of the past. One could have said that the things emitted the odors of a spiritual substance which had impregnated them. "Do I exhalt myself"? he asked himself, at the aspect of the images that succeeded one another in his mind with prodigious rapidity, clear as visions, not obscured by a funereal shadow, but living a superior life. "Is this image my spirit has created of itself free of everything supernatural? Do these things take form in me in the same way as dreams are formed? Do they have the same essence? (143)

The power of such an unspecified visual inventory is that it testifies to the existence of mythic values that cannot be quantified. Experience is coded symbolically, from the perspective of a possible collectivity, through the linking of disparate and contingent realities, as in a dream. Tradition dominates with the force of artifacts that conceal the mysteries of a different time and space. So it is also that Claudio Cantelmo of *Le vergini delle rocce* will thank the ancient masters of Tradition, whose teachings include the need to seek out the neophytes, calling them to action in behalf of a new revelation, disciples who will follow the new Christ on the way to perfection. Such a rudimentary fantasy strengthens the psychic effectivity of the subject, from which emerge figurations of prodigious impulses that invest the dead world of D'Annunzian reality with a formal completeness:

> Qui tutto è morto, ma tutto può rivivere all'improviso in uno spirito che abbia una dismisura e un calore bastevole a compiere il prodigio. Come imaginare la grandezza e la terribilità d'una tal resurrezione? Colui il quale potesse con-

tenerla nella sua coscienza parrebbe a sé medesimo e agli altri invasato da una forza misteriosa e incalcolabile, assai maggiore di quella che assaliva la Pitia antica. Per la sua bocca non parlerebbe il furor d'un dio presente nel tripode, ma sì bene il genio stesso delle stirpi custode funereo d'innumerevoli destini già compiuti. (2:415)

[All is death here, I thought to myself, but all can suddenly come to life again in a spirit that may have a warmth and redundance sufficient to accompany the miracle. How to imagine the grandeur and the terror of such a resurrection? He whose conscience could conceive it would appear to himself and to others invaded by a mysterious and incalculable force greater yet than that which assailed the ancient Pitia. The fury of a priestess in the tripod would not speak from his mouth, but rather the funereal genius itself of guardian races, of innumerable destinies already completed.] (35)

The regenerative powers of myth lay the groundwork for heroic action, promoting a utopian impulse and faith in some ultimate disclosure.

From the standpoint of narrative structure, myth functions as a kind of archetypal event, an antetext containing an exemplary history that exerts its power of attraction over the present. Events recounted in the present are valorized always in relation to a past moment of plenitude, the constitutive elements of which harbor arcane and mysterious essences. D'Annunzio's male protagonists embody always a refined artistic sensibility, attuned to the secret affinities among things. The unifying consciousness of narrative, whether that of Andrea Sperelli of *Il piacere* or Paolo Tarsis of *Forse che sì, forse che no*, reads the world as a transparent emblem, replete with correspondences.

The structure of D'Annunzio's sentences reflects the propensity to recapture a mythical essence, while, through the use of imaginative analogies, it keeps the reader once removed from all specific referents. The result is a kind of looping of the syntactical chain, achieved through a proliferation of units that share in the same grammatical structure and rhythm. Vittorio Roda refers, somewhat negatively, to an architecture of predictable movements and patterns, a stylistic "tautology" that contradicts D'Annunzio's avowal of unconditioned expressive freedom.[6] Certainly, proof of this assertion may be found in all of D'Annunzio's novels, for as long as the primordial holds the center of the poet's interest, repetition, albeit intended to enhance the rhetorical strategy, will predominate as a sort of magical replay of signifiers belonging to a collective psyche. To proceed otherwise would be unthinkable, given the priority D'Annunzio assigns to the evocative function of literature.

Also, from the point of view of thematics, priority is given to a model event of the past against which the present action is framed. D'Annunzio's early novel, *Il piacere*, is ostensibly a story about physical love which, as the title suggests, is equated with sensual pleasure. But the experiences it portrays have much less to do with sexual intimacy than with love as a symbolic act, deprived of every leveling effect associated with physical gratification. Love in *Il piacere* is the love of the mythic Other, the acting out of desire for fullness that can never be fully satisfied. Love exists, for the protagonist, at another time and in another text. At once the object of memory and aspiration, it appears crystallized in an ideal figuration that can never be reenacted in the narrative present. The tension in the novel is created precisely by Andrea's desire to reenact his past love with Elena (a mythical event associated, indeed, with a mythical name), against which the Elena of the present and also her surrogate opposite, Maria (a name equally mythical), appear as illusory metaphors, temporary stand-ins who serve mainly to direct the reader's attention to the ontological ripeness of the original event.

The mythical past cannot be revived, only reinvented. The future holds for D'Annunzio only decadence and death, a state, however, that can be exorcized, made to be yet another locus for experiencing the sacred. Let us take, for example, the portrait D'Annunzio draws of modern technology, particularly that of the airplane in *Forse che sì, forse che no:*

Tutte le tettoie rombarono e soffiarono, gonfie di procella come le case di Eolo. Trascinati a braccia sul campo, trattenuti dalle braccia muscolose, rapiti infine all'astro violento dell'elica, i velivoli partivano l'un dopo l'altro a conquistar il cielo magnifico, taluni giallicci come i capovaccai, taluni rossastri come i fiamminghi, taluni cinerognoli come le gru. Scoccavano come i silvani, volteggiavano come i rapaci, strisciavano come le gralle. Nello strepito imitavano da lungi l'applauso come i colombi, il tintinnio come i cigni, la raffica come le aquile. Tutte le forze del sogno gonfiavano il cuore dei Terrestri rivolti all'Assunzione dell'Uomo. L'Anima immensa aveva valicato il secolo, accelerato il tempo, profondato la vista nel futuro, inaugurato la novissima età. Il cielo era divenuto il suo terzo regno, non conquiso col travaglio dei macigni titanici ma col fulmine fatto schiavo. (2:925-26)

[The rooftops roared and exhaled, swollen as they were with tempests like the abodes of Aeolus. Dragged by hand on to the runway, held steady by muscular arms, captured finally by the violence of the propellers, the planes departed one by one in conquest of the magnificent sky. Some were yellowish in color like vultures, others reddish, like flamingos, others ashen like cranes. They darted forth like sparrows, maneuvered like hawks, glided like gulls. Their noise emulated the crowd's applause, clapping like doves; they jingled like swans, gusted forth like eagles. All the powers of dream filled the hearts of the Earthbound as they witnessed the Assumption of Man. The immense Spirit had stepped over the century, accelerated time, deepened our sight of the future, welcomed in the newest of ages. The sky had become its third realm, conquered not by the labor of titans but with the harnessing of the thunderbolt.]

This is merely one small part of an extensive tour de force in which the degraded and mechanical content of modern aerophysics undergoes mythical reinvention. Roda is no doubt well on target when he notes that, in D'Annunzio's world, the machine's very right to existence depends on its being a replica of the past, a fact that helps quiet the anxiety of an unknown future.[7] Attention in this passage is, in fact, centered much less on the airplane's functional capacities, on what it does, than on its physical characteristics, on what it is like, and what it signifies in terms of the human capacity to conquer and enslave nature. Elsewhere, in order to further alleviate the pain of uncertainty that the mechanical age has heralded, D'Annunzio brings humanity and machine together in the creation of a dual nature similar to that of mythical creatures:

> Giulio Cambiaso non aveva mai sentito così piena la concordanza fra la sua macchina e il suo scheletro, fra la sua volontà addestrata e quella forza congegnata, tra il suo moto istintivo e quel moto meccanico. Dalla pala dell'elica al taglio del governante, tutta la membratura volante gli era come un prolungamento e un ampliamento della sua stessa vita. Quando si curvava su la leva a manovrare contro un colpo un salto un buffo; quando inchinava il corpo verso l'interno del circolo nel veleggio roteante, per muovere con la pressione dell'anca il congegno inteso a inflettere la velatura estrema; quando nell'andare all'arza manteneva l'equilibrio con un bilanciamento infallibile intorno al centro di stabilità, e trovava a volta a volta il modo di trasporre l'asse del volo, egli credeva essere congiunto ai suoi due bianchi trapezii con nessi vivi come i muscoli pettorali degli avvoltoi, che aveva veduto piombarsi dalle rocce del Mokattam o aggirarsi su l'acquitrino di Sakha. (2:924)

Properties of Writing

[Giulio Cambiaso had never felt so fully the harmony between his machine and his skeleton, between his disciplined will and that mechanical force, between the movement of his instincts and that of his machine. From propeller to rudder, the entire flying body was like an extension and expansion of his own life. When he bent over the stick to maneuver against the wind, when he leaned toward the internal circle of his glide to change its direction with the pressure of his hip, when, soaring upward, he maintained stability with delicate balance and from time to time found the way to change the direction of flight, he believed he was wedded to his white wings with living fibers like the pectoral muscles of the vultures he had seen plunge down from the rocks of Mokattam or circle the canals of Sakha.]

It is important to note that, in contrast to futurism, the exorcism here is worked not on the individual but on the machine. Futurism's mythification of the machine involved the stripping away of humanity's false, irrelevant and nonessential cultural overcoat, a peeling away of external layers of socialization to get to its pure and essential core, which, according to the futurist interpretation, was carnal and sensual. In the futurist vision, humankind would be driven by the machinelike forces of its carnal nature, become metalized, its body parts interchangeable like an engine's. Its purpose was to generate speed; human beings were truly alive only when in motion. In the futurist universe, human being and machine were seen as entwined in a beautiful but deadly embrace, plunging upward in a spiral of destruction. The machine generates velocity, humanity and machine in motion generate war, and war turns on its creators, destroying them. Chaos, for the futurists, was humankind's ultimate triumph. From the passage just cited, it is clear that D'Annunzio feared most what futurism exalted: motion in itself, the revitalization of human nature through self-sufficient action.

In D'Annunzio, mythical knowledge has for its object a Tradition of things sacred and mysterious, which constitute the essential core of an elitist fraternity of devotees. To act is to act for something, according to the traditional means/end prerogative. For futurism, knowing involves the destruction of traditional object symbols and their replacement with the symbols of the machine age. The conceptual similiarities between the two cultural projects is based in the common desire to attain—Julius Evola, fascism's high priest of "spiritual" racism, once declared—"per via di simboli ad una percezione di quell'ordine uperstorico nel quale la natura e lo stesso uomo sono, per così dire, allo stato di creazione e che dunque, tra l'altro, contiene il segreto delle energie che agiscono dietro e dentro le cose visibili e la corporeità umana."[8] [by means of symbols the perception of that superhistorical order in which nature and humankind itself are, as it were, at the state of creation and which, therefore, contains the secret energies acting behind and within visible things and human corporeality].

D'Annunzio's concept of Tradition and the mythical thinking on which it is founded allow the reader to experience life in opposition to its rationalization under capitalism. We are aggressively compensated for a market system whose logic stresses quantity, fragmentation, degradation of human value and activity, and the desacralization of objects. By means of the creation of mythical texts where on practically every page we are made to savor ideas and feelings that resist quantification and where we encounter objects to which a sacred essence has been restored, D'Annunzio carries out what has been described by Frederic Jameson as "the libidinal transformation of an increasingly dessicated and repressive reality."[9] To most readers, however, it all amounts to mystification, although a kind of mystification that resists becoming profane. D'Annunzio's aesthetic gestures, his myths of regeneration, appear useless because they cannot be placed in the service of immediate sociopolitical objectives without losing their deep ritualistic significance.[10] No doubt, D'Annunzio's thematics of heroism and brutality were brought down to earth by fascism, but only at the expense of desacralizing them, of contaminating the purity of their inspiration.

It would be wrong, therefore, to take the instances of gratuitous brutality in D'Annunzio too literally and to assimilate them to the utilitarian brutality employed by the fascist squads. In D'Annunzio, brutality, especially the gratuitous brutality of the sexual act, is best understood as a metaphor for death, a reenactment of the Freudian Thanatos. It is the death of desire that Tradition teaches us to approach religiously through commemoration: "Così l'Antico m'insegnò la commemorazione della morte in modo consentaneo alla mia natura, affinché io trovassi un pregio più raro e un significato più grave nelle cose a me prossime" (2:410). [The Ancient taught me the commemoration of death in a way suitable to my nature, in order that I might find a value more meaningful and rare in the things near to me] (26). The quotation, taken from the first book of *Le vergini delle rocce*, signals the protagonist's movement toward rebirth, toward the Imaginary, the domain of images in which the wish for some ultimate fulfillment, unavailable in the everyday real world of Eros, can be realized.

Death's triumph, then, sets us in the direction of a world of aesthetic perfection where the mysterious, demonic power of Style rules supreme: "[L'Antico] mi comunicò infine la sua fede nel demoniaco; il quale non era se non la potenza misteriosamente significativa dello Stile non violabile da alcuno e neppur da lui medesimo nella sua persona mai" (2:410). [The Ancient finally communicated his faith to me in the demonic; which was nothing else but the mysteriously effective power of Style, undefilable, not even by him himself in his own person] (27). Hence, Claudio Cantelmo's quest for a reality that transcends itself, his return to a race on the verge of extinction, to the libidinal space of death, suggests that art and race form an indestructible unity.

It is only in this phantom realm of the Imaginary that desire can be finally put to rest. The desire to father the future king of Rome generates the form that exasperates that very desire by becoming an all-inclusive principle of gratification. Claudio never performs the material act of generation, which is only an imaginative possibility. The three virgins are beyond possession. As aesthetic figurations, they evoke the plenitude achieved in the death of desire, while, simultaneously, the wishful impulse for nonreified experience carries the burden of knowing its own antithesis: "Una grande tristezza e una grande dolcezza cadevano dall'alto nella chiostra solitaria, come una bevanda magica in una coppa rude. Quivi riposarono le tre sorelle, quivi io raccolsi la loro ultima armonia" (2:567). [A great sadness and a great sweetness fell from on high into the solitary cloister, like a magic drink in a coarse bowl. In this spot the three sisters rested, and in this spot I captured their ultimate harmony] (296).

This puts us in a better position to understand the archaic and regressive in D'Annunzio, particularly the thematics of race and its complementary motifs of blood rituals and sacrifice. In an increasingly subjective and psychologized world of relativized values, where individuals coexist as one among many fragments, where one becomes the slave of mechanization, and where the petty aristocracy entertains ever fewer privileges, the model of a presocial tribe whose members are connected integrally by blood and race constitutes an important libidinal device. The myth of race is at once a principle of wholeness and hierarchy (antithetical to fragmentation and relativity) and a reserve of vitality and new energies. Tribal warfare as, say, in *Gli idolatri* serves two basic functions: it prevents the disintegration of the racial community that is sacred by virtue of the violence it propagates, and it shows that ritual violence is a kind of curative procedure because, through vengeance, it compensates for desacralization, restoring the community to health.[11]

Like the author, we, as readers, are simultaneously frightened and fascinated by the brutality and barbarism. We are frightened because we cannot help but transpose tribal conflict into class struggle. We are attracted to the violence precisely because it is ritualistic: that is, purified of all pragmatic impulses, justifiable because it is sacred. Hence, D'Annunzio must appeal to the socially alienated Other by exhibiting the sacred in his own existence and by harnessing the potential for explosion and, through oratory, directing it toward the conservation of his own livelihood.

The "coppa rude" from which we sip the magic potion of aesthetic transcendence is history itself, that repressed subject that continually erupts into D'Annunzio's narratives in the form of unruly crowds and downtrodden popular masses. Whether confronted with the prosaic reality of urban poverty or the forceful vulgarity of petty merchants at an auction, intent on obtaining "oggetti preziosi a prezzo vile" (1:364) [precious objects at a vile price] or attesting to the desecration of Rome, which has suffered "delle più ignominiose violazioni e dei più osceni connubii che mai abbiano disonorato un luogo sacro" (2:411), [the most shameful profanation and most obscene bawdry that have ever dishonored a sacred place], D'Annunzio's protagonists all reveal their author's deep anxieties over the marginalization of his social and intellectual class. D'Annunzio's attachment to historical reality is most revealed at those moments in which the experience of the impersonal Other elicits a response that exceeds every limit of the objective illusion championed by naturalism, to the extent that the very content of representation becomes the figure of expressionistic reaction. For example, at the outset of *Il piacere*, the memory of ecstasy and amorous transcendence fades abruptly into its opposite when Andrea and Elena stop to quench their thirst in a tavern outside Rome:

Si diressero verso l'osteria romanesca, passato il ponte. Alcuni carrettieri staccavano i giumenti, imprecando ad alta voce. Il chiaror dell'occaso feriva il

gruppo umano ed equino, con viva forza. Come i due entrarono, nella gente
dell'osteria non avvenne alcun moto di meraviglia. Tre o quattro uomini
febbricitanti stavano intorno a un braciere quadrato, taciturni e giallastri. Un
bovaro, di pel rosso, sonnecchiava in un angolo, tenendo ancora la pipa spenta.
Due giovinastri, scarni e biechi, giocavano a carte, fissando negli intervalli con
uno sguardo pieno d'ardor bestiale. E l'ostessa, una femmina pingue, teneva
fra le braccia un bambino, cullandolo pesantemente.

Mentre Elena beveva l'acqua nel bicchiere di vetro, la femmina le mostrava
il bambino, lamentandosi.

— Guardate, Signora mia! Guardate, signora mia!

Tutte le membra della povera creatura erano di una magrezza miserevole;
le labbra violacee erano coperte di punti bianchicci; l'interno della bocca era
coperto come di grumi lattosi. Pareva quasi che la vita fosse di già fuggita da
quel piccolo corpo, lasciando una materia su cui ora le muffe vegetavano.
(1:10–11)

[They headed toward the inn on the other side of the bridge. Some carters
were unharnessing their horses, cursing loudly. The setting sun lit up the
group of men and beasts vividly. The people of the inn showed not the faintest
sign of surprise at the entry of the two strangers. Three or four men shivering
with ague, morose and jaundiced, were crouching round a square brazier. A
red-haired bullock-driver was snoring in the corner, his empty pipe still between his teeth. A pair of haggard, ill-conditioned young vagabonds were
playing at cards, fixing one another in the pauses with a look of beast-like ea-
gerness. The woman of the inn, corpulent to obesity, carried in her arms a
child which she rocked heavily to and fro. While Elena drank the water out of a
glass mug, the woman, with wails and plaints, drew her attention to the infant.

–Look, Signora, look at it!

The poor little creature was wasted to a skeleton, its lips purple and broken
out, the inside of its mouth coated with white spots. It looked like life had
abandoned the miserable little body, leaving but a little substance for fungoid
growths to flourish in.][12]

There are at least three distinct but complementary ways of looking at
this passage. First, it may be seen as an attempt to juxtapose the protagonists' elevated spirituality and the peasants' crude material existence; every
avenue of communication between the two is blocked, except that of instinctual binding. The woman exhibits the dying child to Elena, knowing
that, as a woman, she is capable of sharing her grief. Second, the dying
child intensifies the lovers' passion, because it appears against a back-

ground of dissolution and death. An apocalyptic foreboding of destruction is further conveyed by the images of "la campagna accidentata, simile ad una immensità di rovine" [the tormented countryside, similar to an ocean of ruins] and the "torma di cornacchie" (10) [flock of crows] that passes over Andrea and Elena as they head toward the city. But this episode is worth citing mainly because it may be seen to incorporate a fantasy structure that articulates a politically aggressive impulse, which the narrative attempts to displace. The sympathy for the victim of poverty, expressed in Elena's "povera creatura," legitimates the realistic story line but also conceals the genuine emotion of fear and anxiety motivating the entire episode. D'Annunzio's beastlike peasants harbor a destructive energy. They bear the force of their material conditions and appear ready to erupt, the adjectives used denoting at once their instability and excitability ("febricitanti") and their feverish aspect ("giallastri") caused by malaria.

Unlike his naturalist predecessors, D'Annunzio is unable to contain through objectification the real, historical threat represented by the brutish existence of the peasantry. Proletarian Otherness, instead of being controlled or minimized by irony, is here attacked, denounced as brutal and squalid. Andrea's response to the recollection of such misery is visceral; it is as if a nightmare has suddenly erupted onto the scene of his love fantasy. D'Annunzio introduces the episode with a heightened image of human and equine similarity ("Il chiaror dell'occaso feriva il gruppo umano ed equino, con viva forza"). The human suffering present amid the faceless multitude takes the form of the decay of bodily parts ("le membra... di una magrezza miserevole; le labbra... coperte di punti bianchicci, etc.), culminating in a general image of decomposition ("una materia su cui... le muffe vegetavano"). The two terms that emerge, feverish energy and decay, may be seen to identify a causal hypothesis. The child's anatomy is thus to be taken as a metaphor for an unprotected social body left prey to the rise of barbarism. On this reading, the aesthetic reversal provoked by realistic description justifies the need for the kind of aesthetic transcendence formally expressed at all levels in the novel.

This anxiety of dissolution brings us to the very heart of D'Annunzio's ideological system. One principal feature is the isolation of proletarian Otherness. Within the imaginary reality of aesthetic enchantment and valorization, the world of undifferentiated masses is bracketed, its presence as a social reality contained within frames that are separated out of the authentic narration. The only way the peasantry can work itself into the narrative is through the mythification of its instinctual life. Another feature is the distance between the peasantry and the aesthetic, mediated by the equally resentful presence of such bearers of petty middle-class interests as merchants, shopkeepers, and the kind of spiritual rabble who, at the close of *Il piacere*, like vultures, await the chance to grab the spoils of a defeated aristocracy. In contrast to the downtrodden masses, the bourgeoisie exists as an antinomy within the aesthetic space; it is responsible for the degeneration of the city, because it tolerated and supported the arrogance of the mindless peasantry: "L'arroganza delle plebi non era tanto grande quanto la viltà di coloro che la tolleravano o la secondavano" (2:411). [The arrogance of the popular masses was not as great as the cowardice of those who tolerated and encouraged it].

Finally, the aesthetic is valorized only virtually, as a realm of escape or transcendence, for it cannot efface completely the traces of history present in the form of material decay and degeneration and in the psychological discontinuity exhibited by D'Annunzio's exceptional characters. This brings us to D'Annunzio's ideal of the *Ubermensch* and the existential experience of consciousness as portrayed in the novels.

We can do justice to the notion of elitism, generally summoned to describe D'Annunzio's heroes, only if we understand it not as the spiritual substance of superior individuals but rather as an ideal, a symbolic response to a situation in which the subject becomes aware of its own crisis: the realization of existing as an undifferentiated, isolated entity, deprived of the unitary and synthetic principle of Being. There is no need to rehearse all the instances in which the drama of the divided self is played out in D'Annunzio's novels. This situation has already been amply documented by Vittorio Roda. Nor, as Roda has also shown, is the crisis of the subject in D'Annunzio limited to the individual psyche. In *Il trionfo della morte*, D'Annunzio anticipates an entire tradition of modernist skepticism in representing the crisis of the subject in relation to language.[13]

No doubt, D'Annunzio's depersonalized subjects are, in the main, thematic constructs; their lack of substance is literally a pretext for the mythic and aesthetic totalities described above. Unlike the characters in Pirandello, where the crisis of the subject appears, paradoxically, as genuine reality, transcendable only through epiphanic dissolution, D'Annunzio's divided selves are equipped with the powers of poetic self-creation. They refuse to accept as theirs the fragmentary, approximate expressive codes, which, for a writer like Pirandello, were the empty shells of existence, deadweights trapping us in unwanted forms. Instead, D'Annunzio's heroes describe the crisis of the individual subject but refuse to speak its language. As they form verbally the image of their own discontinuity, they employ the language of poetic regeneration, a code that can never be deciphered, that appeals to our emotions and explores the secrets of the universe.

Take, for example, the authorial commentary on Tullio Hermil's psychological predicament in *L'innocente:* "Silenziose onde di sangue e d'idee facevano fiorire sul fondo stabile del suo essere, a gradi o a un tratto, anime nuove. Egli era *multanime*" (1:394–5). [Silent waves of blood and ideas made new spirits flower, by degrees or all of a sudden, on the stable foundation of his being. He was of multiple souls.] At the thematic level, furthermore, the atomistic fragmentation of the human psyche, instead of fostering a sense of weakness and vulnerabilty as the effect of disorientation and displacement, actually becomes a source of power. The world of illusory appearances, the phenomenal reality that for Pirandello was the prime source of existential insecurity and angst and that necessitated the self-deception of his characters' perpetual masquerades, turns into an occasion for celebrating unlimited creative potential:

> I fenomeni innumerevoli che si succedevano nel suo mondo interiore, d'attimo in attimo, gli facevano apparire illimitata la potenza comprensiva della sua anima. Ed ebbe veramente un singolare incanto per lui quell'ora fugace in cui gli parve di scoprire nascosti rapporti ed analogie segrete tra le rappresentazioni del Caso e il suo sentimento." (1:918).
> [The innumerable phenomena that moved within him from moment to moment made the full power of his spirit seem limitless. The fleeting hour, in which he thought he discovered hidden links and secret analogies between the unfolding of Chance and his feelings, was for him a time of unique enchantment.]

D'Annunzio's practice in this context is to translate irrational discontinuity as a linguistic problem. Secret analogies and hidden relations can be revealed only through an instantaneous perception that contradicts the consequential syntax of logical thought processes. But in contrast to the baroque writers, the world's unlimited correspondences are the object not of the mind's ubiquitous eye but rather of the senses. The *mysterious* is, for D'Annunzio, a corporeal reality that can be explored only through the senses. Niva Lorenzini demonstrates that D'Annunzio's analogies and phonosymbolic imagery depend largely on an intricate process of synaesthetic coupling, a rhetorical preference that allows the poet to forge a unity out of the indefinite and equivocal nature of language—according to Lorenzini's own formula, "to give body to words."[14] Such a stylistic practice has a definite bearing on D'Annunzio's exceptional personalities. As a structural device, the D'Annunzian hero is a source of existential unity, in that he embodies the freedom of the symbolizing power of the mind while asserting the radical priority of the individual subject over the material world. He possesses the power to shape the life of humankind, because he exists above and beyond human relationships. Like the synaesthesis he produces, he brings together within himself a multiplicity of meanings and sensations; he is the individual elevated to the highest degree, the sign of signs.

Yet, this very aspiration to unity and plenitude, no matter how successfully it cancels the traces of fragmentation and conflict characteristic of bourgeois reality, no matter how many devices it employs to dismantle the problematic nature of the intellectual hero, and no matter how inventive it becomes in forging new channels of literary communication—this ideal of transcendence and stability springs from the fear of a dispossession at once psychological and social. In this regard, let us return briefly to *Le vergini delle rocce,* the novel that, from the standpoint of both thematics and structure, represents D'Annunzio's most original attempt at creating a "post-bourgeois" or "post-individualistic" reality.[15]

In the early novels, even where the power of mythical thinking and creative self-assertion is exhibited most forcefully, as in *Il trionfo della morte,* the reinvention of the instinctual and the archaic at the hands of a visionary protagonist takes place within the formal boundaries of naturalist prose and the general thematics of the European psychological novel, in which the literal and the figurative levels of representation, although often intersecting, are kept formally distinct. For example, in *Il trionfo della morte,* Giorgio's escape from a society of common values regulated by ironclad economic laws and his revitalization in nature and through direct contact with primitive ritual and violence are part of a itinerary structured within narrative time and fictional history. The figurative dimension of his experience, as stated in the novel's preface, is the object of the reader's understanding, to be derived from the narrative system, which employs naturalistic form to suggest the possibility, embodied in the figure of the *Ubermensch*, of total regeneration through myth.

In *Le vergini delle rocce*, the distinction between the literal and the figurative disappears completely. The impulse toward organic wholeness dominates at the formal as well as the thematic level. Narration gives way to oratory, intent on demonstration and persuasion. The plot takes on a simplicity unseen in D'Annunzio's previous novels; it sheds every residue of the tension between the real and the ideal that is typical of the bourgeois mind-set, to the extent that it dissolves completely in oration and prophecy. Readers are no longer conceived as terms of dialogue. There is nothing in the novel they can recognize as belonging to their world of prose, no objects, no emotions, no characters with whom they can identify. The novel does not provide the readers with a window out onto a different way of feeling and understanding but presupposes their total formlessness, like that of a newborn child. They are vaulted, without any mediation whatsoever, into an alien reality, beyond history, into the realm of the Imaginary, where life begins and everything is possible.[16]

Within the novel's fantasy structure, possession is the dominant theme. The protagonist begins his exile in Trigento, the land of a race on the verge of extinction, because he has been dispossessed of his civilization. A vicious social plague has taken hold of Rome and transformed the mythical seat of Tradition and Value into a sordid marketplace:

Il contagio si propagava da per tutto, rapidamente. Nel contrasto incessante degli affari, nella furia feroce degli appetiti e delle passioni, nell'esercizio disordinato ed esclusivo delle attività utili, ogni senso di decoro era smarrito, ogni rispetto del Passato era deposto. La lotta per il guadagno era combattuta con un accanimento implacabile, senza alcun freno. Il piccone, la cazzuola e la mala fede erano le armi. E, da una settimana all'altra, con una rapidità quasi chimerica, sorgevano sulle fondamenta riempite di macerie le gabbie enormi e vacue, crivellate di buchi rettangolari, sormontate da cornicioni posticci, incrostate di stucchi obbrobriosi. Una specie d'immenso tumore biancastro sporgeva dal fianco della vecchia Urbe e ne assorbiva la vita. (2:432)

[The contagion spread constantly everywhere. In the incessant contact of business, in the ferocious fury of appetites and passions, in the disordered and exclusive exercise of useful activity, every sense of decorum was lost, every respect for the great Past was laid aside; the struggle for gain was fought with an
implacable spite and frenzy without any restraint. The pick-axe, the trowel and
bad faith were the arms; and from one week to another, with a rapidity almost
chimerical, enormous empty cages, surmounted by false entablatures, en-
crusted with opprobrious stucco and riddled with rectangular holes, arose
upon the rubbish-filled foundations. A species of immense, whitish tumor
came forth from the side of the grand old city and absorbed the life of it.] (66)

But under such advanced conditions of degeneration and decay, the
social body cannot hope to be saved. The disease has progressed, the
prospects for recovery are dim: paradoxically, the patient must die in order
to be reborn. He must renounce within himself the human desire and ambition on which the pestilence of industrial civilization feeds. But since that
is impossible, his only hope is to dream of an impossible redemption. The
fact, then, that the mythical coupling of the protagonist with one of the virgins of Trigento never comes about proves that the quest for plenitude was
known from the first to be illusory and that the collective experience of
epiphany or dream, realized through the agency of the artwork, is the only
means through which the repossession of Culture and Tradition can be
achieved. In other words, the part must suffice for the whole, art for civilization. D'Annunzio, perhaps in spite of himself, has acted out a Hegelian
aesthetic principle. He has overcome the universal by the pure activity of
the individual: "This pure activity, conscious of its inalienable force, wres-
tles with the unembodied essential being. Becoming its master, this negative activity has turned the element of pathos into its own material, and
given itself its content; and this unity comes out as a work, universal spirit
individualized and consciously present."[17]
    The character of Claudio therefore, cannot serve to bring about the
ideal of the *Ubermensch* and to initiate a new cosmic cycle from which
artists can emerge as supreme. Were they to do so, they would be, literally,
casting the seed of their own destruction. In a society of regenerated humanity, of the ideal become real, there would be no need for a religion of
beauty, which can arise only through the force of its negation. This may
explain why D'Annunzio views art primitively, as embodying a sacred

power, the force of a supernatural spirit, like that in a fetish. In the play *La Gioconda,* to cite a paradigmatic instance, Silvia's absent hands (lost in a desperate attempt to save her husband's art from destruction) are symbolic at once of fulfillment and privation, the ever-present, essential terms of D'Annunzio's literary dialectic. D'Annunzio's aestheticism and aspiration toward the sublime, very much like the white sleeves covering Sylvia's mutilation, conceal within themselves the projected reality of their irrevocable loss. The timeless mysteries of existence and arcane lineages, of Beauty and Spectacle, that gave substance to the landed aristocracy's privileged existence have been forfeited by the advent of bourgeois rule. Art can exist only in the form of an absent object, the thing possessed by a subject that has disappeared into nature in order to become myth, sensation, music, and legend.

In concluding, we must address the question of D'Annunzio and fascism. The problem is perhaps best viewed against the historical background of what was at once the most heroic and most aesthetic of all of D'Annunzio's gestures: the taking of the Dalmatian city of Fiume and the genuinely revolutionary climate that action engendered. Fiume, seen as a mythical event, is a supreme example of the new model of energy or libidinal apparatus described above that cuts across all political boundary lines to forge a transnational spirituality of heroic citizen-warriors, devoid of every pragmatic or utilitarian impulse and perpetually nourished by a religious and magical communion, by heroic action and prodigious deeds. Fiume illustrates how D'Annunzio's mythical vision was capable of exploding into history, how it addressed class anxieties and determined the containment of utopian dreams and inchoate fantasies.

In D'Annunzio's mind, the raid on Fiume was a prepolitical event, in the sense that it was not determined by practical considerations. The proclaimed annexation of the city was not meant to prove simply that Italy had vindicated her territorial rights and that the liberal state was impotent in deciding the fate of the nation. Instead, the event generated an overarching spiritual reality that summoned together all enslaved peoples of the world in a search for freedom and justice, united against the economic and political interests of the ruling powers. Fiume was beyond ideology; its imperative was not to achieve a settlement but rather to create an existential social reality and generate a compensatory vision of possibility. The mutinous elements of the Italian army who joined the poet in his raid considered themselves a spiritual elite whose heroic action transcended the boundaries separating dream from reality. Together with their *comandante* they repudiated everything that went under the heading of materialism (all the known forms of bourgeois democracy and the conventions and institutions that reflected the capitalist appetite for profit and exploitation). They fought for a mythical, racially cohesive people of workers, whose spirit, rooted in the land, was to be a source of inspiration for all the "weak" peoples and nations of the world.

D'Annunzio's Fiume denounced politics in favor of a new lyrical order that signaled the beginning of a new age of regenerated humanity. Within this libidinal utopia, humanity was free from all forms of dependence resulting from a social order based on class distinctions. Here worker-producers replaced bourgeois citizens; their freedom consisted in the experience of individuality within the plenitude of collective harmony. D'Annunzio's Fiume was a kind of fantasy text, the momentary realization of utopia in the affirmation of poetic imagination. It mesmerized the generally apolitical petit bourgeois intelligentsia, fascinated, as Gramsci once remarked, by genius and the spirit of adventure, for it offered them a channel of mobility capable of defeating its collective condition of displacement and isolation from the structure of organized society.[18]

Emergent fascism embraced D'Annunzio's adventure wholeheartedly but deprived it of its genuinely mythical substance. Mussolini pressed the myths on which it was founded into the service of power politics, class privilege, and political realism, and, as had futurism after its initial revolutionary impetus, D'Annunzianism collapsed, surrendering the logic of its myth structure to the very thing it so forcefully opposed: the glorification not of the people but of the state; and D'Annunzio, dejected by the course of events, retired to Gardone to resume his literary activity.

D'Annunzio, unlike many of his followers, was not a fascist and actually remained until his death anchored to the utopian beliefs that inspired the raid on Fiume. But this fact is of less importance to us than the very positive effect that his brand of mythical knowledge had on the lower, upwardly mobile stratum of the bourgeoisie, the very class that, denounced in the narratives as vile and fetid, became the base and support of fascist hegemony. To understand how D'Annunzio's mythical texts could appeal to the mentality they ostensibly opposed, we must adjust our focus to include the larger social picture.

Like the other modernisms that came into existence in Italy at the turn of the century, D'Annunzio's, and the D'Annunzian phenomenon in general, has its social and ideological roots in the risorgimento. By and large, the risorgimento was a bourgeois assault on traditional social organization. Its objectives were to open up channels of social mobility and loosen the previously rigid class boundaries. The unification of Italy, however, did not lead to greater upward mobility. From 1861 on, the Italian class structure remained essentially unchanged, as existing political and economic elites maintained their power and privileges and new elites, the industrialists, for example, were created. What mobility did exist on a mass scale may be characterized as basically intraclass, as opposed to interclass: rural peasants became urban menial laborers, artisans became skilled laborers, clerks became small entrepreneurs.

The intellectuals who had worked for the risorgimento were all engaged in searching for a resolution of the "social question": how to create a national popular cultural hegemony and increase socioeconomic equality. They, too, experienced a deflation of their aspirations to mobility in the new Italy. An exemplary case in point is that of Giovanni Verga, whose development as a writer from the early patriotic and explicitly romantic novels to the mature pessimism of the *Novelle rusticane* and *Mastro Don Gesualdo* clearly parallels his experience as a literary artist in society having to cope with the problems of identity, support, and recognition. Through their attack on middle-class institutions and morality, the Milanese *scapigliati*, too, as a group, revealed a collective condition of displacement and isolation from the structure of organized society. Having traded commitment to a channel of mobility that ended in a secure (with respect to the true goals of the risorgimento) patronage for a commitment to succeed "in the real world" (i.e., to establish a genuinely active link between artistic development and social change), the intellectuals then found themselves excluded from the possibility of achieving the status they felt they deserved, as moral and spiritual guide for the nation they were working for. They had turned their backs, to a great extent, on traditional academic aspirations, confident, however, of being able to maintain or even improve their lot in the new order. But unified Italy did not recognize the intellectuals as having special sociopolitical value and therefore meriting privileged treatment, and in this sense the intellectuals found themselves displaced. At the turn of the century, the entire cultural sector in Italy was searching for a strategy to reintegrate the intellectual into society on favorable terms.[19]

In this context, D'Annunzio's art, together with futurism and the major modernistic experiences of Pirandello and Ungaretti, may be viewed from a sociological perspective as a means of creating a new interpretative scheme for ranking members of society, whereby social power ensued upon the fulfillment of certain specific existential qualifications. In the case of D'Annunzio, these qualifications may be summarized by the term *Tradition*, understood in the sense described above as a repository for the mysterious and the arcane. Conflict in society was now between people or groups who valued Tradition and those who did not. In other words, power in society, rather than depending on one's external position in traditional hierarchies, now depended on internal psychic dispositions. The social function of this theoretical device in D'Annunzian ideology was to enable it to circumvent traditional conflicts and tensions between social classes and competing elites and to define a new path upward to social power. D'Annunzio's optic on social hierarchy, which provided him as an intellectual an avenue for realizing a meaningful social mandate, then had to be imprinted on the existing social system: thus the "political" activity embodied in the Fiume adventure.

By identifying D'Annunzio's narrative system as mythical in its operations, we can interpret the relation between it and the historical situation in which it found its motive force and specific ideological configuration. In Italy at the turn of the century, the developing nationalist, irredentist, interventionist and eventually fascist tendencies were all premised on utopian thought forms and employed myths in substantiating the basis of their political projects.

At this point, it is useful to distinguish between myths and utopias as forms of thought. As is evident from the sketch drawn here of D'Annunzio's mythical thinking, myth is, in the last analysis, a determination to act, rather than an intellectual product. Its end is a utopian construct consisting of a combination of imaginary elements constituting a model that can be compared to existing society. The D'Annunzian, like the futurist, utopia is a radical, but nonetheless rational, calculable historical vision.[20] It presupposes a goal that can be achieved, yet since it negates utilitarian expediency as its principal condition, its myths are not technicized, that is, not employed as means for realizing concrete political success. They remain as emblematic forces of destruction and regeneration, agents of a possible transformation of reality, preconditions referring to an empty space, the existential abyss of human consciousness, beyond which stands the image of utopian fulfillment.

The relation between D'Annunzio and fascism, therefore, has to be understood as one between competing mythical systems and competing utopias. They differ in the quality of their respective myth systems but share a common response to the historical problematic of displacement which accounts for D'Annunzio's paradoxically large petit bourgeois readership. D'Annunzio's mythical narratives provided a symbolic response to a concrete historical predicament, to which fascism provided a large-scale political and organizational solution. His defense of Art and Tradition explains the potential usefulness of the undetermined social position of the petite bourgeoisie as a working ideology. Belonging neither to the proletariat, to the classic bourgeoisie nor to big business, the petite bourgeoisie sought the missing totality of its existence in a principle capable of transcending the real political order. Futurism, let it be noted, also provided such a principle in its notion of existence as dynamic process. The futurist solution, however, was grounded in a myth system, based on the overvaluing of technology, that was completely at odds with the real social conditions in which it participated. Because of this, its vitalized imagery, conceived for practical ends, could not take hold among the masses.

D'Annunzio's myth of Tradition and his fascination with race and hierarchy provided a principle of control that, without exceeding the boundaries of tradition, countered the structural instability of the petite bourgeoisie. The link between D'Annunzio's art and fascist ideology must be explored, therefore, at the level of structural correspondences between two myth systems that, although essentially different, function in similar ways. The discontinuity and monadic isolation that defined individuality in the age of capitalist expansion is defeated by D'Annunzio not through any process of social exchange but rather through fusion into mythical categories—the same kind of principles underlying the fascist concept of the State, seen as a spiritual and moral fact in itself, and supported by the mythical notions of nation, people, empire, Rome, youth and race.

CHAPTER FOUR

Luigi Pirandello

Epistemology and Pure Subjectivity

If D'Annunzio's fictions aimed at reinventing tradition, the motivation behind Luigi Pirandello's narrative style was the search for a kind of ideological "dead zone," where words appear as the imprints of some dreadful yet
incommunicable experience. The tradition D'Annunzio celebrated was, for
Pirandello, lost forever, and with it disappeared the sublime mysteries of
existence. In the contemporary industrial world of market capitalism, the
literary artist had now become the chronicler of existential death. The sole
compensation left for humanity was to live inside life's empty shell and
play out arbitrarily assigned roles within the fiction of an eternal present.

Like all roles, however, these required gestures to convey the inaccessible significance of the human condition. Rather than elaborate sentences
created to evoke a past beyond comprehension, Pirandello's gestures are
best described as epistemological. They counterbalance and ultimately
nullify the vacuous imprints of language by generating vitalistic impulses
that reassert human existence from within the prison house of words.[1] Pirandellian epistemology functions to promote mythical thinking: it provides a discursive means whereby the Self is deconstructed to the point of

negation, then reconstructed as perpetual life and authentic being.

By general consensus, Pirandello's last novel, *Uno, nessuno e centomila*,[2] is the work of prose fiction that presents the nucleus of the problem of human identity developed in his plays. Pirandello himself believed that the novel advanced an ideal epistemological itinerary and, thus, should be considered the epitome and summary of his entire literary and dramatic production. As a narrative that charts in detail the disintegration of personality, he regarded it as an exemplary text that harbored the positive side of his vision of life, namely, the notion of self-creation as the unique motive force of existence.[3]

It is not by chance, then, that *Uno, nessuno e centomila* consists largely of the discourses of other Pirandellian characters, including Henry IV and the father in *Sei personaggi,* and the authorial voice of *L'umorismo,* the philosophical essay with the most specific consequences for Pirandello's theater and fiction. Giovanni Macchia has described these subtexts as veritable acts of plagiarism, attributable ultimately to the Pirandellian concept of the decomposable character who can be recycled and reused according to need.[4] No doubt, the intersecting planes of collective moral and psychological reality deprive Pirandello's characters of all status as concrete, individual types endowed with specific, historically recognizable identities. *Uno, nessuno e centomila*'s hero, Vitangelo Moscarda, alias Gengè, has been unseated as a traditional narrative subject and resituated in terms of his subjection to the Other. With this new definition of the Self as the Other, of the "one" as "a hundred thousand" and, therefore, as "none," Pirandello questions the certitude of the subject as conceived by modern metaphysics. The truth of Being exists not in its reality but in its possibility. Being is representable only as the "can be," the subject only as a hypothesis, the abstract possibility of Being. In this sense, *Uno, nessuno e centomila* is at once the masterscript of the phenomenology of self-creation and a program for exploring the paradoxical logic that underlies Pirandello's theater.

When asked to comment on the significance of Moscarda's predicament, Pirandello replied: "La realtà, io dico, siamo noi che ce la creiamo: ed è indispensabile che sia così. Ma guai a fermarti in una sola realtà; in essa si finisce per soffocare, per atrofizzarsi, per morire. Bisogna invece variarla, mutarla continuamente, continuamente mutare e variare la nostra illu-

sione."[5] [Reality, I say, it is we who create it. But beware of attaching yourself to only one reality; for you end up suffocating in it, wasting away,
dying. So we must vary it and change it continually, continually change
and vary our illusion.] This representation of human existence is at one
and the same time a philosophical dictum, applicable to all of Pirandello's
mature work and another instance of unspecified quotation. Pirandello has
taken the words just cited directly from Moscarda, but they could well be
the thoughts of any number of his characters. What is significant for us is
not the mimicking or self-plagiarizing in itself that constitutes, as Macchia
puts it, the "grande, interminabile monologo pirandelliano" (51) [the great,
interminable Pirandellian monologue] but rather the ideological effects of
such an outlook on a narrative conceived as both the synopsis and com-
pendium of the playwright's art.

The semantic peculiarity of Pirandello's remarks is their obsessive character. Within a conceptual frame typical of philosophical irrationalism (reality as vital flux, indefinite movement, forceful volition, etc.), we find a
dominant connotation of dread and fear. "Soffocare" [to suffocate], "atrofizzarsi" [to waste away], "morire" [to die] are the syntagmas of the pathological, if not schizophrenic, language with which Pirandello conveys
mankind's laborious struggle for self-verification. What can be deduced
from Moscarda's experience is that human identity does not evolve from
genetic or social predispositions, nor is it conditioned by historical factuality. Being oneself does not amount to the realization of one's innate potential. Instead, the personal identity of the Self is an object to be created.
Man's constructed identity, then, can be seen to converge with the Pirandellian ideal of a humanity devoid of social masks and of a subjectivity that
has not been contaminated by history precisely because it is an aesthetic
construct. As such, it is an ideal consistent with the aestheticization of
collective political life that emerging fascism advanced as a means of
purifying, thus exonerating, the violence and exploitation it fostered. In
this sense, Pirandellian epistemology can be viewed as an ideological act
far more relevant to the political reality of the times than D'Annunzio's
utopian appeal to Race and Tradition.

Over the years, Pirandello criticism has drawn attention to the enormous importance of the mirror in determining Moscarda's outlook. Gian
Paolo Biasin was among the first to argue that Moscarda's genuinely exis-

tential variety of alienation begins in front of the mirror, where he discovers that knowing himself is synonymous with dying.[6] This accounts for Moscarda's renouncement of self-knowledge, thus eliminating the possibility that the thought process could fill the void created by the dismantling of illusion. According to Biasin, Moscarda therefore "rifiuta la sua 'maschera', tutto ciò che è personale, con l'azione opposta a quella da cui la sua storia aveva avuto inizio" (62) [rejects his own "mask," all that is personal, with an operation the reverse of that with which his story had begun].

Moreover, for Biasin, Moscarda's mirror carries out a social function because it is the means through which the reader is made to dwell on the alienating reality of society: "Capovolgendo il termine pazzia in quello di coscienza Moscarda denuncia i rigidi schemi in cui la realtà borghese delimita il comportamento sociale" (63). [Transposing madness into consciousness, Moscarda denounces the rigid limitations that bourgeois reality places on social behavior.] Thus, the theme of madness interests Pirandello not as reference to mental illness but rather as the "affascinante, imperscrutabile lato notturno dell'uomo, presente in potenza in ognuno e pronto sempre a far crollare le costruzioni su cui si regge l'idea stessa della società umana" (55) [fascinating, impenetrable dark side of man, virtually present in every one and always ready to bring down the foundation on which the very idea of human society rests].

Renato Barilli, in more or less the same way, has attempted to couch in economic terms the relation between Moscarda's mirror and his social polemics: "All'atto dello specchiarsi è affidato soprattutto un ruolo negativo: quello di uscir fuori, di estraniarsi dalle parti artificiali in cui siamo collocati: dall'esercizio dell'avere . . . per avvicinarsi piuttosto a quello dell'essere."[7] [The act of seeing oneself in the mirror is given the largely negative function of disaffection and alienation from the artificial dimensions of life: from the operations of having . . . in order to acquaint us with those of being.] The mirror, for Barilli, reflects our false spontaneity and the character we have constructed in order to meet the utilitarian demands of everyday life. Pirandello's purpose, Barilli concludes, is to contest the logic of possession and, thus, to move in the direction of an absolute freedom of Being, which means becoming an integral part of the vital flux of life.

Common to both interpretations is the emphasis placed on the subversive aspect of Pirandello's discourse on madness.[8] Moscarda's cognitive eccentricity, his idiosyncratic and frenetic desire to confirm his identity, are undoubtedly part and parcel of Pirandello's polemics against the traditionally conceived subjectivity of the bourgeois individual. The novel's diaristic structure, furthermore, serves as a paradoxical complement to the disintegration of what was once conceived to be a monadic, self-contained individual, made to plunge headlong into dissolution. From a purely narrative standpoint, however, it would be hard to make a case for the novel as a vehicle of social protest. At the story's conclusion, the reality of bourgeois existence, despite Moscarda's laborious attempts to overcome it epistemologically, offers in effect no way out. The bourgeois model of subjectivity, once deconstructed, is, in turn, reconstituted. This reformation (or "creation") of Moscarda is what Pirandello believes to be the novel's positive side, that is to say, its hopeful and comforting message.

In other words, Pirandello's language of antibourgeois protest is an epistemological attack on the bourgeoisie' existence in history; it strikes to the heart of its mode of perception and its moral and ethical prerogatives. But once decomposed, that same existence is refounded and newly articulated in ahistorical, absolute terms. The ideology embedded in Moscarda the character's schizoid behavior becomes more significant when seen in the light of the philosophical glosses provided by Moscarda the narrator. The absolute freedom of Being, which presupposes the total absence of an objective dimension to existence, cannot be realized except as a fiction; if taken literally as a rule of thumb for life, it is, by definition, madness.

To avoid the difficulties involved in the acceptance of Moscarda's discourse as a literal transcription of experience, it is useful to focus less on the protagonist's story and more on its mode of telling. The story of Moscarda's paradoxical identity begins when, in the guise of narrator, he recalls that one day, as he was looking at himself in the mirror, his wife happened to remark that his nose slants a bit to the right. This apparently innocent and playful comment triggered the anxiety Moscarda defines as his affliction; "quel male che doveva ridurmi in breve in condizione di spirito e di corpo così misere e disperate che certo ne sarei morto o impazzito, ove in esso medesimo avessi trovato (come dirò) il rimedio che doveva guarirmene" (742). [that affliction, which had to reduce me in little time, physically and mentally, to such a miserable and desperate condition, to the point where I would have no doubt died or gone mad had I not found (as I

shall explain), in that very ill, the remedy which was to cure me of it].
What is noteworthy in this passage is that the voice of the narrator does
not originate from without, except when, at a time concurrent to his recollection and writing, he declares himself recovered. Thus, Pirandello's reconstruction of Moscarda's life follows a linear path and gains in intensity
the more it is commented on philosophically as a universal truth.

In the account Moscarda gives of his life, two structural preoccupations
seem to dominate. First, there is the subject's position as the object of
analysis and the continual reiteration and verification of the radically divergent relationship between the "I" of the narrator-protagonist and the
"you" of the others to whom Moscarda addresses his discourse. Second is
the authorial intervention whereby the narrator's endangered subjectivity
is empowered, thus recovered temporally, by means of the division of his
discourse into brief segments ("capitoletti"). Such a technique allows Pirandello to juxtapose existential chaos to philosophical reasoning.

In the articulation of these two structural features, Pirandello relates the
condition we ourselves create when we begin to reflect on the origins of
our experience. When, like Moscarda, we employ our reason to understand
how we exist in relation to others, we see the objective basis of knowledge
to be a chaos devoid of sense. We look into the void at the risk of either
dying or going mad. The death referred to is existential death, and the
madness, a state of ontological insecurity derived from depersonalization.
The terms are interchangeable. They carry the phenomenological burden
of being-in-the-world: namely, that the phenomena of everyday experience do not reveal true Being; from a psychological standpoint, they depict
the loss of the self and the entry into the realm of dream and fantasy, into
the kind of perpetual masquerade, exemplified by Moscarda, of which the
theatrical stage is a powerful allegory. In both structural characteristics, we
can locate the humoristic decomposition of reality, whereby the incongruities of a particular system (in this case, Moscarda's everyday life) are
revealed.

Moscarda's story emphasizes difference by illustrating the fact that his
life is a fiction created by others. Consistent with Pirandello's philosophy
of humor, Moscarda decomposes his own image of Self, which gives him a
glimpse of nothingness (his naked mask). But what prevents Moscarda
from directly confronting the reality of the void he has uncovered, from

falling into the abyss, as it were, is, in effect, his own philosophical discourse or humoristic epistemology. By standing back and commenting on his affliction, Moscarda exercises control over chaos; paradoxically, he gives chaos form, by taking possession of the primordial flux of life and, thus, filling his existential void with a new logic or dialectic of doubt. These formal characteristics regulate the complex Pirandellian thematics of seeing oneself live. "Già subito mi figurai che tutti, avendone fatta mia moglie la scoperta, dovessero accorgersi di quei miei difetti corporali e altro non notare in me. . . . Mi si fissò . . . il pensiero che io non ero per gli altri quel che finora, dentro di me, m'ero figurato di essere" (743–42). [I at once imagined that everybody, since my wife had made the discovery, must be aware of those same bodily defects and notice nothing else about me except them. . . . [The thought struck me . . . that I was no longer for others what up until now I had pictured myself as being.]

Moscarda's remarks, uttered immediately before the beginning of the mirror game, mark two crucial stages of his malaise: first, the moment in which he begins attending to the gaze of other; second, the moment he realizes that others do not share his vision of himself. They point not only to Moscarda's awareness of being the object of another's attention but, more important, to the apprehensive, if not obsessive, nature of that realization. Moscarda is prepossessed by the thought that his body has become a thing for others to peruse: "[Gli imposi il mio naso] a una ferma e attenta osservazione, come se quel difetto del mio naso fosse un irreparable guasto sopravvenuto al congegno dell'universo" (742). [(I imposed my nose on him) so he could examine it carefully, just as if those defects in it represented an irreparable fault in the mechanism of the universe.] Moscarda's initial encounters with the reality of alienation reveal the sense he has of being always visible and, therefore, his fear of being penetrated by the Other's gaze, hence, his vulnerability. To make himself invulnerable, he goes on to objectify his obsession.

This puts us in the position of understanding Moscarda's predicament as the discourse of a schizoid personality, which can be decoded by using the model provided by R. D. Laing in *The Divided Self*.[9] Moscarda's desire to solicit the look of the Other is a sign of his desire to be the center of the Other's attention. In order to dominate, he places his self in a tactical position. At the same time, his desire to hold sway over others is accompanied by guilt and anxiety, a factor that necessitates (and justifies) the humoristic distance assumed in recounting his experience.

Given the unique character of the event that leads Moscarda to take inventory of his entire being, it is legitimate to suppose that its antecedent, or pre-text, is the failed attempt on Moscarda's part to acquire a sense of his own identity. To become aware of himself and to know that others are aware of his existence is a way of defending himself against the dangers implicit in the real absence of identity. If Moscarda were truly "no one" in the clinical sense of schizophrenia, it is unlikely that he could commit himself to the project of recovery.[10]

In recounting his story, Moscarda begins from an extreme point of ontological insecurity not far from the dreaded state of non being (existential death or madness). In the course of his narration, he satisfies his need to assert the concrete fact that he is alive and real by considering himself an object of his own perception. From this derives the functional importance of the mirror.

Moscarda poses the following problem to himself: since he is not in the eyes of others what he is for himself, who is he really? His dilemma is that while he is *living*, he cannot see how he appears to others; and if he stops to look at himself in the mirror, he does not see himself *living*. For capturing being in one particular image deprives it of all its vitality and spontaneity. So Moscarda, in his quest for self-knowledge, is condemned to the futile pursuit of his own image, thus to a life of narcissistic and exhibitionistic behavior:

> andare inseguendo quell'estraneo ch'era in me e che mi sfuggiva; che non potevo fermare davanti a uno specchio perchè subito diventava me quale io mi conoscevo; quell'uno che viveva per gli altri e che io non potevo conoscere, che gli altri vedevano vivere e io no. . . . [Nello specchio] volevo sorprendermi nella naturalezza dei miei atti, nelle subitanee alterazioni del volto, per ogni moto dell'animo. . . . L'idea che gli altri vedevano in me uno che non ero io quale mi conoscevo; uno che essi soltanto potevano conoscere guardandomi da fuori con occhi che non erano i miei e che mi davano un aspetto destinato a restarmi sempre estraneo, pur essendo in me, pur essendo il mio per loro . . . ; una vita nella quale, pur essendo la mia per loro, io non potevo penetrare, quest'idea non mi diede più requie. (750–52)
> [to go in pursuit of that stranger who was inside of me and who escaped my

grasp; whom I couldn't stop in front of a mirror because he immediately became me as I saw myself; that one person who lived for others and whom I could not know; whom others saw live and I didn't. . . . (By looking in the mirror) I wanted to surprise myself in the spontaneity of my actions, in the sudden changes of facial expression caused by every fluctuation of emotion. . . . The idea that others saw in me a person that was not the me I knew; the person that only they could know, looking at me from without with eyes that were not my own and that gave me an aspect of myself destined to remain always alien, inspite of being in me, inspite of being mine for them . . . ; a life in which, inspite of being my life for them, I could never penetrate, this thought kept me forever disturbed.]

But Moscarda's obsession with seeing himself as he appears objectively is already a sign that his self has become an invisible and transcendent entity, knowable only to itself. His being-in-the-world does not verify unequivocally the presence of his self, which does not reside in his body but instead, like a phantasm, exists separated from it, present everywhere but nowhere in particular.

Moscarda's quest is a vicious circle. His reality depends on the possibility of his being seen and recognized by the Other, while at the same time the Other constitutes an insuperable threat to his identity. To resolve this dilemma, he embarks on a series of complex and subtle experiments designed to safeguard his most intimate self. Again in front of the mirror:

Andai, con gli occhi chiusi, le mani avanti, a tentoni. Quando toccai la lastra dell'armadio, ristetti ad aspettare, ancora con gli occhi chiusi, la più assoluta calma interiore, la più assoluta indifferenza. Ma una maladetta voce mi diceva dentro, che era là anche lui, l'*estraneo*, di fronte a me, nello specchio. . . . Non mi vedeva neanche lui, purchè aveva come me, gli occhi chiusi. . . . Era per me quel che io ero per gli altri, che potevo essere veduto e non vedermi. Aprendo gli occhi però, *lo* avrei veduto così come un altro? . . . M'era accaduto tante volte d'infrontar gli occhi per caso nello specchio con qualcuno che stava a guardarmi nello specchio stesso. Io nello specchio non mi vedevo ed ero veduto; così l'altro, non si vedeva, ma vedeva il mio viso e si vedeva guardato da me. . . . Finchè tengo gli occhi chiusi, siamo due: io qua e lui nello specchio. Debbo impedire che, aprendo gli occhi, egli diventi me e io lui. Io debbo vederlo e non essere veduto. E possibile? Subito come io lo vedrò, egli mi vedrà, e ci riconosceremo. Ma grazie tante! Io non voglio riconocermi; io voglio conoscere lui fuori di me. E possibile? Il mio sforzo supremo deve consistere in questo: di non vedermi *in me*, ma d'essere veduto *da me*, con gli occhi miei stessi ma come se fossi un altro: quell'altro che tutti vedono, ma io no. (754–55)

I went ahead, my eyes shut, my arms outstretched, groping. When I touched the glass of the armoire, still with my eyes closed, I waited until I was absolutely calm and indifferent. But within me a damned voice kept saying that even he, the *stranger*, was there in front of me, in the mirror. . . . He didn't see me either because, like mine, his eyes were closed. . . . He was for me what I was for others, because I could be seen and not see myself. But opening my eyes, would I be able to see *him* as if he were another? . . . Many times it happened that my eyes would encounter in the mirror the eyes of someone looking at me in that very same mirror. In the mirror I didn't see myself and I was seen; in the same way, the other didn't see himself but saw my face, and he saw himself looked at by me. . . . As long as I keep my eyes closed, there are two of us: I, here, and he, in the mirror. I have to prevent that, opening my eyes, he becomes me, and I him. I have to see him and not be seen by him. Is it possible? As soon as I see him, he will see me, and we will recognize each other. But thanks! I don't want to recognize myself; I want to know him outside of me. Is it possible? My supreme task consists in this: not to see myself *in me*, but to be seen *by me*, with my own eyes, but as if I were another: that other that every one sees, except me.]

In terms of this mirror game, such an existential dilemma reveals the subject's inordinate preoccupation with his own visibility. And from his own craving to see himself derives his fear of being the object of the Other's knowledge and thus being exposed (made visible) to the enemy who stands ready to divest him of his being. Therefore, the phenomenology of the mirror turns out to be less a symbol of the subject's depersonalization than a strategy that makes out of depersonalization a mechanism of defense. Placing himself continually in front of the mirror is nothing more than a way of taking control of a potentially dangerous situation by transforming it into play. Moscarda's metacritical reflections, transcribed in italics at the end of the novel's first book, summarize the protagonist's real predicament. Against the assault of the Other, neither being seen nor being invisible is sufficient. Only the continual exibition of self, a sign of Moscarda's wish for depersonalization, can provide the therapy necessary to strengthen his security:

Io non ero per gli altri quel che finora avevo creduto d'essere per me; io non potevo vedermi vivere; non potendo vedermi vivere, restavo estraneo a me stesso, cioè uno che gli altri potevano vedere e conoscere; ciascuno a suo modo; e io no; era impossibile pormi davanti questo estraneo per vederlo e conoscerlo; io potevo vedermi, non già vederlo; il mio corpo . . . era per me come un'apparizione di sogno; una cosa che non sapeva di vivere e che restava lì, in attesa che qualcuno se la prendesse; come me lo prendevo io, questo mio corpo, per essere a volta a volta quale mi volevo e mi sentivo, così se lo poteva prendere qualunque altro per dargli una realtà a modo suo; quel corpo per se stesso era tanto niente e tanto nessuno, che un filo d'aria poteva farlo starnutire. (759)

[I was not for others what I had till then believed I was for myself; I could not see myself live; being unable to see myself live, I remained an outsider to myself, namely one whom the others could see and know, each in his own way; and I couldn't; it was impossible for me to confront this outsider, to see him and know him; I could see myself, but could not see him; my body . . . was like an apparition in a dream, unaware that it was alive, waiting to be taken by someone; just as I took this body of mine to be as I wanted myself, so it could be taken by anyone else who would give it a reality in his own fashion; this body in itself was so much a nothing and a nobody that a puff of air could make it sneeze.]

At the root of Moscarda's sophistic reasoning lies a psychoanalytical reality of considerable import, namely, his fixation with being invisible ("io non potevo vedermi vivere") or disappearing ("in attesa che qualcuno se lo prendesse . . . questo mio corpo"). The account Moscarda gives us of his past, particularly of his relationship with his father, supplies the reasons for the vulnerability he converts into ontological insecurity. What characterizes his relationship with his father is his inability to understand the obscure meaning of his father's gaze:

E nei limpidi vitrei occhi azzurini il solito sorriso gli brillava per me, d'una strana tenerezza, ch'era un po' compatimento, un po' derisione anche, ma affettuosa, come se in fondo gli piacesse ch'io fossi tale da meritarmela, quella sua derisione. . . . Quella tenerezza per me, nascosto, m'appariva ora orribilmente maliziosa: tante cose mi svelava a un tratto che mi fendevano di brividi la schiena. Ed ecco, *lo sguardo di quegli occhi mi teneva affascinato* per impedirmi di pensare a queste cose, di cui era fatta la sua tenerezza per me, ma che pure erano orribili. (790; italics mine)

[And in his limpid, almost glassy, pale blue eyes, there shone for me his usual smile, a strangely tender smile, with a hint of compassion in it, a trace of derision as well, but affectionate, as if in the final analysis he was glad that I was the sort of son to deserve his derisiveness. . . . That hidden tenderness for me now appeared horribly malicious, so many things it at once revealed to me that sent shivers up my spine. And yet *the stare of those glassy eyes held me fascinated* in such a way as to prevent my thinking of those things that went to make up his tenderness in my regard, but that were nonetheless horrible.]

The ambiguity of his father's gaze makes Moscarda question the true nature of his father's love, and since his own identity is inextricably connected to that gaze, the hostility he senses there but that he does not thoroughly comprehend returns later in life in the form of an ontological conflict between the Self and the Other. The resurfacing of the conflict is symbolically realized in front of the mirror, which, with the disappearance of the father, becomes the only possible source of Moscarda's identity:

Davanti al padre sentii . . . tutto lo sgomento delle necessità cieche, delle cose che non si possono mutare: la prigione del tempo; il nascere ora, e non prima e non poi; il nome e il corpo che ci ha dato. . . . E sentiamo la nostra vita come lacerata tutta, meno che in un punto per cui resta attaccata ancora a quell'uomo. E questo punto è vergognoso. La nostra nascita staccata, recisa da lui, come un caso comune, forse previsto, ma involontario nella vita di quell'estraneo, prova d'un gesto, frutto d'un atto, alcunchè insomma che ora, sì, ci fa vergogna, ci suscita sdegno e quasi odio. E se non propriamente odio, un certo acuto dispetto notiamo anche negli occhi di nostro padre, che in quell'attimo si sono scontrati nei nostri. . . . Quel seme gettato ch'egli non sapeva, ritto ora in piedi e con due occhi fuoruscenti di lumaca che guardano a tentoni e giudicano e gl'impediscono d'esser ancora in tutto a piacer suo, libero, *un altro* anche rispetto a noi. (792–93).
[In front of my father I felt . . . all the terror of blind necessity, of things that cannot change: the prison of time; being born now, and not before or after; the name and the body he has given us. . . . And we feel our life as if all torn apart, save for a point for which it remains attached to that man. And that point is a shameful one. Our birth, detached, cut off from him, as a common case, was possibly foreseen, and yet it was an involuntary thing in the life of that stranger, the proof of a deed, the result of an action, something, in short, that now, yes, causes us shame, arousing in us contempt and almost hatred. And if not exactly hatred, there is a certain sharp contempt that we note even in our father's eyes, that in that moment happened to meet our own. . . . That seed which he unknowingly sowed, now erect on his feet and with two snaillike bug

eyes that stealthily look him over and judge him and prevent him from being wholly what he would like to be, free, *an other* even with respect to us.]

It becomes all the more evident that not seeing himself live is a strategy employed by Moscarda to ward off his real fear of being invisible, a fear that grew with his father's death and that now he has recast into the image of his own death, that is, of the *Other* that steals his self. In orthodox Freudian terms, Moscarda has taken hold of the anxiety deriving from his fear of nonbeing through the repetition, either in the form of outright play or humoristic detachment, of his discourse on invisibility. In other words, being invisible is one and the same as taking cover or disguising oneself as a means of defending against the imaginary aggression of the Other. Hence to emphasize, as criticism has done, Moscarda's existential anxiety and his desire to go beyond the temporal and spacial limitations of his condition, although no doubt true, adds nothing to what the narrating voice endeavors to have us understand.[11] Instead, if Moscarda's wish to escape from his reality is taken as a symptom of his desire not to be seen, it is thoroughly consistent with the hero's ultimate point of arrival, namely, his epiphany. It is here, in the novel's final paragraph, that we find the meaning of the subject's circuitous intellectual rambling. Moscarda is at the end of his rope. His anguish has led to his ruin and he must now withdraw from life. His retreat to a hospice for the mentally ill indicates his repudiation of the world over which he has lost his power. His dialectic has canceled all objective reference, save that of his name. Now, it too, must be effaced:

Non è altro che questo, epigrafe funeraria, un nome. Conviene ai morti. A chi ha concluso. Io sono vivo e non concludo. La vita non conclude. E non sa di nomi, la vita. Quest'albero, respiro tremulo di foglie nuove. Sono quest'albero. Albero, nuvola; domani libro o vento: il libro che leggo, il vento che bevo. Tutto fuori, vagabondo. . . . Pensare alla morte, pregare. C'è pure chi ha ancora questo bisogno; perchè muoio ogni attimo, io, e rinasco nuovo e senza ricordi: vivo e intero, non più in me, ma in ogni cosa fuori (901–2).

[A name is nothing but an epigraph on a grave. Something for the dead. I am alive, and I do not conclude. Life does not conclude. Life knows nothing of names. This tree, tremulous pulse of new leaves. I am this tree. Tree, cloud; tomorrow, book or wind: the book I read, the wind I drink. All outside, wandering. . . . There are still people who need to think about death and to pray. I die at every instant, and I am reborn, new and without memories: live and whole, no longer inside myself, but in everything outside.]

Here, Pirandello describes a condition of pure subjectivity, whereby the Self, existing outside of time and space, is everything. Moscarda speaks the paradoxical language of schizoid fantasy, according to which living is equivalent to self-annihilation. By merging with the landscape, Moscarda forfeits his individual autonomy, and, by losing that self that the scrutiny of others puts into question, he accomplishes the paradoxical task of evading non-being by eluding Being.

Like his more tragic counterpart, Henry IV, Moscarda has willed his own exile to the realm of the inessential, achieving being as absolute possibility. Like Henry IV, he is always the Other, never himself, always neutral and impersonal; not what anyone sees but rather an abstraction of unlimited but altogether abstract possibility. But unlike Henry IV, Moscarda does not realize that true pretense may consist in the act of pretending and that in effect he has fallen into the very state of nonbeing he so vigorously tried to avoid. Such a condition was, in fact, inevitable from the moment he renounced his objective existence. For if non being is equivalent to Being, the desire for absolute freedom outside of society leads him, paradoxically, to the abrogation of all liberty.[12]

Having cast Moscarda's rebellion in these terms, let us now turn to his actions, because, from a narrative standpoint, only through what he actually does (as opposed to his thinking) can he achieve his desired state of being a pure subject. Why does Moscarda act, instead of remaining isolated within the fortress of his dialectic? Let us consider briefly his reflections on acting:

> Quando un atto è compiuto, è quello; non si cangia più. Quando uno comunque abbia agito, anche senzache poi si senta e si ritrovi negli atti compiuti, ciò che ha fatto, resta come una prigione per lui. . . . Compiamo un atto. Crediamo in buona fede d'esser tutti in quell'atto. Ci accorgiamo purtroppo che non è così, e che l'atto è invece sempre e solamente dell'uno dei tanti che siamo o che possiamo essere, quando, per un caso sciaguratissimo, all'improviso vi restiamo come agganciati e sospesi: ci accorgiamo, voglio dire, di non essere tutti in quell'atto, e che dunque un'atroce ingiustizia sarebbe giudicarsi da quello solo, tenerci agganciati e sospesi a esso, alla gogna, per un'intera esistenza, come se questa fosse tutta assommata in quell'atto solo. (798–99)

[When an act is complete, it is what it is; it can change no more. Anyway, when one has acted, even if he doesn't feel or find himself in the completed act, what he has done remains like a prison for him. . . . We complete an action. We believe in good faith that we have put ourselves wholly in that action. We realize, however, that it is not the case and that the act is instead always and uniquely one of the many that we are or that we can be, when, unfortunately, suddenly we find ourseleves hooked and suspended. I mean to say that we realize that we are not altogether in that act and that it would be a gross injustice to judge us by that act alone, to keep us hooked and suspended on it, as in a pillory, for our entire existence, as if that existence were summed entirely in that one act.]

In spite of his analytical rigor, Moscarda is still speaking the language of madness. The act is an impediment to freedom; it is a trap into which the self aspiring to indeterminacy can fall. The simplicity and resoluteness of the act inhibit the expression of an elusive and transcendent being. The act puts an end to possibility, subjugating the self to the mercy of the Other. An action, therefore, cannot be but a ruse, a fiction, a misrepresentation, rather than an authentic product of the self. To act at all, then, is tantamount to acting, in the theatrical sense of the word. Instead of verifying the subject's intimate reality, the act, in a paradoxical twist of Pirandellian logic, serves to defend that reality from contamination. It is by means of the fiction of acting that Moscarda reaches the open and nonconclusive state of being he exhalts at the end of his story. For this reason, the deeds that lead him directly to the hospice cannot be measured according to motivations within his historical life but rather only against the background of his existential dilemma. Let us consider two examples: Moscarda's theft of the documents regarding Marco di Dio's estate and his foiled attempt at intimacy with Anna Rosa, for both are essential stages of the subject's journey toward dissolution and reconstruction.

Moscarda's actions are strategic because they are largely symbolic acts, designed to give material substance to his defenses. In the case of Marco di Dio, the contradictory acts of eviction and endowment are not motivated by any real feelings on Moscarda's part. He, in fact, refers to them as experiments: "Incamminandomi verso quel primo esperimento, andavo a porre graziosamente la mia volontà fuori di me, come un fazzoletto che mi cavassi di tasca. Volevo compiere un atto che non doveva esser mio, ma di quell'ombra di me che viveva realtà in un altro" (813). [Moving toward that first experiment, I went ahead to situate graciously my will outside of myself, like a handkerchief out of my pocket. I wanted to realize an act that wasn't mine but that belonged to that shadow of me, which lived in the reality of another.] According to Moscarda's intentions, this act succeeds in subverting the logic of the circumstances in which it takes place. But most of all, it expresses Moscarda's desire to dominate his situation by means of paradox, evident from his posing of the problem in terms of an insoluble dilemma.

So even if Moscarda's act is characterized by his detachment from it, the sense of power he derives from distance does not help fill the void of his existence. On the contrary, since it is impossible for him to participate in life without renouncing his being, he must remain always divided from the Other, his relatedness being only indirect and contrived. Through interaction, Moscarda's rapport with the Other takes on a highly peculiar character, for he tries to obtain what he wants without relinquishing his authority over the process of exchange. So by stealing the documents, Moscarda gets what he wants while remaining still elusive. However, the theft as an act of vindication is not complete because the very act of stealing causes Moscarda to fear again his own vulnerability. The system of defense he has so carefully built has its weaknesses and is still subject to danger: "Mi sentii in quel bujo una volontà che si smarriva fuori d'ogni precisa consistenza; e n'ebbi un tale orrore, che fui per venir meno anche col corpo" (830). [In that darkness, I felt my will losing all of its consistency, and I was so horrified that I was about to pass out.]

The symbolic dimension of Moscarda's act is once again revealed in the episode's final sequence, when, he reports, "uno scarfaggio non ben sicuro sulle zampe sbucò in quel punto di sotto lo scafale, diretto verso la finestra. Gli fui subito sopra col piede e lo schiacciai" (831) [a cockroach on wobbly legs came out of the wall right beneath the bookshelf and headed toward the window. I was immediately on it, crushing it with my foot]. The language used in describing this act is one of both projection and defense. Moscarda is both the cockroach with uncertain legs and the person who crushes it. As Laing might put it, by crushing something, he avoids being crushed, just as renouncing his identity in front of the mirror is a way of safeguarding his autonomy and just as by stealing he shows his fear of being stolen.[13] Although it is possible to read the entire episode of Marco di Dio in light of Moscarda's relationship with his father, my intention is not to make the novel into a case of clinical pathology, but rather to draw attention to the structures underlying the narrative, to better understand the ideology produced by the text. So even if the interesting episode of Moscarda's encounter with Anna Rosa lends itself to a Freudian reading, its ideological value consists in the way it preserves intact the mechanism the subject employs to avoid entrapment. Anna Rosa is a neurotic who carries her dead father's pistol with her wherever she goes. By accident, the gun goes off, wounding herself and Moscarda, whom she tries to embrace in the bedroom of a convent where she is convalescing.

Moscarda recounts his bizarre relationship with Anna Rosa immediately before the concluding section of the novel, devoted to his dissolution. Against the suggestive backdrop of a cloister, the threads of Moscarda's desperate philosophizing are brought together in a far-reaching synthesis that affects not only the private world of his own disillusionment but also the world of the Other. We hear Moscarda's subversive theses rehearsed once again, but now, as they are spoken to another person, they take on a different function:

> Lei non può conoscersi che atteggiata: statua: non viva. Quando uno vive, vive e non si vede. Conoscersi è morire. Lei sta tanto a mirarsi in codesto specchio, in tutti gli specchi, perchè non vive; non sa, non può o non vuol vivere. Vuole troppo conoscersi, e non vive. . . . Non si può vivere davanti a uno specchio. . . . Procuri di non vedersi mai. Perchè, tanto, non riuscirà mai a conoscersi per come la vedono gli altri. . . . Sono certo che anche a lei, come a me, dopo quel discorso e dopo quanto le avevo già detto di tutto il tormento del mio spirito, s'apre davanti in quel momento sconfinata, e tanto più spaventosa quanto più lucida, la visione dell'irrimediabile nostra solitudine. L'apparenza d'ogni oggetto vi s'isolava paurosamente." (890–91)
>
> [You can only know yourself when you strike a pose: you are then a statue; you are not alive. When one is alive, one lives and does not see himself live. To know oneself is to die. You spend so much time looking at yourself in that mirror because you do not live. . . . One cannot live in front of a mirror. . . . Try never to see yourself. Because, in any case, you would never know yourself as others see you. . . . I am certain that after this speech of mine and after I had told her of all my spiritual torments, there opened up before us in that boundless and frightfully clear moment the vision of our irremediable solitude. The appearance of every object took on a terrifying isolation.]

Moscarda is still in search of some kind of ontological security. In order to validate his own sincerity vis-à-vis his uncertain self, he must threaten the security of the Other. Again, Moscarda defends against the presence of the Other. But why should he protect himself from Anna Rosa? The epistemology in the passage just cited plays a particularly interesting role: it suspends, and thus rarifies, the episode's literal theme of Anna Rosa's sexual provocativeness: "Sotto le coperte s'indovinavano procaci le formosità del suo corpo di vergine matura. . . . Certo, standosene così col viso nascosto, pensava ch'io non avrei potuto fare a meno di guardare il suo corpo come si disegnava sotto le coperte. Mi tentava" (887). [Under the blankets the shapeliness of her mature virginal body could be seen. . . . Certainly, as she lay there with her face hidden, she was thinking that I could do no less than stare at the outlines of her body under the sheets. She was tempting me.] But at the very moment Moscarda's erotic fantasy demands a complementary discursive action, the hero's mind abruptly swerves off track on to the subject of existence: "Nella penombra della cameretta in disordine, il silenzio pareva consapevole dell'attesa vana d'una vita che i desideri momentanei di quella bizzarra creatura non avrebbero potuto mai far nascere né consistere in qualche modo" (887). [In the semidarkness of the disorderly little room, the silence seemed conscious of the vain expectancy of a life which the momentary desires of that strange creature would never be able to satisfy nor to have any sort of consistency.]

The original erotic impulse is further degraded as Moscarda's reflections take on a metaphysical dimension: "Avevo indovinato in lei l'insofferenza assoluta d'ogni cosa che accennasse a durare e stabilirsi" (884). [I had perceived in her an intolerance for everything that gave the impression of continuity and solidity.] After the epistemological musings first cited, we pass to the *discours manqué* of a seduction sequence, dramatically interrupted by Anna Rosa's strange and unpredictable act:

> Non so precisamente come avvenne. Quand'io, guardandola da quella lontananza, le disse parole che più non ricordo, parole in cui ella dovette sentire la brama che mi struggeva di donare tutta la vita che era in me, tutto quello che io potevo essere, per diventare uno come lei avrebbe potuto volermi e per me veramente nessuno, nessuno. So che dal letto mi tese le braccia; so che mi attrasse a sé. Da quel letto poco dopo rotolai, cieco, ferito al petto mortalmente dalla piccola rivoltella ch'ella teneva sotto il guanciale. (895)

[I don't know exactly how it happened. When looking at her from that distance, I said things I don't remember, words in which she must have sensed my consuming passion to give her all of the life within me, all that I was capable of being, in order to become the person that she would have wanted me to be, and for myself truly no one at all, no one. I know only that from the bed she stretched out her arms to me; I know that she drew me to her. From that bed, a moment later, I rolled off, blinded, mortally wounded in the chest by a small revolver she kept hidden under the pillow.]

This episode reveals an entire process of repression and sublimation of instinct into thought. The existential defense first proposed helped divert attention from the sexual object, at once feared and desired, by suspending it in the abstraction of possibility. The act of shooting harbors a complex symbolic dimension, which can be summarily illustrated according to two archetypal events. The first is the woman's appropriation of the masculine function of control and domination: shooting is symbolic ejaculation, which is symbolic death (the intentional death of the male). The second is the fear of sexual contamination, expressed on two parallel levels: the wound (blood), fainting (death); and defloration (the contamination of the womb and birth). The highly stylized character of the incident contains all the elements typical of a castration fantasy. To be nobody is annihilation, death, seen as the appropriation (castration) of being. To ward off the condition of nonbeing, to safeguard the "man" in Moscarda, it is necessary to protect, according to the logic of paradox, the one hundred thousand Moscardas.

If the ambiguity of the narrative is an integral part of the subject's existential defense, it lends itself quite naturally to interpretation according to an existentialist model. Pirandello's exemplary description in *Uno, nessuno e centomila* of the modalities of the solitary self (the losing of the self in the They) and the process by which the self relinquishes its central position as the subject of representation has a striking likeness to the more contemporary canonical texts of philosophical existentialism and to the Heideggerian variant in particular.

Like Moscarda, practically all of Pirandello's characters are literally "thrown into the world." We find them in unwanted situations, victims mostly of past events that determine their future and slaves of an impersonal collectivity and the dictating presence of the Other. They all choose particular ways of being-in-the-world, but their choice is only a pretext for questioning the ontological status of the Self. Their role as dramatic characters is to show that Being, experienced as relational, is doomed to becoming entrapped in an insoluble subject-object problematic. Their way out is, like Moscarda's, through the conquest of self beyond temporality.

La realtà che io ho per voi è nella forma che voi mi date: ma è realtà per voi e non per me; la realtà che voi avete per me è nella forma che io vi dò; ma è realtà per me e non per voi; e per me stesso io non ho altra realtà se non nella forma che riesco a darmi. E come? Ma costruendomi, appunto. (779)
[The reality I have for you is in the form you give me: but this is reality for you, not for me; the reality you have for me is in the form I give you; but it is reality for me, not for you; and for myself, I have no other reality save for the form I give myself. And how? By constructing myself, that's how.]

These remarks constitute the hermeneutical circle of Pirandellian logic. The terms of such a dialectic of existence in the world are the "io" and the "voi," which, seen objectively, become the Heideggerian Dasein and the They. The passage interprets the novel's meaning as the subjugation of Dasein to the pervasive dictatorship of the They. The reality of Dasein depends on its constant appropriation by and for the Other and vice versa. No one is oneself, and everyone is the Other. The relativism of interchangeable perspectives intensifies the control exercised by the They: I am as you see and judge me, but, conversely, you are as I see and judge you. "I can become you" translates into "Dasein can become the They." The fact that I exist with the Other means that my "being-there" is, as Heidegger puts it, my being of the "Others".[14]

Against this subjection to the They, Moscarda explicitly affirms the impossibility of exiting from the circle of paradox: "Io mi costruisco di continuo e vi costruisco, e voi fate altrettanto" (779). [I construct myself continually and I construct you, and you do the same.] The They (or "voi"), like the being- there (or "io"), has no exact point of reference. "You" is not this or that person, nor does it refer to a specific historically and socially founded collectivity. But rather, since your identity is mine and mine yours, you and I are neutral, impersonal entities. We exist at the mercy of an impersonal other. For Pirandello, this is human existence as it appears to consciousness: a vicious paradoxical circle. When we give meaning to phenomena, we are asserting what we already know; the understanding we presuppose in making judgments about the world is already part of common knowledge. Moscarda cannot and does not learn anything more about himself than what is dictated by the Other. In his search to become the Other while holding on to the shadow of his selfhood ("Il mio sforzo supremo deve consistere in questo: di non vedermi *in me*, ma d'essere veduto *da me*, con gli occhi miei stessi ma come se fossi un altro" (755) [My supreme task consists in this: not to see me *in me*, but to be seen *by me*, with my own eyes but as if I were another]), he excludes any and every possibility of self-knowledge.

But Gengè Moscarda does not remain trapped within the paradoxical logic of this hermeneutical circle. He cuts the knot by refusing to look in the mirror ever again. Reasoning about existence has led him to become a nonperson. He must now recover his being by other means. The conclusion of "not concluding" discussed above is at once the third leg of a negative syllogism constructed by his desperate reasoning and the death of his being. In the place of a conclusion, he introduces an intuitive leap into the All by which he purifies and safeguards his subjectivity. "Being-in-the-world" becomes "being-of-the-world," no longer in conflict with the They, outside the sphere of social existence, in an uncertain zone of absolute, objectified Being where subjectivity and objectivity are no longer opposed. The course Moscarda resolutely follows can be best described phenomenologically as the course of *Dasein* toward death. From a Heideggerian perspective, death is the dissolution of all conflict into sameness, the end of Being-there. In the process, the person is at once forgotten as a historical entity and rendered eternal as a concept. Again in Heidegger's terms, Moscarda could be said to be an "existential" rather than an "existence" (33).

Moscarda's experience derives from the conviction that living requires, necessarily, the playing of roles. In this sense, his story addresses the problematic of selfhood at the base of Pirandello's theater. Pirandello's characters are all lucidly conscious of the roles they play. Their dramatic function consists in convincing themselves of the reality of their experience. Their way of coming out ahead in their conflict with the Other is to attempt always an ultimate fiction, to create still another truth in order to elude the simple and direct realization of their alienated objectivity. We cannot help

notice in this process a certain structural inconsistency, one that characterizes both Moscarda's story and Pirandello's theater as a whole: namely, the
author's impulse to protect the identity of his petit bourgeois characters by
criticizing the representative aspects of classical bourgeois ideology.
Moscarda's life cannot be represented, simply because he has no life of his
own; but still, it is his degraded and abstract being that Pirandello endeavors to safeguard. As a result, the criticism he levels at the logic of liberal
capitalism is decentered and ambiguous; the only thing that is certain is the
prevailing impulse to create an irrational totality.[15]

Capitalism, as Pirandello saw it, was not just an economic system but
also a civilization of liberal individualism that in order to survive had to accommodate the interests of the popular masses. Particularly in the case of
Italy, this was a society open to reform from below as a means of protect-
ing itself against the threat of revolution. The fundamental characteristic
of liberalism was its stated ideal of a rational social unity composed of the
diversity of particular interests. Pirandello shared with fascism a profound
antagonism toward the liberalist ideology of the particular. (Fascism saw
itself as the radical negation of this concept of bourgeois individualism and
argued for the subordination of particular interests to the natural and organic unity of the nation.) His critique consisted in demonstrating that the
individual, in spite of his ability to become what he wished, was always
something else; his essence was his otherness. The ideological relevance of
this critique consists in its capacity to repress history, to efface the social
and political determinants of everyday life and to replace them with an ontology of subjectivity.

To make the crisis represented in Pirandello's work intelligible from a
historical standpoint, we must include what has been canceled from the literary register, namely, the crisis of a social class. On the one hand, Pirandello's work is both a symptom of and a response to the isolation and political ineffectiveness of the lower and middle strata of the Italian bourgeoisie
that resulted from the development of industrial society. On the other, it
attests to the severe limitations a unified Italy placed on the intellectual's
traditional role as ideologue. Estranged from the processes of legitimization and consensus, the intellectual (as represented by Pirandello's pervasive philosophical voice) becomes the negative critical consciousness of the
bourgeoisie. He invalidates the liberal ideological principles that facilitated

industrial development and the creation of mass society. At the same time, by absolutizing subjectivity, he safeguards the economic base and class structure of that very same social order his criticisms are designed to weaken. The effect of questioning the rational certainty of liberal individualism is one of vulnerability: the self as seen and judged by the Other. In order to escape the precariousness of existence, the Self must desolve into the All. Individuality is, by Pirandellian definition, indistinctiveness.

We can now advance some general conclusions with regard to the politics of Pirandello's exemplary text: first, that its rejection of the rational consciousness of the traditional bourgeois intellectual is a variant of the petit bourgeois subversiveness common in Pirandello's times; second, that its critique of the liberalist subject is shared not only by "revolutionary" fascism but also by fascism after 1925; third, that the restructuring of consciousness according to an irrational imperative, whereby conflict is resolved by means of intuition and myth, is a solution to the crisis of personal reality consistent with that advanced by emergent fascism in relation to the crisis of society; and fourth, that the Self as an aesthetic construct constitutes a logical basis for fascism's aestheticization of politics.

Yet, through its stock of obsessive images and through its repetitive narrative and dialogic sequences, Pirandello's art could be said to demonstrate the limits of the ideology underlying its own generative forces. But its assault on all forms of existential closure ends up by creating an ontological closure in which particular and universal are one and the same. Nevertheless, it is the process of desperate questioning, which undermines conventional logic, that appears to take us beyond the imposed structure and finality of the texts themselves. This is perhaps why Pirandello has influenced such truly radical dramatists as Jean Genet and Samuel Beckett, whose aesthetic and social ideologies fall at the opposite end of the political spectrum.

It would be, indeed, tempting to conclude that, in spite of Pirandello's allegiance to fascism and the many affinities that exist between his work and fascist ideology, his work subverts the absolute control and total closure that was the essence of fascist practice. But fascism, let us not forget, also was subversive; it too endeavored to lay in plain sight the fallacies and inconsistencies of liberal democracy. Its early ideology, which finds an analogue in Pirandello's thought, waged war against the unvarying and changeless, against a lifeless and stagnant reality, in the name of vitality and life. It too, like Pirandello's Moscarda, rejected the notion of existence as interaction and exchange among individuals, and it too endeavored to reconstitute the bourgeois subjectivity it attacked and degraded in the form of mythical alternatives.

CHAPTER FIVE

Italo Svevo

Contradiction and the Borders of Modernism

Analytical, introspective, and realistic are the adjectives most often used to describe Italo Svevo's fiction and to situate it in a cultural space far removed from the literary production of his then better-known contemporaries.[1] Svevo shares no fundamental structural, stylistic, or thematic feature with either Giovanni Verga or Gabriele D'Annunzio. And, although his ironic frame of mind suggests an affinity with Luigi Pirandello, the events and emotional states he creates have little, if any, of the playwright's metaphysical urgency. In sharp contrast to Pirandellian humor, Svevian irony emphasizes that reality, rather than being a horrific abyss, is an endless field of possibilities, an occasion, in a truly modernist sense, for intellectual free play. Pirandello's narrative dialectic was based on the question of either seeing or not seeing, accepting or rejecting, which involved a process of distinction and elimination. From Moscarda's phenomenological experience of subjectivity emerged a totally abstract human entity, distinct from the empirical individual, a being capable of endless transformations but only beyond the borders of rational consciousness and social interaction, in some rarified, ontological sphere.

As a result, the structural coordinates of human subjectivity are made accessible to us only in the form of ambiguity and inauthenticity. Moscarda's experience was based on the conviction that to live meant, necessarily, to pretend or to play a part. Pirandello's many characters share Moscarda's point of view, in that they all try to convince themselves of the reality of this or that thing or event. Their way of winning the battle with the Other is to attempt an ultimate fiction in order to avoid facing the elementary truth about themselves, namely, that their fate is to live ungrounded in a world of common, quotidian existence.

From Zeno Cosini's perspective, seeing and not seeing and accepting and rejecting are noncontradictory, coextensive terms, placed side by side and given prominence precisely because they evoke contradictory situations. The ambiguity which Moscarda dreaded, and which sent him headlong into a spiral leading to existential death, is Zeno's vital fluid. Zeno's realities are real, his parts are genuinely *his*, and his fictions are the genuine facts of his existence.[2]

The voice of Zeno's narrative is that of an old man who is trying to deceive his pyschoanalyst. Zeno recounts selective episodes from his life; The text he thus produces is the object of Svevo's story. *La coscienza di Zeno* is the story of the deception that is Zeno's reality, a story that reflects in its "agrammatical syntax" the illusive mental processes by which the "text" is produced.[3]

The primary effect brought about by Zeno's writing is the realization that he is a captive individual, for his entire life is conditioned by desires over which he has little if any control. His narrative (ironically psychoanalytic) recounts what appears—we never know to what extent Zeno is telling the truth—as a tortuous rambling through life in search of some kind of stability, a presence of mind and emotional composure that, he knows, will always escape him. Well-off financially, Zeno is firmly installed in a world of dull yet gratifying bourgeois values (conscience, duty, truth, legality, etc.), which he admires for the sense of well-being they foster, and at the same time exposes as facades, manufactured to give an air of respectability to one's needs and drives. Zeno's unique gift (the great psychoanalytical talent he appropriated from Doctor S.) is an unrelenting consciousness that discloses at every turn of the narrative the modes of deception he himself creates in order to safeguard desires he can never thoroughly satisfy.

There is no need to rehearse all the paradoxes, contradictions, and ironies that make Zeno's autobiography so appealing to contemporary tastes. Nor is it necessary to explore once again the deep psychoanalytical dimensions of the narrative as a blueprint for modern existence. Behind Zeno stand both Nietzsche and Marx as theoretical buttresses to his material struggle for survival, as well as to his skeptical hermeneutics. From Freud, Zeno has learned not only about the vicissitudes of desire, but also that the pleasure of humor is perhaps our best defense against reality's many provocations. Svevo criticism has resourcefully explored these and other lines of influence and affinity but has left largely unattended the entire area of the politics of Zeno's relation to a world in which he, unlike Moscarda, is very much at home.

As the more perceptive readings of *La Coscienza di Zeno* have argued, Zeno's neurosis is a means of knowledge, and in this respect it is one and the same with the literary text. Writing helps Zeno unearth the forces behind his malaise; it helps him convert his handicap into a powerful hermeneutics that sets in clear light all the contradictions and fictions lurking behind appearances. Yet at the same time, writing also deceives, actually perpetuating a whole system of deception that keeps him, as well as his reader, from objective knowledge. Language, then, is a form of duplicity, the false coloring we give to our thoughts and feelings. There is nothing Zeno can write about himself that is true; what is true is only desire and its offspring: contradiction and equivocation. The most characteristic feature of *La Coscienza di Zeno* is the heightened quality of its deceit. Numerous studies have examined in depth and with subtlety the novel's many levels of ambiguity, centering on the processes of revelation and deformation that safeguard the logic of Zeno's desire.[4] Such a course of inquiry is justified explicitly in Zeno's confession that every word he has written in Tuscan is a lie ("Con ogni nostra parola toscana noi mentiamo")[5] [We lie with every word we speak in the Tuscan tongue]. Since Zeno's confessions are all written in Tuscan, they, too, must be lies. Fiction, after all is fiction, and the memoirs Doctor S. has vindictively published are nothing but the literature of Zeno's life.

Hence, the very first thing we learn about the life recounted in Zeno's text is that its account is uncertain and equivocal; because of this, it cannot be coherently portrayed as representative of a reality existing beyond its own textualization nor can it be understood within the interpretative scheme deployed by Doctor S. In the book's final chapter, Zeno accepts, ironically, the ephemeral and fragmentary character of his experience, which he juxtaposes to the solidity of the images he invents in evoking it: "Ma inventare è una creazione, non già una menzogna. Le mie erano delle invenzioni come quelle della febbre, che camminano per la stanza perché le vediate da tutti i lati e che poi anche vi toccano. Avevano la solidità, il colore, la petulanza delle cose vive" (445–46). [But invention is a creative act, not merely a lie. My inventions were like febrile hallucinations, which walk about the room so that one can survey them from all sides and even touch them. They had the solidity, the color and the movement of living things] (352). These are images created by Zeno's desire; they are artful and authentic, irreducible. Rather than mirrors of Zeno's past, they are its artifical reconstruction and, as such, can only refer to themselves.

The brief passage just cited brings us to the heart of Svevo's modernism. The images Zeno invents for the doctor's consumption are the substance of both his conscience and his consciousness. The thematic presence of psychoanalysis in the novel can be seen, therefore, as the site at which the struggle to produce a work of art takes place. It creates and justifies the conditions of the battle, objectifies the chaos, and sets the narrative rules for its decipherment and transformation.

If we consider the text from Svevo's standpoint, we can see how the story raises questions not only about life in modern bourgeois society but also about the status of art. In D'Annunzio and Pirandello, we have noted the different ways in which art becomes an end in itself, detached from social and political restraints, and how it incorporates thematically the subversive freedom and power that modern capitalism has denied the artist. These writers' responses to the alienation and reification of the artist's cognitive function were those of outsiders looking in, estranged from the processes of legitimization and consensus. From such a perspective, art is a means of escape into a completely different realm, namely, the aesthetic. D'Annunzian myth and Pirandellian epiphany reconstitute the organicity that the capitalist division of labor has torn into fragments, but with the effect of hypostatizing cognition at the expense of history and morality. History is fused into an eternal present of sensual correspondences and transcendence. Morality becomes one with the aestheticization of the self.[6]

Svevo, by contrast, is an insider who, much like Zeno, reaps the benefits of a society he at once loves and hates. In political terms, he harnesses a progressive, liberalizing outlook, an optimism that recognizes the creative potential of the bourgeoisie at the same time that he exposes its faults. He produces its metaphor in the form of Zeno who, as both its conscience and its consciousness, embodies the mentality necessary for its survival. In many ways, he understands its logic better than any of its official representatives do. The Pirandellian subject is resolute in its endeavor to determine itself; in this sense, it is the last, degraded vestige of classical liberal thought. The Svevian subject obeys different laws, unlike its Pirandellian counterpart, it is not at all caught up in the romantic problematic of self-realization, it knows well the limits of self-creation. A deeper structure dictates the laws regulating its survival, one that, in fact, thinks and speaks for it. In Zeno's narrative the controlling force is the Unconscious. Svevo rescues the fractured Pirandellian subject, so to speak, at the last moment, when it is ready to reconstitute itself in myth, while he ignores the whole process of desperate self-interrogation, on the presupposition that the subject has within its conscious power the ability to understand itself and that no other forces are at work in determining its activity.

By composing his autobiography, Zeno puts himself in a position to regulate totally its events and predicaments while at the same time giving himself over to the Other, which operates within him as a kind of second nature. The contradiction is glaring but endemic to being a subject in the world of monopoly capitalism, that is to say, a kind of commodity that continually exchanges itself for itself, that differentiates among its many postures (patient, son, husband, lover, rival, businessperson, writer, etc.) elaborating, with slight variations, the same story. Like the commodity, Zeno has taken possession of time and space. Every moment of his story is regulated by his consciousness, which acts like a market indicator, showing the fluctuations of a system that can never be totally understood.

Zeno's story ends on a particularly ironic note: of all things, the war, which enabled him to profit in business, provides the necessary cure for his malady. He is now in a position to reflect on the fate of humankind in general. At this point in the narrative, Zeno's and Svevo's voices conflate.[7] Zeno's everyday experiences in all spheres have led him to envisage human life as a prison of disease from which there is no escape. Life, he writes in the final note of his diary, is ultimately a terminal illness: "A differenza delle altre malattie la vita è sempre mortale. Non supporta cure" (479). [Unlike other diseases, life is always mortal. It admits of no cure] (377). The social order in the age of machines, he concludes, is immutable. All that is left is the hope of annihilation, which will free the world of "parasites and disease."

Zeno's fatalism stems, perhaps, from his first hand knowledge of the logic of capitalist production: "Gli ordigni si comperano, si vendono e si rubano" [Implements are bought or sold, or stolen], while people become "più furbo e più debole" (479) [weaker and more cunning] (378). Exchange value has invaded and captured the human community; it spreads its lethal disease behind the facade of convention and respectability to the point where its human products, weak and spectacled, will fashion humankind's ultimate destruction. It is senseless for Zeno, a victim of alienated labor, to rebel against it, for machine-age technology has become omnipotent, and the natural world it has poisoned has succumbed to its rule. Like Pirandello, Svevo has abandoned all hope in human perfectibility. Man in his final assessment is incorrigibly evil and aggressive; as a result, civilization is doomed:

> Forse traverso una catastrofe inaudita prodotta dagli ordigni ritorneremo alla salute. Quando i gas velenosi non basteranno più, un uomo fatto come tutti gli altri, nel segreto di una stanza di questo mondo, inventerà un esplosivo incomparabile, in confronto al quale gli esplosivi attualmente esistenti saranno considerati quali innocui giocattoli. Ed un altro uomo fatto anche lui come tutti gli altri, ma degli altri un po'più ammalato, ruberà tale esplosivo e s'arrampicherà al centro della terra per porlo nel punto ove il suo effetto potrà essere il massimo. Ci sarà un'esplosione enorme che nessuno udrà e la terra ritornata alla forma di nebulosa errerà nei cieli priva di parassiti e di malattie. (379)
> [Perhaps some incredible disaster produced by machines will lead us back to health. When all the poison gases are exhausted, a man made, like all other men, of flesh and blood, will in the quiet of his room invent an explosive of such potency that all the explosives in existence will seem like harmless toys beside it. And another man, made in his image and in the image of all the rest but a little weaker than them, will steal that explosive and crawl to the center of the earth with it, and place it just where he calculates it would have the maximum effect. There will be a tremendous explosion, but no one will hear it, and the earth will return to its nebulous state and go wandering through the sky, free at last from parasites and disease.] (377)

This ending demands to be read literally, as a terrifying vision uttered with all the urgency and weight of prophecy. Practically every commentator has remarked that the cataclysm Svevo predicts for the modern world springs from his deep knowledge of human weakness, of disease, of man's chronic vulnerability and precariousness, and of his general ineptitude, which causes him to develop weapons as extensions of himself. In this sense, it heralds the end of Zeno, who is Svevo's representative of a social order grown weak and meaningless.

But there is another way to look at this ending: not so much as a prophecy of a future apocalpyse unleashed by industrial society but as an allegory of the new conditions of life and of a new consciousness of the subject in that very same society, which, in the wake of the great imperialist war, is doomed to a mode of rootlessness and chaotic activity typical of the commodity form. The more Zeno presents himself as inept and fragmented, the more his condition begs for some kind of redemption or transcendence. When Zeno decides to stop looking at himself, he gains, paradoxically, the health and wholeness he, like Moscarda, has so resolutely sought. The only thing that now matters for him is the present; in abandoning psychoanalysis and thus discarding his past, Zeno has given up any hope of understanding himself. He has entered, in other words, the perpetual present of commodity time, in which all connections with one's origins and formation have been effaced. He will now dedicate himself wholeheartedly to his business activity: "Come tutte le persone forti, io ebbi nella mia testa una sola idea e di quella vissi e fu la mia fortuna" (477–78). [Like all strongwilled people, I had only one idea in my head, and on this I lived and made my fortune by it] (376). Time and space now consolidated, bound in the perpetual mutation of the commodity (a replaying of the same old story), Zeno is forced to live out a life without meaning. To this condition Svevo gives the imprint of messianic time: the day of judgment, the ultimate catastrophe.

The itinerary schematically charted here is the loop of the modern capitalist sensibility, which begins in the consciousness of contradiction and then, embattled, doubles back upon itself to equate fragmentation and perpetual mutation with life itself, ruling out all other solutions save that of total annihilation.[8] Seen in this light, La Coscienza di Zeno can be read as an advanced form of modernist fiction, one that borders on what we have come to know as postmodernism.[9] It is no accident that the strong sympathies readers evidence today for Zeno are largely founded on the nature of his psychological response to life and the manner in which that response is expressed. The remainder of this chapter is devoted to the questions of meaning and interpretation that Zeno's self-analysis raises in relation to modern and postmodern sensibilities.

Unlike Pirandello, Svevo does not base his literary ideology on the destruction of reason, and, as we have said, he has no dream of escaping the capitalist social order. On the contrary, Zeno delights in his quest for profit, his breast swells with pride at the outcome of his first capital investment: "Nel momento in cui incassai quei denari mi si allargò il petto al sentimento della mia forza e della mia salute" (478). [When I pocketed the money, my breast swelled at the thought of my strength and abounding health] (414). The contradictions that the capitalist economic order generate are left unresolved, as part of the human condition itself, and, paradoxically, are signs of both its health and its decay.

But while Svevo seeks to convert chaos into art by valorizing images and dramatic gestures, he responds to the aura of creativity he gives to his enterprise in a very particular way. Instead of trying to define or rationalize his imagemaking, he invests it with an uncertain status. The doctor notes and records everything Zeno tells him, but Zeno is aware that he has told him nothing at all: "'Abbiamo avuto questo, abbiamo avuto quello'. In verità, noi non avevamo più che dei segni grafici, degli scheletri d'immagini" (446). ["We have had this, we have had that," though we had really had nothing but graphic signs, mere skeletons of images] (352).

Zeno has produced a number of texts, pictures of his life, visions or dreams, which the doctor seeks to unite into a tidy narrative in much the same way that a literary critic illustrates a hypothesis by arranging various pieces of data and attributing significance to them. But, unlike the doctor, Zeno understands that his words cannot say what he means, the images he evokes intersect with other images, to the extent that his imagemaking has a life of its own. There is no one text but, instead, an interweaving of images whose meanings are equivocal and unstable because they are controlled by impulse and desire. The doctor, on the other hand—and, by implication, Svevo's readers—are free to recombine Zeno's texts as they wish, to impose meaning on them.

A kind of deconstructionist *avant la lettre*, Zeno calls into question not only the doctor's Oedipal interpretation but also, most importantly, the methodological conviction on which that interpretation is based: namely, that there can be a fixed system of representation. But despite his uncertainty about the truth value of his images, he still aspires to a unified representation of life. Such a unity can be attained, however, only after the last piece of the puzzle has been put into place. Zeno utters his final thought on the unresolved question of interpretation just before Svevo speaks out on the fate of mankind: "Il dottore, quando avrà ricevuto quest'ultima parte del mio manoscritto, dovrebbe restituirmelo tutto. Lo rifarei con chiarezza vera perché come potevo intendere la mia vita quando non ne conoscevo quest'ultimo periodo" (478). [When the doctor gets the last part of my manuscript, he will have to give me back the whole. I should be able to write it all over again with absolute certainty now; how was it possible for me to understand my life when I did not know what this last part was going to be?] (377). There are two preoccupations in this statement that seem to interconnect: the impulse to create a true picture of his life, and the desire to do so by means of the performative act of rewriting. Hence, the impulse to a totality full of connections is tempered by the awareness that such a unity is nothing but another text. The texts contained in Zeno's manuscript all dissolve into an illusory master text, thus deferring meaning until the life they symbolize has in truth ended.

It is, therefore, consistent with his outlook that Zeno should exhibit a preoccupation with the instability of language. Words for him have a life of their own; they do not always say what he means; yet he does have some measure of control over their effects, if not their meanings, a control regulated by his desire, by a foundation of need that he refuses to face squarely and accept for what it is.

This brings us to what is, perhaps, the novel's principal theme, the problematic status of Zeno's identity. Zeno is not only a subject whose motivation and behavior are continually at such odds that the language he speaks is inherently ironic; since his text is written as a confession, he is also in a position to evaluate, ironically, the effects of his deception. When Carla asks Zeno if Augusta is very pretty, he replies that it is a matter of taste and then comments:

C'era qualche centro proibitivo che agiva ancora in me. Avevo detto di stimare mia moglie, ma non avevo mica ancora detto di non amarla. Non avevo detto che mi piacesse, ma neppure che non potesse piacermi. In quel momento mi pareva di essere molto sincero; ora so di aver tradito con quelle parole tutt'e due le donne e tutto l'amore, il mio e il loro. (233)

[Some restraining principle was still at work in me. I had said I had admired my wife, but I had not said that I did not love her. I had not said that I thought her pretty, but neither had I said that I might not think her so. At the moment it seemed to me that I was being very truthful; now I know that in those few words I betrayed all women and all love, both mine and theirs.] (188)

This is one among numerous examples of the logic of Zeno's desire and of his ability to distance, however slightly, the deceit involved in safeguarding his identity.

Zeno is always devising strategies to make his life better but is constantly frustrated. He conceives of himself as alienated from a principle of health and stability. Does his self have an essential meaning? Can he identify that meaning? These questions, which generate and regulate the narrative, anchor the hermeneutical impulse evinced by the text solidly within the frame of modernism. Yet the effect of Zeno's preoccupation with language is to foreground the signifier, to the extent that it appears detached from its unifying frame, that is, from Zeno's historical past and from an achievable future. It is from here that we get the sense of a fragmented subject and of an identity in the process of being constructed.

But, *La coscienza*, in contrast to postmodern fiction, does not reduce experience to a series of pure and unrelated presents. Zeno does not experience himself as a spectacle, ephemeral and without density; nor does he express anywhere disbelief in the epistemological foundation of his thought, and nowhere can we find the kind of "contrived depthlessness" that Jameson has identified with postmodernism.[10] Yet Zeno places emphasis on the power of his words to deceive, creating as he does images of the self that may have nothing to do with its true identity. Such a tack would appear to suggest a shift from the experience of Being-in-the-world as a unified and essential phenomenon to a sense of the self as image or public identity.

Zeno has been coached by his doctor to produce or, as it were, to reproduce desire. His literature, the doctor hopes, will offer access to Zeno's unconscious motivations, bringing them into the light of day and, therefore, curing the neurotic patient of his obsessions. But since Zeno is in a position to comment on his deceit, his confessions are seen as texts that produce, rather than reflect, the subject's identity. These are images of the self, accumulated from the past and distributed eclectically over the course of the narration, images that compress the subject's history into an overwhelming present ("presente imperioso") devoid of spatial and temporal barriers. Space is the locus of the writing event, and time is the materialized movement of desire, both well contained within that economy of telling about the self with which Zeno markets his identity. Zeno's text and thought process are one and the same, and together they eclipse any sense of a personal history that the succession of events may evoke. In effect, Zeno's reality is his only problem, at once specific and absolute; it is the text of his presence in history, a presence made visible by writing.

The instruments Zeno employs in producing and recognizing himself are psychoanalysis and his resistance to it; these, too, are texts he manipulates in such a way as to conceal any trace of real linkage to himself. Paradoxically, psychoanalysis enables Zeno to position himself in front of his life and, therefore, outside of his own history.[11]

The site of the game is established right from the beginning. Zeno relaxes after lunch, paper and pencil in hand:

> Il mio pensiero appare isolato da me. Io lo vedo. S'alza, s'abbassa . . . ma è la sua sola attività. Per ricordargli ch'esso è il pensiero e che sarebbe suo compito di manifestarsi, afferro la matita. Ecco che la fronte si corruga perché ogni parola è composta di tante lettere e il presente imperioso risorge ed offusca il passato. (24)
>
> [I seem to be able to see my thoughts as something quite apart from myself. I can watch them rising, falling . . . their only form of activity. I seize my pencil in order to remind them that it is the duty of thought to manifest itself. At once the wrinkles collect on my brow as I think of the letters that make up every word. The present surges up and dominates me, the past is blotted out.] (27)

From the very first word of the introduction, "vedere," Zeno posits and cancels the truth basis of his search for the origin of his alleged ills. It is not that his childhood cannot be seen but rather that, since its images are obscured, it becomes the subject of divergent possibilities, materials from the past signifying something we cannot master because they resist placement in a pattern of development. Scenes from Zeno's past will collapse upon each other to form Zeno's life; a life, that, since it is organized with the fragments of a partially illusory history, escapes becoming romanticized. Therefore, Svevo begins his novel by endowing Zeno with an awareness ("coscienza") of being an individual subject confronted with a multiplicity of discontinuous realities to which he will endeavor to give some kind of figuration.

A slightly different way of looking at Zeno's strategies of self-building and preservation is to view them from the standpoint of what they allegedly reject, namely, psychoanalysis. The reader's sense of Zeno's life derives principally from how Zeno represents himself to himself and from how pleasure, fantasy and dream are the real substance of his human existence. His art of narrating his self is inseparable from the libidinal processes it recounts. For all of Zeno's resistance to Doctor S.'s method, his parodic banalization of Freud's doctrines of free association and Oedipal yearnings, Zeno writes a preeminently Freudian text, a narrative that unmasks the subject as a contradictory and unfinished entity. In doing so, Svevo executes a vision that has, for the narrative heritage it addresses, the same subversive effect that Freudian psychoanalysis had on the Western aesthetic tradition. Like Freud, Zeno interrogates the humanist subject and by concrete illustrations reveals its dream of health and subject integrity to be a libidinal fantasy. If, as Terry Eagleton states, "psychoanalysis examines what takes place when desire is given tongue, comes to speech" and if it is equally true that "speech and desire can never consort amicably together, as meaning and being continually displace one another,"[12] then Zeno's text is quintessentially psychoanalytical; not because it reduces the protagonist's experience to a psychoanalytical matrix but rather because, in its process of telling, it demystifies the subject, shattering its pretensions of wholeness. Accordingly, Zeno's text conflates pleasure and reality, showing that the rationale for its construction is inextricably linked to the subject's drives. Zeno's reality is his pleasure: the practical achievements of his marriage are his pleasure; his business is his pleasure. The distinctions that bourgeois society makes between culture and value, on the one hand, and appetite or the libidinal, on the other, no longer apply.

In narrative terms, Zeno's desire becomes an obstacle to representation, despite his attempt to represent his life. By endowing Zeno with a critical consciousness that is the propelling force of the narration, Svevo is saying that there are no hidden areas of the self, no invisible font from which human actions derive. Hence, he realizes an important shift in perspective from the unconscious to the conscious mind, and to the effect of Zeno's corporeal needs and drives on both his consciousness and his conscience.

Zeno's consciousness is nothing more than an occasion for his and our pleasure. The pleasure derives from humor, and the humor from Zeno's refusal to be distressed by the provocations of his reality. His ego triumphs, reasserting at every turn his invulnerability.

The process involved in Zeno's many triumphs is one of reversal. Zeno renders himself impervious to the threats made against his ego by transforming his body, which experiences distress, into a mind that dominates it, erasing in one swipe of logic the provocations of reality. At the death of his mother, Zeno substitutes poetry for tears and compensates for the loss by transmuting it into an occasion for comfort. At the death of his father, Zeno converts the material fact of his father's last punishing gesture into a fictional representation, persuading himself that the slap he had given him at the point of his death could not have been intentional.

There is something plainly hedonistic about Zeno's maneuvers. Yet, although the pleasure principle dominates his reasoning from beginning to end, it does so in such a way as to leave indelible traces of the reality it endeavors to supplant: namely, the body, that mode of being, couched in the problem of health motivating Zeno's narrative, which cannot be transcended and which is at the root of Zeno's world. The body is the means by which Zeno's psychological and irrational needs are articulated as texts. These texts constitute a total picture of the subject, full of connections; at the same time, they show that these connections are really continually shifting fragments, entities, manipulated and fetishized, that unwittingly display the illusionary nature of all coherent representation. That is to say, Zeno himself can be taken as a metaphor for language and literature; he himself is an unstable entity, a character whose very existence is emblematic of our contemporary, fragmented world.

It would be incorrect, however, to equate the fragmentation of personal identity with the fragmentation of social reality into autonomous small narratives constituting a heterogeneous network of different voices, devoid of a center or global principle of organization. In the Trieste of Svevo's time, the crisis of capitalist relations of production no doubt affected the authority of the entrepreneur and the structure of his enterprise.[13] But at the same time, no alternative viewpoints emerged to challenge his authority, just as Zeno, despite his uncertain identity, enforces his perspective at every turn of the narrative. His consciousness is a closed world that can reflect only upon itself; it never intersects with other realities and, like the commodity form described above, functions like a forever changing substance. In other words, there is an ultimate consistency and coherence to all of Zeno's instabilities. That is why the overall effect of his consciousness is density rather than the depthless sensationalism characteristic of many postmodern fictional characters, a density that lacks all luster and ostentation, remaining just as "gray" and internal as the landscape in which it is set.[14] Moreover, the images that Zeno presents of himself are not superimposed on the surrounding narrative space; they do not implode upon us. Zeno knows his place in a world that has remained relatively stable. His search for a personal identity is, ultimately, no search at all. For right from the beginning, he is aware that it is his pleasure, rather than his identity, that is at stake.

So, although Svevo's quest for totality amid chaos turns upon itself ironically in *La Coscienza di Zeno,* producing a totality of fragments, the epistemological ground of modernist writing remains solidly in place. Zeno is constantly seeking to interpret his world and his place in it. He is repeatedly concerned with the modalities of knowing. To what degree is knowledge of the world and of the Other reliable? To what extent can we know the meaning of our actions? These questions make possible Svevo's use of a typically modernist perspective in the creation of a single consciousness through which are filtered the thoughts, presumed and real, of the other characters.

Zeno is described at the beginning of this chapter as a captive individual, his entire life subordinated to the demands of his desire. His imprisonment, however, is not altogether complete, for the laws he obeys are more the laws of production than of consumption. That is to say, his desires are related to his need to compete for survival in a hostile world of imperialist expansion and not yet those created by the capitalist rationalization of society and culture. But if this is true, what then creates the novel's metafictional effect? It is the book's diaristic form, which takes hold of Zeno's entire enterprise, placing on it conditions dictated by the contingency of external events. Thus writing, which cannot help but be a discourse on language, takes the place of those events and, more important, is a surrogate for that act the author cannot perform: namely, the production of a true and genuine book, the modern epic, the ideal book much heralded by D'Annunzio (1:653), which perhaps only Joyce was able to realize fully.

CHAPTER SIX

Carlo Emilio Gadda

Travesties

In *Young Törless*, Robert Musil describes his protagonist as living in a time brought to ruin ("in einer erstörten Zeit").[1] A similar assessment could be made of the life of Carlo Emilio Gadda's characters, especially Gonzalo Pirobuttiro, who is mortally obsessed with living in a world devoid of rational and moral foundations. The only difference is that, for Gonzalo "time" refers mostly to his own being-in-time, rather than to an epoch and a civilization. It is a "time" characterized in *La cognizione del dolore* as "consumato" [ravaged], "dissolto" [dissolved], and "doloroso" [painful]; a time that invades the "vacuità degli spazi" [the hollowness of spaces] and the "tenebra delle cose" [opaqueness of things].[2]

With this sense of vandalized existence, Gadda developed his work as a writer. In much the same way as Musil, he based his fiction on the conviction that traditional rationality and morals do not account for the incomplete, dark side of human cognition, which does not operate according to the rules of causal necessity or logic. Since the early twenties, when he began his lifelong courtship with philosophy, the problem foremost in Gadda's mind was that of entanglement; the psychological and metaphysical knot that becomes more intricate the more one attempts it. Gadda refers to such a condition of Being as "il grottesco che alberga nelle cose" [the grotesque that resides in things] or "la baroccagine del mondo" (32) [the baroqueness of the world]. This depletion of Being into intrigue generates its own principle of expression, the *macaronic,* a form of writing designed to subvert conventional forms of cultural and literary knowledge. The macaronic exposes the deceptive nature of canonized phenomena, thus striking back at the abuses of history and its fraudulent discourse. But it also explores what Gadda calls "gli strati autonomi della rappresentazione" [the autonomous strata of representation] and reinvents existence as vulgar spectacle.[3]

Gadda's pronouncements on such matters border on the obsessive. His reflections on the nature of the world and of writing, on the interrelations of cognitive and literary systems, and on the limitless expressive potential of the written word have no equal in twentieth-century Italian literature. Each of his numerous texts is metalinguistic and metanarrative in the most rigorous sense of the terms. They all submit language and literature to a merciless tribunal, presided over by a judge eager to prosecute the most cherished of idols and unafraid to submit the integrity of his own juridical identity to the most artful and unrelenting of investigations.

But in taking account of Gadda's striking originality, it is not enough to describe the mechanisms and configurations of his investigative process; it requires also that one enter into the interspace of lacunae and fissures that constitute a large part of the senseless reality, of the devastated and dolorous time, he so rigorously abjures. The title itself, *La cognizione del dolore,* is a powerful marker, meant to sound an alarm at the very time it endorses the need to track down the elusive referent it invokes. *Quer pasticciaccio brutto de via Merulana,* a work equally remarkable, capitalizes on the form of the detective novel to distance the anxiety that in *La Cognizione* derives from the subject's entrapment, producing what is at once a parodic replay of the original trauma of *La cognizione* and its means of repression. Our reading of Gadda focuses on the processes of displacement in both novels, which ensure the containment of an unspeakable personal trauma within the bounds of literature; the Gaddian strategy parodies the way literature manipulates reality, the way it investigates and assigns guilt.

In part 1 of *La cognizione del dolore,* during Doctor Higueroa's visit to the

Pirobutirro villa, Gonzalo says that he has dreamed a "frightening dream." This comes at a crucial moment in the exchanges between the doctor and him, when, tormented by the thought of never occupying first place in his mother's affection, he confesses his frustrated need for maternal love and care: "Sono stato un bimbo anch'io. . . . Forse valevo un pensiero buono . . . una carezza no; era troppo condiscendere . . . era troppo!" (119). [I was once a child myself. . . . Then I deserved perhaps a kindly thought . . . no, not a caress; that was condescending too far . . . it was too much!] The account the novel has already given of Gonzalo's experience and actions describes plainly his untenable position of entrapment in the life of his mother, the dynamics of which we now expect to see disclosed in the dream.

Our anticipation is heightened furthermore by the ironic conflict of opinions on the dream's potential significance. In another fruitless attempt to relieve his patient's anguish, the doctor attempts to depreciate the event, calling it a mere bewilderment, a "momentary phantasma" (119), while Gonzalo, undaunted by the physician's solicitude, regards the vision philosophically, as a means of extricating himself from the enslavement of reason, of breaking the holds of power exercised by dialectical argumentation (i.e., definition, categorization, abstraction): "È rifiutare le sclerotiche figurazioni della dialettica, le cose vedute secondo forza." [(To dream) is to reject the sclerotic figurations of dialectical reasoning, things seen according to the logic of force.]

He then expands this thought, using a familar Pirandellian image:

La forza sistematrice del carattere . . . questa gloriosa lampada a petrolio che ci fuma di dentro . . . e fa il filo, e ci fa neri di bugie, di dentro . . . di bugie meritorie, grasse bugiardosissime . . . e ha la buona opinione per sé, per sé sola. . . . Ma sognare è fiume profondo, che precipita a una lontana sorgiva, ripullula nel mattino di verità. (119)

[The systematizing force of character . . . this glorious oil lamp that smokes within us . . . and leaves its streak, coloring us black with lies, inside us . . . big, fat greasy lies . . . and has a good opinion of itself, of itself alone. . . . But dreaming is a deep river that rushes to a distant spring, bubbling into the morning of truth.]

The dream is then likened to the guile of a snake:

Un sogno . . . strisciatomi verso il cuore . . . come insidia di serpe. Nero. [A dream . . . streaking toward my heart . . . like the cunning of a snake. Black.]

So, according to Gonzalo, truth and treachery are entangled in the dream process. The manifest dream gives solace in the resolution of the dilemma engendered by the mutually opposing actions of desire and repulsion, immersing the dreamer into the deep river of human prehistory; but its latent content is nonetheless terrifying.

The text prefacing the dream narration may be taken as a cautionary measure, for it allows a kind of uncertainty to be created in its readers as to whether they will confront in the dream the real world of Gonzalo's destructive instincts or whether the "glorious lamp" of reason will again smudge them with lies. Gonzalo's preemptive statements prevent us from accepting as intimate truth what is remembered of his dream, while they simultaneously justify the form in which the dream will be reported: not as a chronicle of events to be decoded and transformed into the dream's latent meaning but as a relatively free wandering of the character's mind in connection with those events. In other words, if Gonzalo's sense of the falsity of logical discourse is correct, he must recreate the dimension from which truth will emerge, knowing that his recreation is a veil much like that which conceals the face of the tall, dark figure of his dream.

Gadda introduces the dream into his story within the context of Gonzalo's fragmented thoughts about his mother's age and ill-health: "La mamma è spaventosamente invecchiata . . . è malata" (119). [Mother has aged frightfully . . . she's ill.] There follows a displacement of the mother's sclerosis to the "figurations of the dialectic," which, according to Gonzalo, the dream occurrence is capable of rejecting. "[Sognare] è rifiutare le sclerotiche figurazioni della dialettica." [(To dream) is to reject the sclerotic figurations of the dialectic.] In this metaphor, as in the dream, the boundaries of logic have been violated. Such a figurative operation, which demonstrates the arbitrariness of signs and of the language-thought condition of possibility, may be considered as just another Gaddian expression of the world's inherent baroqueness.

But keeping more in tune with the novel's overriding Oedipal theme, the mother-dialectic equation, generated by verbal displacement, reflects the neurotic subject's desire to locate his own position within the established social order. The mother and the dialectic are both figures of power; they both occupy for Gonzalo places of dominance within the Oedipal territory of repression. Dreaming eludes these Oedipal codes by resisting fixity with flow ("fiume"), surface with depth ("profondo"), being with becoming ("ripullula"), death with birth ("mattino"). *La cognizione del dolore* embodies the signifying process of which Gonzalo's dream is a particular, symbolic instance: the tension toward schizophrenizing, that is, the impulse pervading the text to destroy the Oedipal ego and, with it, the countless forms of Oedipal repression through the freeing of narcissistic desire. In other words, Gonzalo's predicament, his double bind as it were, consists in the fact that he is forced to remain within the sphere of Oedipal domination by either accepting a neurotic identity or internalizing the social world, that is, becoming normal. The only way of escaping this neurosis-normality impasse is through the dissolution of the self by withdrawal into the adirectional flow of desire.[4]

In the dream account, Gadda presents, rather than a narrative, a series of repeated images meant to expose the forces within Gonzalo's mind that generate them. The images are related dynamically, through exclamation and ellipses, as if to reproduce the anguish involved in the process of simultaneous telling and concealing.

The text emphasizes certain associations through compulsive repetition. Gonzalo's dream experience is conveyed in images of hopelessness and desolation: for example, "Gli anni erano finiti. . . . Ogni finalità, ogni possibilità, si era impietrata nel buio. . . . Il tempo era stato consumato. . . . Ogni mora aveva raggiunto il tempo, il tempo dissolto" (120). [The years had ended. . . . Every finality, every possibility, turned to stone in the darkness. . . . Time had been consumed. . . . Every flower had reached its time, time dissolved.] Everything has already come to pass for Gonzalo; there is no future, no possibility. Past and future have turned to stone. From the empty house and prevailing darkness emerges the dark figure or shadow of a woman. The principal association is between the darkness and emptiness of the outside world and the motionless, veiled woman who, the reader presumes, is Gonzalo's mother. We may notice, however, that the relationship between her and the dreamer dissolves in the oxymoron of "oscura certezza" (120) [obscure certainty]. Is it Gonzalo's mother? Is the dream a premonition of her death, from which she is returning? Or is the woman mourning the death of another? Is the horrific, superhuman force that prevents her from loving the same force that crushes her?

The fact that Gonzalo is both the dreamer and the interpreter makes it impossibile for us to see his vision clearly without the overcoding recriminations of his conscience. What we have are the fragments of a dream; the fragmenting serves to distance us, while the metaphors of darkness, silence, shadow, and petrification are attempts to soften the terror of the vision. The narrator will, in fact, try to distract us more by breaking the unity of the dream account with the suggestion (to the reader) that it may all be just tragic literature: "Sotto il cielo di tenebra . . . Veturia, forse, la madre immobile di Coriolano, velata." (82). [Under the sky of shadows . . . Veturia, perhaps, the motionless mother of Coriolanus, veiled.]

But the precision with which Gonzalo reconstructs his dream—the varied diction and syntax of the death theme, full of assonances, repetition, and literary allusions—and its symmetrical organization in three stratified moments give the text the appearance of a stylistic paradigm designed to prove the impenetrability of the mystery it encloses.[5] Yet at the very moment this stylistic overloading conceals, it forces us to dwell on the importance of the procedure, on the act and manner of disguise itself.

La cognizione del dolore offers, in fact, a number of structurally relevant patterns of dissemblance, beginning with its imaginary South American setting in which the people, institutions, geography, and history of early twentieth-century Italy (chiefly Lombardy) are easily recognizable. The protagonist Gonzalo wears the transparent mask of autobiography, covered by the more concealing disguise of grotesque caricature that produces a tragi-comic deformation of the self—a form of baroque objectification meant to disclose only some traces of what is claimed to be the subject's extraordinary experience. In this vein, it can hardly go unnoticed that Gadda comments on his story in the form of an imaginary dialogue between author and editor. By giving the impression that the writing belongs to someone else, he skirts the problem of outright deception, while at the same time creating a boundary between his self-portrait and his personal history, the true essence of which he portrays as absent, as a story that cannot be written.

So, it is not by chance that, in the novel's first part, the theme of the threatening quality of reality emerging from Gonzalo's "delirio interpretativo" (37) meshes and concludes with the comic ruse of Palumbo Mahagones's feigned deafness. Consequently, Gadda releases his readers from the grip of Gonzalo's delirium, placing before them, on the threshold of his presentation of the mother, a more sustained diversion. The tragic biography (or autobiography) at the novel's core is potentially too revealing, too full of unconfessable subject matter; so it must be controlled through the modalities of disguise: in general, by its transformation into literature. For by being revealed as literature, it displaces the reader's attention from the coordinates of tragic existence expounded in the story to the alienating functions of the artifice. This form of masking produces a double, or split, textual identity that cannot be reconciled with or reduced to either of its component parts.

But if this is so, to what extent can the text deliver a coherent message? Romano Luperini has pointed out that Gadda uses literature primarily as a means of estrangement, his immediate purpose being to prevent the reader from viewing the literary work as anything but an artificial construct, essentially linguistic in character, which produces knowledge by revealing the contradictions and unexpected connections among things.[6] Literature as such depends on the relativity of empirical data and thus, according to Luperini, is incapable of offering syntheses. Gadda's narratives are, then, to be understood as a court of law before which the signifying capacity of literature is made to account for itself. They retain a degraded cognitive potential, generated by an overriding nostalgia for plenitude, which Gadda expresses in spite of his clear awareness of the liability of such an impulse. The tragic and sublime style of Shakespearean drama, mimicked throughout *La cognizione del dolore*, indicates Gadda's concern with recapturing the unity of the classic vision, while its position within the narrative confers on it the function of parody. That is to say, Gadda's concern with totality as a lost ideal appears as one among other languages, objectified and estranged by assignment to the characters, whose identities Gadda is careful never to fuse with his own. In this sense, Gadda's texts constitute a metalanguage that reveals the cognitive limitations of the very realities it expresses.

But even if, following Luperini, we account for Gonzalo's dream as a discourse on the limitations Gadda places on any attempt to appropriate the Unconscious, we cannot help but notice that the estrangement produced by the dream, because of its obsessive stylization, calls attention back to the protagonist's desire to reveal himself at the very moment he shows his need for disguise. Thus, the danger of being found out or exposed, rather than being nullified, becomes dramatized. Gadda's metalanguage may then be seen as a symptom of self-concealment, as a way of depersonalizing the text, draining it of its subjectivity, conferring on it a figurative death, analogous to the all-engulfing death expressed in the dream's end-of-time fantasy.

From a psychoanalytical standpoint, the dream's network of imagery and illusion reproduces the impulses and deep emotions that characterize Gonzalo's love-hate relationship with his mother. Using the setting of the terrace and deserted house, Gadda conveys first his character's sense of exclusion, then his more complex feelings of loss and abandonment. The deaths of Gonzalo's father and brother, his immediate rivals for maternal affection, commit the hero to a situation of desperate longing for the mother they have had and he has not; on the other hand, this feeling is offset by guilt and remorse for his unconscious wish for their deaths, promoted by either the desire to possess his mother or the recognition of his not being in her womb, which makes him sad and fearful. The emptiness of the house symbolizes the absence of maternal love; more important, it is a sign of existential desolation and solitude: Gonzalo's inner emptiness, the deadness he experiences from his lack of an autonomous identity, from his inability to dissociate himself from the life of his mother.

The Senora carries in her son's life the functions of object and Other; she is the bearer of pleasure and the missing part of his self that he desires to claim. Her death would then spell the rupture of this dependence. But in Gonzalo, object and Other have become inextricably enmeshed as two mutually dependent aspects of the same entity. This is why Gonzalo feels the all-embracing power of deadness, of "possibility . . . turned to stone." While he wishes for his mother's death as a means of liberation, he cannot extricate himself from it, that is, from her. The concluding dream image shows that the force of death falling upon her originates in Gonzalo and is generated by him: "Questa forza nera, ineluttabile . . . più greve di coperchio di tomba . . . cadeva su di lei! come cade l'oltraggio che non ha ricostruzione nelle cose. . . . Ed era sorta in me, da me!" (120) [And this black ineluctable force . . . heavier than a tombstone . . . fell upon her! as the outrage falls, beyond all reparation. . . . And it had risen in me, from me!]

The metaphor combines the opposing desires of possession, conveyed in the sexual nuance of "falling upon" and "covering," and the annihilation of the threat to his identity his mother represents. In order to fill his own emptiness, he must destroy the Other, but he cannot destroy the Other without killing his self. At the dream's end, in fact, the impulse to kill his mother is equivalent to existential self-destruction: "E io rimanevo solo" (121). [And I remained alone.] This return to isolation confirms Gonzalo's acceptance of nonbeing, the preservation of Oedipal dependence in the memory of grief, namely, of the signs of Oedipal dominance, "gli atti . . . le scritture di ombra . . . le ricevute" [the documents . . . the scriptures of shadow . . . the receipts]. Emptiness wins out: the dream account finishes elliptically as to indicate absence which is also omission or deletion.

The plenitude Gonzalo longs for can only be achieved by literally filling in the gaps, supplying the meaning that his fragmented discourse willfully omits. Such an operation entails removing the mask of language, which is equivalent to the renouncement of isolation. Gonzalo must exist separated from his mother because he is so absorbed in her. To accept integral relatedness with her means passing from a neurotic identity, characterized by uncertainty and fear, to a psychotic union with the Other. It is this fullness that is terrifying.

A difficulty we confront in reading *La cognizione del dolore* is establishing the distance that separates the narrator from the author and his major characters. Gadda produces in the figure of Gonzalo an external image of his self, projected in the form of impulses and instincts that are contained and determined by a specific history. He extends this self-image to include its presence in the minds of others as it has been perceived, reflected on, and systematized by his ego. This latter mode of self-projection is the novel's narrating voice, which functions as a screen between the instinctual world of Gadda-Gonzalo and the reader. Thus, the narrator, as the Gaddian ego, calibrates the operative distance between author and public; as the ego, it helps safeguard the author from direct exposure through the filter of ironic estrangement. The degree to which the psychological distance can be maintained by means of narrative control depends on the gravity of the impulse. The narration, which absorbs both narrator and character, is determined wholly by the forces of passion and not by any predetermined schema.

The styles of *La cognizione* hinge on the degrees of difference that separate the narrator emotionally from Gonzalo's object relations. The geographical and social setting and the episodes relatively extraneous to Gonzalo's inner world are written with various kinds of humor, ranging from ironic understatement to more direct and engaging forms of comic incongruity, such as the listing of tricks unsuccessfully played on Pedro in order to catch him at his game of deception. But as we are brought closer to Gonzalo's personal world, in the social context of the country villa, grotesque caricature and outright derision predominate. The narrator produces the deformation as the expression of Gonzalo's perspective, just as the deformed perspective of others generates the caricature of Gonzalo. As Gadda probes the center of this world of perverted images, he focuses on the tragedy of mother and son, on their isolation, loneliness, and frightful dependence on one another. At this psychological juncture of deep emotional involvement, the distance separating narrator and characters abruptly diminishes, causing a seepage of one existential perspective into the other, so that the original, fictional distinctions between narrator and characters have all but disappeared.

Although the doctor's presence in the first part of the novel ensures the integrity of the narrating ego's monitoring role, in the second part we are brought into unmediated contact with Gonzalo and the Senora. The narrator speaks with the same deep consciousness present in Gonzalo's account of the dream, a consciousness that is now projected on the mother. He literally plays the part of the Senora, focusing on his identity through her eyes. As in the dream account, death occupies center stage. The Senora's thoughts are filled with memories of her youngest son, killed in the war. Here, as elsewhere, Gadda structures his fiction as the double of his own experience. The crucial feature of his representation of Gonzalo's mother is the persistent sense of futility her figure expresses. The death of her son left her hopeless, confined to emptiness and isolation. The narrating voice charts her movements to indicate her next-to-death-like being. She wanders about the villa aimlessly, "come cercando il sentiro misterioso che l'avrebbe condotta ad incontrare qualcuno: o forse una solitudine soltanto, priva d'ogni pietà ed'ogni imagine" (168) [as if seeking the mysterious path that would have led her to encounter someone: or perhaps only a solitude, shorn of every compassion and of every image]. She is compared to the suffering King Lear, while outside a storm, at once the extension of her prolonged agony and the symbol of her self-destructiveness, rages against her.

In this position of isolation and despair, the Senora shows a curious resemblance to her son. The first-person narration of Gonzalo's dream and the narrator's description of the mother as described by the narrator, share the same phenomenology of the self. In both cases, existence is depicted in images of terror, darkness, death, and, particularly, abandonment. The separate dimensions of mother and son thus find unity in the narrator, who, as the voice of Gonzalo's ego, manages the figure of the mother so as to ensure that the reader's perception of her conforms to Gonzalo's.

Up to now, we have considered the figure of Gonzalo primarily in relation to its Oedipal object. But as protagonist he is also a narcissistic subject. Gadda's continual preoccupation with narcissism suggests that it may be a highly appropriate sphere of reference for understanding not only how the hero absorbs the conditions of *dolore* but also how he reacts to them—in a word, how Gonzalo attempts to overcome his Oedipal fate.

In *La cognizione del dolore*, narcissism performs a dual function. Thematically, it appears as a type of Nietzschean ego-inflation which the narrator presents as an index of psychopathological delusion. From the standpoint of style, narcissism is also the primary expressive mode of the narrating subject, who often falls prey to an "interpretative delirium" or narcissistic rage. For example, when the doctor suggests that the ailing Senora leave the villa to be examined by a specialist in a nearby town, Gonzalo, aware of her refusal to do so, unleashes a fierce tirade against the grandiose inflation of the ego:

Bel modo di curarsi! . . . a dire: io non ho nulla. Io non ho mai avuto bisogno di nessuno! . . . io, più i dottori stanno alla larga, e meglio mi sento. . . . Io mi riguardo da me, che son sicura di non sbagliare. . . . Io, io, io. . . . Il solo fatto che noi seguitiamo a proclamare . . . io, tu . . . con le nostre bocche screanzate . . . con la nostra avarizia di stitici predestinati alla putrescenza . . . io, tu . . . questo solo fatto . . . io, tu . . . denuncia la bassezza della comune dialettica . . . e ne certifica della nostra impotenza a predicar nulla di nulla . . . dacché ignoriamo . . . il soggetto di ogni proposizione possibile. (123–24)
[A fine way to take care of yourself . . . to say, "There is nothing wrong with me. I've never needed anyone! . . . The farther away the doctors stay from me, the better I feel. . . . I can take care of myself: that way I am sure not to make

mistakes. . . . I, I, I. . . . The mere fact that we go on proclaiming . . . I, you . . . with our uncouth mouths . . . with our avarice of the constipated, predestined to putrescence. . . . I, you. . . . this very fact . . . I, you . . . reveals the baseness of the common dialectic . . . and guarantees our impotence in preaching anything about anything . . . since we ignore . . . the subject of every possibile proposition.]

In a typically Freudian manner, the associative process is meant to lead us to the real subject of Gonzalo's aggression, "il soggetto di ogni proposizione possibile": the father, whose name it is useless to take in vain. The logical constraints of language have no fixed truth value, because they are instruments of an oppressive code imposed by a tyrannical father. To predicate the meaning of something means to reaffirm this authority and, as a result, to retain the separation between the I and the Other. Predication nourishes the narcissistic self by objectifying the Other. Gonzalo then, indicating the paternal subject, turns his rage against its historical symbol, the bell tower:

> Quello [il suono] che ha appena finito di venire fuori di là . . . dalla matrice di quelle mènadi scaravoltate a pancia all'aria . . . col batacchio per aria. . . . Bestie pazze! per cui ho patito la fame! Cinquecento pesos! cinquecento: di munificenza pirobutirrica: cinquecento pesos! con la maglia rattoppata. . . con i geloni ai diti . . . i piedi bagnati nelle scarpe . . . i castighi! perché i diti non potevano stringere la penna . . . col mal di gola sul Fedro . . . con sei gradi di amor paterno addosso . . . e un fumo da far inverdire le meningi . . . perché il caro bataccio venisse buono . . . buono agli inni e alla gloria. (124–25)
> [What just finished coming out of there . . . from the matrix of those maenads hurled belly-first into the air . . . with clapper hanging out. . . . Mad beasts! And I went hungry because of them, as a child hungry! Five hundred pesos! Five hundred: Pirobutirro munificence: five hundred pesos! With my jersey patched . . . chillblains on my fingers . . . my feet wet inside my shoes. . . . Punishment because my frozen fingers couldn't grasp the pen! . . . With a sore throat over the Phaedrus . . . with six degrees centigrade of paternal love upon me . . . and enough smoke to make my gray cells turn green . . . so the dear clapper would turn out well . . . good for anthems and glory.]

According to Gonzalo's story, at a time of severe financial hardship his father donated five hundred pesos to the town for the construction of a bell tower. In this hysterical outburst, the father's narcissistic character and tyrannical authority are relived and negated through the sexualization of their repressive symbol ("batacchio per aria . . . a intronare"). In a preceding diatribe, Gonzalo had transformed the bells into monstrous penises that ejaculate their sound on the plush and sultry countryside. But more important, Gonzalo's invectives against the narcissism of paternal authority are also a way of reestablishing his relationship with the father in terms of power. Not being able to tolerate his father's selfish, fanatic attachment to the countryside and villa (both figurations of the mother), he seeks to belittle that devotion. Paradoxically, the balance of power falls to the side of the son, as he exhibits narcissistically the omnipotence of his pen, the one once rendered impotent by his father's prodigality.[7]

In approaching the manifest psychoanalytical content of *La cognizione del dolore*, we are confronted with the problem of reducing the text to an illustration of something beyond itself, in particular, to a form of pathology. To what extent does pathology explain the novel? On the one hand, the continual flashing throughout the work of Freudian signifiers encourages a psychoanalytical reading of the text. On the other, the very transparency of psychoanalytical content in the surface narrative modifies the terms of the problem. The point is not that beneath the text's literal meaning exists a latent psychoanalytical content and that the text is its evidence but rather that the literal meaning and its psychoanalytical content are equivalent. The fact that the text demands a psychoanalytical response from the reader complicates the methodological question. Are we to find the text's ultimate meaning in the rationale provided for Gonzalo's malaise?

The surfacing of deep meaning, produced by Gadda's psychoanalytical writing of the text, has an important historical function. It can be seen as a response to fascist Italy's rejection of Freudian ideas: both intellectually, at the hands of Crocean and Gentilean neoidealism, and culturally, according to the popular myth of Latin purity and decorum.[8] In this sense, there is no other literary text of the 1930s that compares with *La cognizione* for its outright subversiveness. Gadda's negation of maternity, family, and community, the basis of institutionalized society, strikes to the heart of fascism's grand objective to reinstitute order and obedience as fundamental social values.

But what we know about Gadda's support of fascism (a reality that most commentators tend to ignore) bids us to be cautious in discussing any outright renouncement of fascism on his part before 1943.[9] In fact, Gadda's politics, which are supported to a large extent by psychoanalytic thought, are conservative and authoritarian and full of references to the hysteria of the popular masses and, particularly, of women. But still, there are some ways in which Gadda's Freudian (meta-psychological) polemics against the father and the law in *La cognizione* are extendable to fascist culture. Gadda's principal objective is to direct the reader's perception to realities outside of, or beyond, the world of appearances, particularly to that part of Gonzalo's mind behind the phenomenal self, which the protagonist can never know directly but which profoundly influences his sense of self. In this respect, let us consider what is perhaps Gonzalo's fiercest and most creative tirade, directed against the tolling of the bells:

Dodice gocce, come di bronzo immane, celeste, eran seguitate a cadere una via l'altra, indeprecabili, sul lustro fogliame del banzavois: anche se inavvertite al groviglio dell'aspide, molle, terrore maculato di tabacco. Vincendo robinie e cicale, e carpini, e tutto, le matrici del suono si buttarono alla propaganda di sé, tutt'a un tratto: che dirompeva nella cecità infinita della luce. Lo stridere delle bestie di luce venne sommerso in una propagazione di onde di bronzo: irraggiarono la compagna del sole, il disperato andare delle strade, le grandi verdi foglie, laboratori infiniti di clorofilla: cinquecento lire di onde, di onde! cinquecento, cinquecento!, basta, basta, signor Francisco, ma questo qui non fa male . . . di onde, di onde! dalla torre: dal campanile color calza, artefice di quel baccano tridentino. Furibondo sicinnide, offerivano il viscerame o poi lo rivoltavano contro monte, a onde, tumulto del Signore materiato, baccanti androgine alla lubido municipalistica d'ogni incanutito offerente. (110–11)
[Twelve drops, as if of monstrous bronze, celestial, had gone on falling, one after the other inexorable, on the shiny leaves of the *banzavois*—even if unperceived in the tangle of the aspen, soft, tobacco-speckled terror. Overcoming locusts and cicadas, and hornbeams, and everything, the matrices of sound were flung into self-propaganda, all of a sudden, which burst forth in the infinite blindness of the light. The chirping of the animals of light was submerged in a propagation of bronze waves: they irradiated the sun's country, the desperate progress of the roads, the great green foliage, infinite laboratories of chlorophyll: five hundred lire of waves, of waves! Five hundred, five hundred! Enough, enough Senor Francisco, but this can't do any harm . . . of waves, of waves! from the tower: from the stocking-colored spire, artificer of that Tridentine din. Furious Sicinnis, they proffered their entrails and then turned

Properties of Writing

them back against the mountain, in waves, tumult of the Lord made matter, androgynous bacchantes at the municipal libido of every gray-haired offerer.]

Here, even the most cautious of amateur Freudians would not hesitate to show how a particular stimulus has opened the door to the Unconscious, from which explodes a fury of resentment and guilt that derives from sexual repression. At the center of the description we find, moreover, an insertion that further substantiates the Freudian hypothesis: "cinquecento lire di onde, di onde! cinquecento, cinquecento! basta, basta signor Francisco." As the only segment of the passage without a narrative referent, we must follow the clue provided by the name Francisco. Given the autobiographical character of the story, our quest is easily satisfied: senor Francisco, Gonzalo's father, can be no other than Francesco Ippolito, Gadda's father. The outburst expresses the anatagonism between Gadda and his father. The free associative process brought about by the bells has revealed the existence of a psychic reality that the mind has removed from consciousness because of its unpleasant or unconfessable content. Following the Oedipal model, we can reduce the narrator's hysteria to its underlying cause. The bells, symbolic of paternal oppression, activate the invective directly against the father's sexual predominance. The narrator's narcissistic reaction displaces attention from the real object of Gadda's contempt, his father and, by extension, the Father, metonymized into the phallus.

Yet in following such a line of reasoning we run the risk of making Gonzalo into a psychoanalytical generalization. The kind of experience from which his figure derives, however, has a particularly historical feature, which must be reconstituted lest we diminish the social value of Gadda's isolated characters, who regard the external world as a menace to their freedom. In the passage just cited, the narrator's imprecation is interrupted by what amounts more or less to a looseness of association: the mention of Senor Francisco in relation to "five-hundred lire of waves." As the punctuation suggests, the sentences are meant to be complementary; the narrating mind, rather than wandering away from the point at which it began (as is typical of schizophrenic discourse), moves toward a concreteness of association: that relates Francisco, money, and the countryside. Senor Francisco's unsuccessful investment has caused the family's bankruptcy and, therefore, its separation from an organic and productive rela-

tion with the community. Humiliation destroys Gonzalo, forcing him to retreat to the villa, where he becomes an isolated, narcissistic individual.
This situation describes the insecurity that affects the family under capitalism. It derives from the breakdown of mutual dependency, which conditions the elaboration of narcissistic object relations.[10]

Several critics have argued that the world Gadda is writing about, albeit
disguised in an imaginary South American setting, is, in effect, the world
of Italian fascism, and that the narrator's numerous spells of verbal aggression are actually directed toward fascism. Piero Pucci was among the first
to discuss fascism's oblique presence in the story, arguing that the tolling of
the bells is a "metaphor for fascist propaganda" (a rite heralding the arrival
of a party hierarch or an imminent radio broadcast by Mussolini) and that
Gonzalo's tirades reflect "the spiritual atmosphere of disgust and, at the
same time, of impotence which is the exact transcription of a sentiment diffused in the Italian anti-fascists between the two wars, conscious either of
the uselessness of their animosity or of that which was to happen."[11] Along
the same lines, Enrico Flores suggests: "Si tratta dello 'straniamento' ot-
tenuto con la creazione di un 'milieu' ispanizzante che serva da maschera ai
riferimenti alla realtà italiana durante il fascismo, e quindi in questo modo
di fuggire la censura fascista."[12] [The estrangement achieved through the
South American setting masks the references to Italian social reality during
fascism; it thus escapes fascist censorship.] More recently, Luperini has
posed the question of the quasi identity of the Mother with fascism. In the
affection the Senora displays toward others, Gonzalo sees both the betrayal
of his frustrated desire for love and her submission to the bourgeois self as
a means of gaining the admiration of her fellow citizens and thus coercing
them into relationships of dependence. Thus, Luperini brings together the
psychological and social aspects of Gonzalo's malaise: "Nevrosi e rabbia
sociale sono in Gonzalo due facce di una stessa realtà. Esse sono presenti
anche quando i motivi del 'dolore' potrebbero sembrare del tutto privati e
riguardare solo l'individuale nevrosi del protagonista."[13] [Neurosis and
social polemics are for Gonzalo two faces of the same reality. They are present even when the ground for "dolore" appears totally private, concern-
ing only the protagonist's own personal neurosis.]

Besides contradicting Gadda's real, however misguided, politics, interpretations such as these sidestep the complex structure of the text, leaving

unexplained the anxiety present in the text's aggressive verbalization as well as its modalities of deception, which include the transgressed ego boundaries between narrator, Gonzalo and the Senora. Keeping in mind Gadda's attachment to fascism, the only coherent political reading of *La cogniᵼione del dolore* would have to regard the novel as a kind of exorcism, as a means of driving out the fascism within Gadda-Gonzalo.[14]

In Freudian terms, Gadda saw represented in fascism a nonsublimated erotic-narcissistic impulse, whose causes are to be found in the pulsations of a libidinally contaminated ego. If, on the one hand, this proposition is correct (as confirmed in *Eros e Priapo*), on the other, it is incomplete, because for the sake of a clinical diagnosis it ignores a number of social and cultural references contained in Gadda's polemics. Furthermore, if we view Gadda's apparent anti-fascism strictly from a Freudian standpoint, we are forced to conclude that it was Gadda's intention to represent all forms of autosexuality as manifestations of an arrested sexual development contrary to normal sexuality, whose objective is procreation and, therefore, the inclusion of offspring into the social order. But Gadda's polemics are much too radical and pessimistic to be considered simply a psychoanalytical critique of fascism. (Gonzalo, let us not forget, suffers from a malady that cannot be medicated.) Instead, the theme of narcissism in Gadda's works goes beyond its direct references to fascism and possesses a character that is more philosophical than psychological. At the outset of his essay, "L'Egoista," Gadda writes:

> Chi immagina e percepisce se medesimo come un essere "isolato" dalla totalità degli esseri, porta il concetto di individualità fino al limite della negazione, lo storce fino ad annullarne il contenuto. L'io biologico ha un certo grado di realtà: ma è sotto molti riguardi apparenza, vera petizione di principio. La vita di ognuno di noi pensata come fatto per sé stante, estraniato da un decorso e da una correlazione di fatti, è concetto erroneo, è figurazione gratuita. In realtà, la vita di ognuno di noi è una "simbiosi con l'universo". La nostra individualità è il punto di incontro, è il nodo o groppo di innumerevoli rapporti con innumerevoli situazioni (fatti o esseri) a noi apparentemente esterne. Ognuno di noi è il no di infiniti sì, e è il sì di infiniti no. Tra qualunque essere dello spazio metafisico e l'io individuale . . . intercede un rapporto pensabile: e dunque un rapporto di fatto. Di una libellula vola a Tokio, innesca una catena di reazioni che raggiunge me.[15]

[Whoever imagines and perceives himself as a being "isolated" from the totality of beings carries the concept of individuality to the point of negation, he deforms it to the point of nullifying its contents. Our biological self has a certain degree of reality, but in many respects it is just appearance, a genuine petition of principle. The life of each of us, considered as a thing in itself, separated from the integration and correlation of elements, is a mistaken concept, a gratuitous image. In truth, the life of each of us is a "symbiosis with the universe." Our individuality is a meeting point, it is the knot, the gnarl, of innumerable relations with innumerable situations (events or beings) apparently external to us. Each of us is limited in infinite directions by a dialectical counterpart: each of us is the no of infinite yeses and the yes of infinite noes. Between any being of metaphysical space and the individual self . . . intercedes a thinkable relationship; therefore, a de facto relationship. If a dragonfly flies in Tokyo, it sets off a chain of reactions that reaches me.]

These general notions respond to the problem of fascism in a more historically particular way than the psychoanalytic perspective, inasmuch as they identify narcissism in relation to the fragmentation and atomization of social life characteristic of modern capitalist development. Pathological narcissism in this sense can be seen as a metaphor for contemporary mass culture, which was heralded by the fascist system of cultural communication. The narcissistic object in Gadda may be viewed, thus, not only as a complex of activities that celebrate individual needs and drives but also as the structuring of desire by means of forms of self-gratification, which is symptomatic of mass culture. Gonzalo himself illustrates the dialectic of narcissism, inasmuch as he resists the weight of patriarchal domination (villa, wall, Nistituto, society) by creating his own grandiose self that rebels against deformation through narcissistic eccentricity. Narcissistic isolation is Gonzalo's refusal to accept repressive society; the real or figurative killing of his mother, in addition to its deep psychoanalytical significance, signals his rebellion against the lure of reintegration, that is, the search for ego gratification by participation in commodity and labor markets. Thus, the Oedipal ground of repression, the family as represented in the social images of society, has been violated by Gonzalo's pervasive desire.

It is not difficult to find the roots of *Quer pasticciaccio brutto de via Merulana* in *La cognizione del dolore*, which ends with a murder and the beginning of an investigation. Also, if it is true that Gadda's principal aim in *La cognizione* was, as he himself states in his preface, to probe the grotesque that nests "nel fegato macchinatore della universa realtà" (237) [in universal reality's machinating liver], then *Quer pasticciaccio* can be seen as the formalization of this investigative process. But why investigate if we know beforehand that the world is evil, that everyone is guilty of something, even the humble and the downtrodden, who, Gadda remarks, are also part of our "bestiaggine comune"? Why investigate, if entanglement is an integral part of both nature and history?

Two aspects of the form of *Quer pasticciaccio* stand out immediately.[16] As Gadda himself defines it, the novel is a *giallo,* and thus it uses the structure and many of the strategies of detective fiction. Two crimes, a burglary and a murder, set into motion an investigation headed by a detective. The process of detection and interrogation lead the reader into a world without boundaries, where everything and everyone is to some degree suspect. The principle of suspicion generates an overriding sense of causal ramification. As we attempt to disentangle the scheme of things, we learn not to dismiss any detail; everything is potentially relevant and meaningful, nothing is safe, nothing can be spared scrutiny, everyone is vulnerable, everyone is guilty.

At the same time, Gadda's novel is very much a comic spectacle, both verbally, in that it parodies spoken and written Italian, and socially, because it subverts social norms and hierarchies. Mockery and derision are its privileged modes of expression. It is Rabelaisian, in the sense Mikhail Bakhtin has given to the term, because it materializes, degrades, violates, deforms, and vulgarizes conventional forms of existence and desecrates treasured idols of rational efficiency.[17] Rabelaisian is the authorial self in its various disguises that Gadda does not leave behind in his travels *ad inferos,* through his world turned inside out. *Quer pasticciaccio* is the twentieth century's greatest monument to Rabelais and the Rabelaisian tradition. But it is a memorial cast in the spirit of nihilism. There is nothing festive or liberating in the chaos and absurdity Gadda describes; his word games and abusive metaphors have as their target not one particular tradition of linguistic dominance but all language, popular as well as official, that usage has fossilized. Gadda's carnival is a totally negative spectacle, with no prospects for renewal and no utopian longings. It ends, as it begins, in death and interrogation, while the reader, following authorial directives, continues relentlessly the search for meaning that reality repudiates.

Although Gadda has often stated his indebtedness to detective fiction (to Conan Doyle, in particular), his giallo, despite its retainment of certain external features of the genre, subverts the relation between order and dilinquency on which the classical detective story is based. D. A. Miller has given us some important insights into the epistemological structure of the genre which have a strong bearing on Gadda's case. He argues that, while the form of traditional detective fiction is based on the premise that no detail can be ruled out in the solution of the crime, its operative strategy is one of dissolving hypothetical significances in favor of selective meaningfulness. "Though the detective story postulates a world in which everything might have a meaningful bearing on the solution of the crime, it concludes with an extensive repudiation of meanings that simply 'drop out.'"[18] The purpose of the investigation, to identify and capture the criminal, underlines both the innocence of the community and its vulnerability. By repairing the fabric of normalcy that the otherness of delinquency has shorn, detectives display their power of policing within the form of the narrative itself: they set the limits, which become one with the narrative structure, and thereby reassure the community that the disruptiveness of the investigation is an exception to the routine social order. The general ideological effect of such a structure is, according to Miller, the illusion that the community is "'outside' the network of policing power" (37).

The main dimension of *Quer pasticciaccio* that sets it apart from the classical detective story is the proliferation, rather than condensation, of significances. Everything under the narrator's gaze is considered but not necessarily as a detail employed in an orderly process that eventually will lead us to the truth. Objects of meaning in Gadda's deliquent world hold a significance that in most instances has no bearing whatsoever on the case. They belong to a different register and dissent from the game of detection, deflecting the reader's eye from the supposed object of inquiry.

Another function of the traditional detective story was to foreground the detectives' exceptional wisdom and acumen, which they exercised in a commonplace world of petty occurrences. Their great capacity to penetrate into areas inaccessible to the ordinary mind was exceptional and was regarded as such by the community. In *Quer pasticciaccio*, Don Ciccio Ingravallo belongs to this gifted class of super sleuths, but he does so parodically, as a caricature of himself: "Ubiquo ai casi, onnipresente su gli affari tenebrosi ... nella sua sagezza enunciava qualche teoretica idea (idea generale si intende) sui casi degli uomini: e delle donne. A prima vista, cioè al primo udirle, sembravano banalità. Non erano banalità" (5). [Ubiquitous as the occasion required, omnipresent in all tenebrous matters ... in his wisdom he enunciated some theoretical idea (a general idea, that is) on the affairs of men, and of women. At first sight, or rather, on first hearing, these seemed banalities. They weren't banalities.] Moreover, Gadda's detective, in contrast, say, to Sherlock Holmes or Dupin, falls short of carrying out the traditional role of monitoring the course of the narration. This function is carried out thoroughly by the narrator, whose probing eye, deprived as it is of one particular object on which to focus, concentrates on everything it sees. As a result, the narrative elements proliferate into a thickening and protraction of meanings.

Two paradigmatic instances of this process can be found in Don Ciccio's awakening the morning of the novel's final day and Biondone's visit to the marketplace in search of Tina's friend. These examples illustrate a process whereby the narrator suspends an action having a more or less precise objective because his eye is attracted to something else. The plot is thereby displaced, opening up an unlimited space of comic and grotesque correspondences. Even if Don Ciccio succeeds in tracking down the criminal, thus concluding an inquiry that substantiates the community's innocence, the activity of the narrator, because it does not coincide with the activity of the detective, accentuates not the innocence but rather the guilt of the entire community. The narrator surveys, controls, and punishes, everything that Don Ciccio cannot do. And at the end of the story, even if the detective seems to have solved the crime, the criminal, in spite of the police's intimidation of the witness, is not named. The investigation breaks down, paralyzed in interrogation. With this absence of a denouement, we return to the entanglement with which we began. Ingravallo thinks he knows who Liliana's murderer is, but, more than ever, the source of the evil eludes him.

Gadda criticism has agreed that the overriding sense of *Quer pasticciaccio* is to be found in its detailed reproduction of chaos, in its representation of the evil of everyday life during fascism, and in its all-inclusive indictment and condemnation, from which only the murdered Liliana (for the most part absent from the action) and a few lower-class female characters are saved. Furthermore, according to Gian Carlo Ferretti, *Quer pasticciaccio* represents "un deciso e quasi programmatico ritorno al romanzo come intreccio, come strumento di rappresentazione e interpretazione della realtà, e in particolare al giallo come indagine dentro il *disordine,* come processo di ristabilimento di un *ordine*[19] [a decisive and almost programmatic return to the novel conceived as intrigue, as a means of representing and interpreting reality, and in particular to the detective story as inquiry within the realm of *disorder,* as a process for establishing an *order*].

Although what Ferretti (and others) say may be true, it does not address the problems foregrounded by such a characterization, namely, Gadda's crossbreeding of the detective story and the macaronic, of the order aspired to and the disorder represented, of the tragic account of a senseless murder and the comic spectacle in which it is set. We are dealing with a highly composite narrative structure truly difficult to understand.

These contrasting features are based on the fundamental juxtaposition of identity and difference, norm and deviance. The detective story is meant to restore order, while the macaronic's purpose is to destroy order; tragedy provides density and coherence, while comedy is founded on incongruity. To which of the opposing terms should we give preference? Gadda has made his own choice indisputably clear, as all of his theoretical essays spotlight invention and polyphony. Gadda's formula, in *La cognizione del dolore,* "barocco è il mondo, e il G ha percepito e ritratto la baroccaggine" (32) [the world is baroque and G. has perceived and depicted its baroqueness], would appear, then, to be the most suitable guide to an understanding of his work. But why is the world baroque? Why is the grotesque part and parcel of the nature of things?

The only way to get free from Gadda's justificatory logic is to move on to a different register, one that enables us to consider *Quer pasticciaccio* as not so much a caricature of the reality of life under fascism (which it also is) as a manner of perceiving and describing that at once represents and deforms, unmasks and conceals, constructs and disguises, that reality. To do so, we must abandon the mimetic or realistic hypothesis on which Gadda bases his narration in favor of a psychoanalytic hypothesis, because from Gadda's point of view it is the only hypothesis that will lead us to history proper. "Una felice espressione o dizione," Gadda writes, "si raggiunge, a quanto sembra, più veramente lungo i misteriosi cammini di una sintesi inconscia, che non per grammaticali o lessicologiche deliberazioni."[20] [Successful expression or speech, it seems, is achieved more directly through the mysterious paths of unconscious synthesis than by means of grammatical or lexicological deliberation.] This is one of many instances in which Gadda indicates the area to be explored without, however, providing any specific directive to follow.

In its form as a detective story, *Quer pasticciaccio*, too, is a kind of signal that tells us to carry out an investigation, which for Gadda is the function of criticism: "[radunare] le cose disperdute nei mille momenti e dispositivi dell'impianto, e [coordinare] questi in una struttura totale"[21] [(to collect) things dispersed in the numerous phases and dispositions of a system and (to arrange) them in a total structure]. And if, as Gadda believes, chaos generates order, perhaps it would be useful to proceed backwards in an attempt to reconstruct the chaos. To do so, we must first dwell briefly on two crucial features of the narrative: the notion of entanglement and the use of dialect.

From the very beginning, the notion of a twisted, ensnarled reality is given so much prominence that it appears almost as a parody or caricature of itself. And although the novel presents numerous knots to be unraveled, these are mainly complications of an emotional or sexual character. The entanglements on which Gadda founds his investigation is the relationship between Liliana and her young domestics, between Liliana and her husband, and between Liliana and her cousin Giuliano. In the traditional detective story, the notion of intrigue or imbroglio was not presupposed, as in *Quer pasticciaccio*, but rather issued from and was verified by the action. Complication was, in fact, an exception to the normative ideal of social harmony. Moreover, the established order that entanglement disrupts, given the ontological nature of evil in *Quer pasticciaccio*, is only apparent, while in the conventional police story, order is an unassailable given on which the illusion that the community is healthy and does not need to be policed is based. The innocence of the social community for the Freudian Gadda is an outright lie, and the scene of analysis, which is the investigation, will illuminate the unstable and contradictory reality behind the mask of appearances, in much the same way, according to Gadda, that psychoanalysis dismantles "l'idea sintesi che noi ci formiamo di noi stessi"[22] [the idea synthesis we form about ourselves].

The entanglement on which the giallo is based, therefore, can be nothing else but the extension and enlargement of the entangled relationships existing, according to Gadda, "tra il bambino e la madre, tra il bambino e la balia" (45). [between the child and his mother, between the child and his wetnurse]. It is an entire system of culture and civilization that must be subjected to the interrogation and complex inquiries of the detective-analyst and his collaborators. They, however, do not occupy a neutral position beyond the parameters of the investigation but are also subjects to be examined, knots to be unraveled. Here, the narrative strategy is to conflate the object of investigation and the concept used to study it, so that the truth of the text coincides with the narrative perspective. But what if the opposite were true: that the truth of the narrator, that is, the metahistorical entrapment of the child in the existence of his mother, which in *La cognizione del dolore* takes hold of practically the entire narrative, has been diffused into the labyrinth of universal guilt. To put it another way, the "groviglio" (7) instructs us to investigate, examine, interrogate, and unravel at the same time that it conceals the true subject of investigation: the authorial self that cannot and must not be identified. Hence, *Quer pasticciaccio* can be considered a pretext containing only traces of the master text from which it is generated; the form of the detective story puts us on the right track, but at the same time it leads us afield in a hunt for something else.

Why dialect? Gadda himself supplies the best answer: because "il linguaggio del popolo è largamente intriso di libertà psicanalitica: più duramente esperto del bene e del male, il popolo trascende più facilmente dei retori a chiamare pane il pane e vino il vino, un po' come Freud se pure al di qua di una terminologia clinica o di una sintassi metodologica" (49). [the language of the common people is largely permeated with psychoanalytic freedom. More hardened by the experience of good and evil, the common people tend more easily than academicians to call a spade a spade, a little like Freud, even if not in clinical terminology or scientific prose]. Dialect, in Gadda's view, is a channel for the unconscious. Juxtaposed to official speech, it becomes a means to explore the relation between reality and fiction. In *Quer pasticciaccio*, dialect carries a dual function. On the one hand, it represents the linguistic awareness of the common people, their spontaneity, as well as their alienation from normative speech. In this sense, its use enables the reader to savor the mentality of Gadda's ordinary characters, whether they actually belong to Rome's urban proletariat or are just peripheral representatives of a culturally and linguistically subaltern world.

On the other hand, dialectal speech, paradoxically, contributes to distancing the reader from the narrative; this is its principal function. One of the most original features of *Quer pasticciaccio* is linguistic contamination, which extends even to the official, learned voice of the narrator, as for example, in the following remark: "Li funerali, contro l'aspettativa o pe mejo dì de la speranza de la polizzia, nun fecero fa un passo avanti a l'indaggine, ma sortanto a le chiacchiere" (153). [The funeral service, contrary to the expectations or rather the hopes of the police, did not help the investigation in the least but only caused more chatter.] This is much more than a case of authorial mimicking, which presupposes detachment and control; the narrating voice itself, as it conveys the details of an event, cannot escape being polluted by popular speech. In this sense, Don Ciccio, who from time to time assumes the authorial optic, "contaminando napolitano, molisano e italiano" (7) [contaminating Neapolitan, Molisan, and Italian], acquires the value of a metanarrative sign of the universal entanglement Gadda aims to represent.

Given the presence of a linguistic norm shared by author and reader, the effect of dialectal contamination is one of comic incongruity. Thus, language, too, in *Quer pasticciaccio* works against the grain of normalcy in a way analogous to the form of the detective story and to the contents it generally includes. The result is a parody of the linguistic norm, which capitalizes on the reality of Italy's regional cultures as well as on fascism's pretentious objective to standardize ordinary speech. The comic effectiveness of Gadda's parody depends on the eccentricity of dialect with respect to the linguistic norm; at the same time, it underlines the spontaneity of popular speech as well as the communicative ineptness of a language that falsifies the inner realities of its speakers. Linguistic parody, whether aimed at ordinary speech or at literary style and syntax, is a typically Gaddian form of negation. The object of negation is the world of appearances, as the narrative voice of *La cognizione del dolore* puts it, "le figurazioni non valide . . . da respingere, come specie falsa di denaro" (165) [figurations that are not valid . . . to be rejected like counterfeit money]. But what lies behind the negation is the reverse image of the thing negated. The object ridiculed through parody is reconstructed and transferred on to a lower plane; thus, it acquires a new temporal and spacial consistency, it becomes—to use Bakhtin's suggestive formula—"the other side of the new object which has taken its place" (410).

Quer pasticciaccio, therefore, can be considered a "scene" at once negated and renewed, an enlargement or dilation, not of conflict and trauma but of a strategy employed to distance the fear of nonbeing, which exhibits similtaneously certitude and equivocation, connecting these notions to the outside world of objects and events. The "dolore" to which Gadda refers in his first novel as "il male oscuro" (204) is a typically schizoid condition of disassociation, according to which things perceived appear not to be real and relationships with others are all to some degree removed. In Gadda, however, we are dealing much less with the conflict between a true and false self than with a kind of integral duality, a dual identity for which the boundaries between self and other are completely obliterated. We have seen how in *La cognizione del dolore* to what extent Gonzalo and his mother are one and the same person. To negate her as a vacuous image was, for Gonzalo, tantamount to negating himself. For this very reason, the matricide with which Gadda had obviously planned to end his novel was in the last analysis discarded. In order that he not annihilate himself in the "rapina del dolore" (the metaphor is significant as it connotes at once theft, violation, and depredation), he must resort to ridicule ("scherno"), knowing well that it too is a mask (204).

In *Quer pasticciaccio* Gadda cloaks the image of self (Gonzalo), which in *La cognizione del dolore* had become a "maschera tragica sulla metope del teatro" (204) [tragic mask on the metope of the theater] in three different characters: Ingravallo, Commendatore Angeloni, and Liliana Balducci. This last disguise is crucial, because it represents much more than comic distancing. While Don Ciccio and *sor* Filippo are caricatures of some well-known Gaddian trademarks (amateur philosopher, celibate, gourmand, etc.), the figure of Liliana involves a much more complex and, in many ways, paradoxical dymanic: the negation of being (actualized in her murder) is Gadda's means of safeguarding the ontological foundation of womanhood. In other words, Liliana is the "self" that must be terminated in order that the authorial voice disentangle itself from muliebrity, from being *donna* and thus, potentially, *madre*. To free itself from its Other means putting an end to the anguished existence of someone who, like Gonzalo, is forced to live within his mother in the shadow of paternal oppression. It is from this conflict that the narrative, as well as Gadda's fierce polemics against Mussolini and fascist Italy, ultimately derive.

Gadda describes Liliana's violated body thus:

> Un profondo, un terribile taglio rosso le apriva la gola, ferocemente. Aveva preso metà il collo, dal davanti verso destra, cioè verso sinistra, per lei, destra per loro che guardavano: sfrangiato ai due margini come da un reiterarsi dei colpi, lama o punta: un orrore! da nun potesse vede. Palesava come delle filacce rosse, all'interno, tra quella spumiccia nera der sangue, già raggrumato, a momenti; un pasticcio! con delle bollicine rimaste a mezzo. Curiose forme, agli agenti: parevano buchi, al novizio, come dei maccheroncini color rosso, o rosa. "La trachea," mormorò Ingravallo chinandosi, "la carotide! la iugulare . . . Dio!". . .
>
> Le mutandine nun ereno insanguinate: lasceveno scoperti li du tratti de le cosce, come du anelli de pelle: fino alle calze, d'un biondo lucido. La solcatura del sesso . . . pareva d'esse o Ostia d'estate, o ar Forte de marmo de Viareggio, quanno so sdriate su la rena a cocese, che te fanno vede tutto quello che vonno. Co quele maje tirate tirate d'oggigiorno. (63–64)
>
> A deep, a terrible red cut opened her throat, fiercely. It had taken half the neck, from the front toward the right, that is, toward her left, the right for those who were looking down: jagged at its two edges, as if by a series of blows, of the blade or point: a horror! You couldn't stand to look at it. From it hung red strands, like thongs, from the black foam of the blood, almost clotted already; a mess! with some little bubbles still in the midst. Curious forms, to the policemen: they seemed holes to the novice, like red-colored little maccheroni, or pink. "The trachea," murmured Ingravallo, bending down, "the carotid, the jugular! . . . God!" . . .
>
> The underpants weren't bloodied; they left uncovered two patches of thigh, two rings of flesh: down to the stockings, glistening blond skin. The furrow of her sex . . . it was like being at Ostia in the summer, or at Forte dei Marmi in Viareggio, when they are lying on he sand cooking themselves and they let you glimpse whatever they want. With those tight jerseys they wear nowadays.]

The distancing and dedramatizing effects of language disassociate the narrative voice from the dead woman's body, surrendering it to the crude scrutiny of others. The spectators now possess Liliana, simply because the narrator has renounced his point of view. The linguistic distancing works to objectivize the author's schizoid perspective, transforming it into a general entanglement, a "pasticcio." The language employed by the narrator is not truly his; it belongs to the other, just like Liliana. The speaking self is empty; it desires an autonomy and a plenitude it can never truly attain.

Gadda presents Liliana's body to the reader in three distinct moments or dimensions: covered by the unrefined gaze of photographers and police agents; reflected on by Don Ciccio as "una decomposizione estrema dei possibili, uno sfararsi di idee interdipendenti, armonizzate già nella persona. Come il risolversi d'una unità che non ce la fa più ad essere e ad operare come tale, nella caduta improvvisa dei rapporti, d'ogni rapporto colla realtà sistematrice" (77) [an extreme decompounding of possibles, an unfocusing of interdependent ideas, formerly harmonized in one person. Like the dissolving of a unity that cannot hold out any longer, the sudden collapse of relationships, of all ties with organizing reality]; and sublimated by the authorial voice in flashes of lyricism geared to soften the rigid and unassailable materiality of the scene: "Il dolce pallore del di lei volto, così bianco nei sogni opalini della sera, aveva ceduto per modulazioni funebri a un tono cianotico, di stanca pervinca." [The sweet pallor of her face, so white in the opaline dreams of the evening, had given away through funereal modulations to a cyanotic tone, a faded periwinkle.]

From a point of view at once allegorical and psychoanalytical, the distancing applied in this scene separates the narrative voice from its Other, that is from the principle of muliebrity that that voice has murdered but that now lives in the form of a dead body, simultaneously possessed and spiritualized into an unfaltering, deathless evil: "Il male ... sembrò esistere: a maturare i giorni e gli eventi: da sempre: muta forza o presenza in un pandemonismo della campagna e della terra, sotto cieli o nuvole che non potevano far altro se non rimirare, o fuggire" (292). [The evil ... seemed to exist: to ripen days and events, since always; silent force or presence in a pandemonium of the country or of the earth, beneath skies or clouds that could do nothing but look down or flee.]

Thus, the author of the story cannot disentangle himself completely from the author of the crime, no matter how many alienating strategies he puts to use. For if Liliana is, as she is, always present as the force generating the narrative, then the principle of guilt, which the narrative voice underwrites, cannot be repealed. In other words, with the death of Liliana Gadda destroys the Oedipal object with which he identified. He escapes, therefore, the anguish of entrapment. Now that the purity and innocence of womanhood has been violated, killed with a stroke of the pen, Gadda can address the phallic principle, the transcendental law, which the subject has internalized and which is the basis of his authority and autonomy.

In *Quer pasticciaccio*, the authority of the subject passes over to the narrative voice, which, in an attempt to topple the rule of law (in Freudian terms, the superego), inveighs against its dehumanizing effects. In a manner consistent with Freud's teachings, Gadda portrays the law, grotesquely embodied in fascism, as no more than a manifestation of desire. He ruthlessly attacks its ever-present hedonistic pathology, its terrorism and despotism. His hostility toward Mussolini and his regime knows no limits. But, perhaps also on account of Freud, Gadda cannot forget that he too was once emotionally attached to fascism's coerciveness, that he too had contributed to the diffusion of the myths in the name of which it violated and ravaged.

Seen in this perspective, the murder of Liliana is the same as the destruction of the metaphysical foundation from which derive the ideals of culture and civilization that fascism proclaimed to defend. The metaphysical heritage that her figure evokes does not disappear, however, but remains as a violated norm, as a kind of theoretical utopia, which the authorial voice from time to time summons nostalgically and which finds its material correspondences in the privileged, consoling figures of Liliana's young domestics, whose "gem-like eyes, a child's" like those of Ines, "enunciarono a tutti quei maschi di poca cena il nome d'una felicità tuttavia possibile; d'una gioia, d'una speranza, d'una verità superordinata alle cartoffie, ai muri squallidi, alle mosche secche del soffitto, al ritratto del Merda" (178) [enunciated to all those men, still without their supper, the name of a happiness that was yet possible; a joy, a hope, a truth superior to their papers, to the squalid walls, the dried flies on the ceiling, the portrait of the shit] or in the "dignita naturale e intrinseca" (286) [natural, intrinsic dignity] of the recovered jewels.

In terms of literary style, Gadda's Freudian struggle against the law and against the metaphysical dimension of human existence turns into a battle against the aesthetic ideals of bourgeois realism and its veristic and neorealistic variants. The formula, championed largely by the *neoavanguardia*, of "creational realism" brings us face-to-face with the materiality of Gadda's writing practice. Angelo Guglielmi's remarks that Gadda's writing provokes rather than represents and that his exclusively material realities exist in a neutral state, can be productively used to understand how Gadda reproduces stylistically the constitutive aspects of his historical experience.[23]

The principal characteristic of Gadda's style is that his images do not imitate any form of objective reality; rather they exhibit objects, already culturalized by use and convention, that are lodged as ideal constructs within the collective psyche. The result is that actions and characters are twice removed from the real, for what Gadda parodies is not their reality, which remains intact and constant as a violated norm, but their cultural representation in language. The impression we get of materiality stems from their existence as things exhibited. The object appears deformed because Gadda parodies not the thing but the discourse that gives it notoriety. Central to this process is the particularly Gaddian notion of the literary work as the *mise en oeuvre* of an unnamed truth exhibited in disguise. It is this masquerading that gives Gadda's works the carnivalesque aura of reality as spectacle, at the same time that it indicates the locus of a crime and the impossibility of disentanglement.

CHAPTER SEVEN

Antonio Pizzuto

The Subject of Narrative

In the sixth chapter of Antonio Pizzuto's *Signorina Rosina,* the protagonist Bibi, thumbing through his manuscript entitled *Ravenna* and relating to his parish priest Don Zazzi the long time and many troubles involved in writing it, refers to a certain Signor Karlebach, a deceased industrialist who, he remarks, was the only person who might have understood his novel. He is quick to add, however, that he could also have been the only person who did not understand it: "L'assoluto, in fondo, consiste nel relativo."[1] [The absolute, in the final analysis, consists in the relative.] While taking notice ironically of the general difficulty of comprehending his own fiction, Bibi's paradoxical observation sets forth the heuristic principle on which Pizzuto's work is based: that particular and relational entities are constant in themselves and there is no center or source for their meaning.

Mr. Karlebach, to whom we cannot appeal for the verification of what he might or might not have understood was perhaps not by accident an industrialist. As such, we assume, he may have championed multinational capitalism, advertising, and the rapid rhythms associated with modern economy and contemporary cultural industries. Moreover, Mr. Karlebach, like Bibi, belonged to a postwar society and a particular social system whose logic emphasized the present and the elimination of what futurism used to refer to as sacred memories.

Karlebach, no doubt, saw something new in *Ravenna*, perhaps a break with the literature he was accustomed to reading: a shift of focus from the subversive thematics of modernist writings to an ideologically neutral space in which meaning retreats before the captivating presence of sensations and objects. But to say that Karlebach "understood" presupposes that there was something to understand and that he was in a position to understand it. Maybe it was the logic of the way he himself perceived and apprehended the world, reproduced by *Ravenna*, that he thought he understood, or maybe this was the very thing that prevented his understanding.

The *Ravenna* referred to was Antonio Pizzuto's third regularly published novel and the first in which he attempts to create a pastiche of sensation and emotion, intended to reflect the garbled, incomprehensible world that at once beseiged and haunted him. In *Signorina Rosina*, *Ravenna* (drafted, or at least projected, at the time of *Rosina*) can be seen as an ironic sign of chaos, inscribed on a fabric that nonetheless exhibits some measure of rational interlacing. Nothing Bibi says about *Ravenna* is useful for deciphering the delirium it encompasses, except perhaps the fact that its title, like the name of a person, tells us nothing about what is inside the book: "Era intitolato 'Ravenna'. Storico forse? No. Una guida della città? Neanche. Perché mai quel nome, dunque. Così. Come uno può essere chiamato Giacomo o Carlo. Secondo il suo gusto, quello era il titolo: libro e titolo erano nati insieme, l'uno per l'altro" (42). [It was entitled "Ravenna." A historical novel, perhaps? No. A traveler's guide to the city? Not even that. Why that name, then. For no reason. Like someone could be called Giacomo or Carlo. According to one's personal taste, that's the title: book and title were conceived at the same time, one for the other.] A name is a name is a name. It has nothing to do with the book; it responds to our practical need to name things, to distinguish them from what they are not named.[2]

Ravenna denotes the landscape of a nonexistent locus, a space deprived of time and continuity to which we, as victims of both history and existence, are hopelessly condemned. Within its boundaries we seek our peace; amid the cars and television sets, we dream of a new, consumer-oriented society that urges us to forget our past and our identity. The absolute non-referentiality of Ravenna, is a starting point for our discussion of *Signorina Rosina,* for it, too, is concerned ultimately with disconnected things and experiences, and it, too, is given a name that tricks the reader into looking in the direction of a person, place, thing, or event that might serve as a focal point for meaning and understanding.

Signorina Rosina would appear to indicate the subject of a narrative, like Madame Bovary, Mastro don Gesualdo or Le sorelle Matterassi, all individuals equipped with private identities, visions of the world, and unique, unmistakable intellectual and emotional features. Signorina Rosina is, too, a person. We meet her early on in Pizzuto's narrative. She is an old relative of the main character, Bibi; we assume she is an unmarried aunt. When we come upon her, she is dying, reduced to a mere trace of what she once was. The care and sensitivity with which Bibi treats her suggests something more than familial regard. However, we learn nothing of their relationship except that Bibi, in spite of the cost involved, is intent on respecting her wishes to be buried in the family tomb located at the opposite end of the peninsula. As soon as Signorina Rosina is introduced, she dies. Her death ("Per lei fu tre sospiri" [21] [For her just three sighs]) is related with such an economy of affect that the reader, already confused by Pizzuto's sudden narrative transitions, is likely to miss it altogether. She then begins her journey by train, alone amid her flowers, by night, over trestles and through tunnels, to a burial destination awaiting her 951 kilometers away.

This Signorina Rosina, the original, fictionally historical Rosina, reappears to Bibi, at the end of the book's penultimate chapter, at the cemetery where she was buried. At dusk, in the "hour of love," Bibi sees the shade that has called his name: "Zia Rosina, egli balbettò, zia Rosina, signorina Rosina. E insolitamente pianse. Non doveva guardarla, né toccarla. Poter rammentare le sue parole. Tanto viaggio perché? Ma ritornerà, zia Rosina? Ritornerà? Basta pensarmi. Pensare è chiamare" (140–41). [Aunt Rosina, he stuttered, Aunt Rosina, Miss Rosina. And he cried, unexpectedly. He should not have looked at her, nor touched her. If he could only remember her words. Why so much traveling? Will she come back, Aunt Rosina? Will she return? All you have to do is think of me. Thinking is calling.] Her words convey an essential message that involves, somehow, the need to preserve a personal history and a tradition, which the protagonist's present experience tends to efface.

But in the space between these two rather direct experiences the reader has of the real Signorina Rosina, Pizzuto refers to at least six other Rosinas whom Bibi encounters in his travels. Signorina Rosina is a gypsy woman he meets by chance at an amusement park, who sews a button on his coat (37); Signorina Rosina is the woman who prepares meals at Don Zazzi's house but is never seen (45). Rosina is the name given to the donkeys used to transport Bibi and a group of students around the site of an earthquake ("Si chiamavano tutti Rosina, col latte e senza latte" [58]. [They all, weaned or unweaned, were called Rosina]); Rosina is the name of the ship whose captain prevents Compiuta, Bibi's companion, from sailing on to get to the island penitentiary where Bibi was on assignment (86). Signorina Rosina is the daughter of the head guard at the island pentitentiary where Bibi is sent to inspect the restoration of a wall, to whom Bibi addresses the question: "Ma le monache, signorina Rosina, possono forse cantare? e cantare Arriva la banda?" (125) [But the nuns, Miss Rosina, could they perhaps sing? sing "The Gang is Coming"?]; finally, Signorina Rosina is the name of a girl who sings a litany in church and who brings Bibi the news that the director of the penitentiary, who had taken him to trial for negligence, had been removed from office (134–35).[3]

The extension of Signorina Rosina's name to different textual referents is no doubt the most salient aspect of the novel's structure. Ruggero Jacobbi, one of Pizzuto's more discerning critics, sees the different figures of Rosina as a kind of *flatus vocis,* a minor apparition that alludes to the loss of traditional values and social stability. For Jacobbi, Rosina is much more than a sign of eccentricity ("il dato inutile che costantemente interviene nell'apparente utilità della vita"[4] [a useless piece of data that constantly intrudes into the apparent usefulness of life] or a symbol of the woman never totally possessed.[5] He interprets Rosina as the object of Bibi's anxiety for universal truth: "Congiungersi amorosamente a sifatta creatura sarebbe ritrovare l'identificazione universale, ma è cosa a lui negata, forse impossibile in sé."[6] [To consummate his love for such a person would be to recover a universal identity, but for him this is prohibited, perhaps impossible.] Elsewhere, Jacobbi remarks that, although Bibi has a family, Pizzuto focuses on his solitary existence and on his rootlessness as signs of his character's awareness of belonging to the ancestral world of the Italian Mezzogiorno, whose vestiges are gradually being obliterated.[7] Pizzuto's Rosinas, then, are traces of an order (a system of values, a way of life, structures of feeling and thinking) that has passed away and whose loss is ever more felt as his character experiences Being in fragments of pleasure and temporary fulfillment.

It would be wrong, however, to view Bibi's experience as a search on Pizzuto's part for a metaphysical foundation to life. The anxiety Jacobbi notes can be referred to as a kind of postmodern anxiety of abandonment: How will it be possible to overcome Rosina, to go beyond the truth and comfort she once represented? How is it possible to overcome a tradition and its postulates of truth and value? From a narrative standpoint, these implicit questions involve a whole series of dialectical oppositions on which the modernist tradition was based (subject/object, space/time, reality/fantasy, art/life, past/future, tradition/innovation), oppositions that have been legitimized by culture and that are part and parcel of the tradition of Italian literary modernism, from Pirandello to Gadda. Pizzuto's art is an attempt to liberate the reader from narrative structures that depend on such dichotomies and to thereby create a new postmetaphysical and posthistorical perspective, one whose formal features express the rationale of a new social system that marked Italy's entry, in the wake of the economic boom of the fifties, into the world of late capitalism.[8]

What is most disturbing about Pizzuto's narratives is that, while scenes of utmost familiarity abound (bourgeois city life, family settings, people on vacation, children playing games, gossip, office interiors, bureaucracy), we have no way of capturing the narrative significance of these settings and actions. They are at once intelligible and distant, existing as material items (signifiers) catalogued in the mind of a viewer who releases them arbitrarily, in a disconnected, discontinuous manner. The result is that they appear as things seen or heard at a distance (the estrangement is justified objectively), about whose reality the narrator is ultimately uncertain. The present time of Pizzuto's narrative, moreover, does not seem to be part of a context, whether historical or psychological, that unifies or centers its perceptions. The picture we receive is undifferentiated, in the sense that places, characters, and events, although fully recognizable in themselves, from a narrative standpoint have no distinguishing characteristics. The reader is forced to reread Pizzuto's sentences over and over again, not because they contain mysterious references or difficult vocabulary but rather because they set no direction for our mind to follow. The narrator moves from sentence to sentence without giving us any hint whatsoever that his focus has changed, that the subject we were expecting to find has been replaced. And, since his perspective is not one of omniscience, we can only piece together the information he gives us to form a picture of what he is seeing.

Take, for example, the novel's first chapter. It tells of the return of Bibi (Alberto Conte, a middle-aged, petit bourgeois, socially maladjusted dreamer, employed by the state as a civil engineer) to his (unnamed) city from one of his usual (but unspecified) business trips. Compiuta is at the railway station to meet him. The action, which covers the space of little more than four pages, consists largely of a rather banal lovers' quarrel. Compiuta wants some assurance that Bibi loves her; she weeps, threatens to go to his wife, is appeased momentarily by his "Ti voglio bene" (9) only to be aggravated again by the knowledge (not explicitly conveyed to the reader) that he is about to embark on another trip. Their quarrel is interrupted twice by moments of reverie, solicited by things done (eating an ice cream) or seen (chefs working in the kitchen of a restaurant).

Our first impulse is to look for a context in which to place the experience and events recounted, to attend to meanings signaled by what we learn of the characters (Bibi's behavior is enigmatic; Compiuta is hungry for some sense of the future of their relationship), and to isolate signs of a line of thematic movement. The vision we get, however, is, from a narrative standpoint, undifferentiated. The speech and behavior of the characters are recorded and interpreted, but at the same time they are displaced by images and sounds that strike the narrator with a vivid charge of affect. The eye of the narrator is much like that of a movie camera that records the hard edge of objects, endowing them with a hallucinatory and compelling quality. The situation and the surroundings are familiar, but since their meaning is absent or lost, it is their materiality that holds our attention:

> Tutto quel che restava della signorina Rosina era lì, a sinistra, rattrappito sotto la luce velata non oltrepassante il lettuccio. L'avambraccio consunto aveva qualche lieve mossa; a tastarlo sembrava di toccare un cavolo. Con un fil di voce la chiamò per nome. La chiamò anche, come nei tempi lieti, Signor Rosolio. Non gli riusciva di frenare le lacrime. Ella schiuse le palpebre. Forse lo ri-

conobbe. Disse che voleva un po' di rosolio. Giungevano rumori di stoviglie e posate. Le umettò la bocca. Uscì. (13)

[All that remained of Miss Rosina was there, on the left, deadened under the faint light that did not extend beyond the small bed. Her decrepit forearm moved just slightly; it had the feel of a cabbage. A hardly audible voice called her by name. Mr Rosolio, in happy times, also called her. He couldn't hold back his tears. She opened her eyes. Perhaps she recognized him. She said she wanted a bit of rose oil. Noises of dishes and silverware. He wet her mouth. He left the room.]

Pizzuto's portrayal here is both ironic and obsessive. His sentences capture an individuality that has been reduced to nothingness by the immobilization of the object of his description, in a series of separate, lifeless observations designed to intensify the material traces of a subject that has all but disappeared. They hold no visibile pattern and make no claim about the significance of what they describe. Signorina Rosina, as the subject of Pizzuto's narrative, exists here in the form of remains, elements of physical matter occupying a familiar space among familiar gestures and sounds. But these surroundings are present as an inventory of signs that, once mentioned and catalogued in the reader's memory, seem to lose all their resonance. Whether Pizzuto, like a film director, wants to emphasize the separate existence of narrative facts or the impossibilty of ordering them in a total pattern of explanation is not altogether clear. The effect achieved, however, is a haunting silence caused by the seeming impossibility of one sentence to generate a sequel. Each, complete in itself, strikes the reader in all of its threatening materiality. At the same time, we are made aware of how the ground of referentiality can shift to destroy the illusion that we can fully embrace a reality—in this case, the reality of Signorina Rosina, which moves, just enouth to evade our grasp, from Signor Rosolio to "il rosolio," the balm, that mitigates the pain of living.

Contained in the realistic illusion is the life of Bibi: the humdrum, solitary existence of a socially maladjusted, impractical dreamer, a misfit not because he comes from the fringes of society but, rather, because he has been brought up and educated according to the highest middle-class values, in a culture whose rhetoric he takes all too seriously. His uncertainty as to what others expect of him and his general inability to understand the social code are direct effects of truly believing in the ideals of a humanist culture. Bibi, in fact, carries that culture around with him, on his sleeve, so to speak, in the form of that unfinished book, *Ravenna*, which, ironically, causes others to regard him with suspicion.

Bibi has accepted the bourgeoisie as the hegemonic social class; he has adopted its culture of individualism, engraved in the institutions of civil society, and, with it, the notion of autonomous subjectivity. In this respect, the disillusioned, maladjusted protagonist sets his unique self apart from his culture while accepting its principle of rule. He awakens our consciousness by juxtaposing his unique vision of the world with its opposite, thereby revealing his own private code of being and the fragility and contingency that designate his need to hold on to the power and authority of his ancestors, symbolized by the figure of Rosina, whom he has dispatched to a distant burial site.

There is no doubt that, as a character, Bibi possesses all the features of a modernist antihero. The name Bibi itself, lovingly transformed by Compiuta into Cibib or Bibicin, suggests littleness in importance, power, and force, as well as the endearing qualities attributable to a pet. He exists, in fact, on a small scale, a being to which society pays little attention. In fact, the narrator tends to overlook him as well, for in the middle of the book, without any warning, Bibi drops out of sight for six chapters. His reappearance toward the end of the novel suggests that we have completed an inconclusive, paralogical journey that is always about to begin again. Furthermore, through the protagonist's equally unexpected disappearance and reemergence, Pizzuto shows that, rather than a character in his own right, Bibi is the image of a character, a photographic reproduction of a character type. His fictional life belongs to the text of the modernist antihero, a text already written and made possible by the belief in the reality of a norm against which modern characters, from Leopold Bloom to Gonzalo Pirobuttiro, stand as a basis for parody.[9] As the character of another text, Bibi can only be looked upon with nostalgia. He exists outside of the actual fictional history he is supposed to experience, as a purely aesthetic representation of the author's vision of life; he is, the allegory of that vision.

This puts us in a better position to understand the primary importance of the form of *Signorina Rosina* in the development of Pizzuto's work. One of the most significant features of the novel is the way Pizzuto deals with the conventional notion of narrative subjectivity. The subject of narrative is generally construed as the locus of consciousness, the point of view or vision of reality that organizes the world of phenomena and interacts with it. In narrative fiction, the subject has always occupied a position of extreme cognitive and epistemological importance as bearer of meaning.[10] Its function in modern Italian fiction has been to identify and define a kind of problematic that, through the process of writing and structuration, it brings under the control of its authority. Whether we are reading Manzoni, Svevo, or Gadda, writers of extremely different narrative styles and disparate ideologies, our first critical impulse is to locate a controlling consciousness, that is, the subject of the narrative whose purpose it is to "subject" the reader to its meaning. In *Signorina Rosina*, Pizzuto begins a process whereby the subject of narrative—whether understood as the subject-individual to whom the author assigns individual qualities (in this case, Bibi) or as a totalizing consciousness that the book imposes on the reader (generally realized in themes or motifs, as, for example, in the potential of Signorina Rosina to be emblematic of a way of looking at the world)—loses its force as a representational mode, becomes decentered or peripheral, and eventually ceases to exist altogether.

To illustrate the means by which Pizzuto realizes such a distinctively postmodern condition, it is useful to return for a moment to Gadda. Gadda and Pizzuto are generally associated on account of their biographical similarities and for the highly experimental and subversive character of their narrative styles. But in terms of the crisis of subjectivity, the difference between them deserves greater emphasis. There can be no doubt that Gadda's *La cognizione del dolore* was designed to put into question the problem of selfhood and personal identity. Through a single center of consciousness, established by a narrator who projects the author's vision of chaos and objective baroqueness onto the mind of Gonzalo, Gadda realizes a biting parody of the individualist subject.

We need not return to the dynamic movement of caricature and satire in the novel; nor do we have to remark again on how the real subject of Gonalo's aggressive verbalization, of his tirades against the grandiose inflation of the ego, is the paternal subject, the father-phallus, who fixes the constants of an oppressive linguistic code Gadda endeavors to explode. While he denounces violently the world around his characters, he is at the same time locked into it; and his verbal mockery and parody depend largely on his belief in the uniqueness of a way of speaking or acting. He can only put himself in the place of his characters, either with sympathy (Gonzalo, Ingravallo) or malice (Mussolini), because he acknowledges the existence of a norm opposed by the world he presents to the reader. So, paradoxically, the crisis of subjectivity expressed in his declamation of individuality, as, for example, in the case of Gonzalo, becomes a vehicle for reinforcing the transgression of the norm and, therefore, retaining, albeit in a critical state, both norm and transgression.

With *Signorina Rosina* we are in a very different situation. Pizzuto, unlike Gadda, does not put up to reality the deforming optic of a circus mirror; he does not subject the world to his judgment. Rather, he establishes between the observer and the world observed a blank or neutral space, devoid of affect, in which representation is destabilized by virtue of the fact that, as Jameson would put it, there is no longer a norm to respect, no longer a society that exhibits the absurdities of existence, no longer individuals displaying unmistakable personalities engaged in conflict, no longer existential and stylistic mannerisms that constitute the basis for deformed or thoroughly subjectivized representation.[11] Pizzuto's characters are dead identities, that is, figures whose significance as characters has been effaced. They inhabit no system save that of the literary text, and each exists only as one among many objects in a world to which the observer accords at times a glance, at times a sustained measure of pleasurable response or philosophic interest.[12]

From the standpoint of the crisis of subjectivity, Gadda's work is a desperate cry for expression, an attempt to forge a highly personal, explosive style amid the chaos of the world and the rubble of existence. It implies a past of other values and the hope of a new beginning after the purge. Pizzuto begins with the death of the subject and of its representation; he takes Gadda's revolution for granted and builds upon its effects. He is a dispassionate Gadda, a true disbeliever in symbolic worlds and in the fictional totalities in which they are expressed.[13]

In this sense, the images of Signorina Rosina do not coincide with a particular substance (for example, womanhood, life's eccentricities, a lost and irrecuperable past) but rather refer back to other signs through which narrative subjects are codified. In other words, Rosina is a trace of what was once a center of consciousness. For Pizzuto, such a center, like all symbols, is an arbitrary construct; it implies the identification of a point of view with the events narrated and a system of logical causality that regulates the succession of events and the order of perception. To destroy such a center, Pizzuto must replace the objective temporal dimension with a succession of events that depends wholly on the preferences of memory.[14]

Although the narrator's memory regulates the course of the narrative in *Signorina Rosina*, Pizzuto does not focus on the act of remembering and is not concerned with giving an accurate transcription of things past. Unlike stream-of-consciousness narratives, the text does not attempt to establish correspondences between past and present. The past recalled, and pressed into service for the story, is a past that occupies the author's mind in the form of disconnected things and events that, in the moment of narration, are linked together spontaneously, as in a collage.

In *Signorina Rosina*, however, we are still able to determine a kind of rationale or organizational principle for the form the materials of memory assume. It consists in grounding the experiences of Bibi and Compiuta in familar surroundings, which are at once affectionately transcribed and distanced through a heightened perspective. The accumulation of naturalistic detail, as in the episode of the life and death of Camilla the Siamese cat, serves the purpose of tracing some undefinable, nostalgic object destroyed by the passing of time, but which now must be made to exist beyond history. In this recovery, time and event coexist in chronological sequence, but not in order to mirror a reality thoroughly appropriated by a narrator intent on registering an irrevocable fact of existence. Rather, Pizzuto's objective is to safeguard the experience of memory by intensifying its moments and materiality to emphasize its loss:

> Lo videro rifugiarsi nello stanzino. La sua coda era enorme, gli occhi spalancati come quella volta in caserma. Il mattino appresso furono somministrate a Camilla con una siringa gocce di latte, di acqua. Non aveva più bava. Stette accovacciata, sempre composta nella sofferenza come nella gioia. Era circa la mezzanotte quando finalmente mandò un gemito, quasi un rauco belato. Doglie? Oh, era dunque sul punto di liberarsi. Forse morti. Camilla scorse la mamma china su di lei. Con un inatteso scatto le si aggrappò addosso, su su fino alla spalla; le unghie aggranfiarono lo scialletto, dovettero esserne staccate ad una ad una. Si lasciò rimettere com'era. (53)
> [They saw her take refuge in the closet. Her tail was enormous, her eyes agape

like that time in the barracks. The next morning, drops of milk and water were administered to Camilla with a syringe. She had no more saliva. She stood crouched, composed as always, in suffering as in joy. It was around midnight when, finally, she let out a cry, almost a hoarse bray. Had labor begun? Oh, she was about to give birth. Perhaps the kittens were dead. Camilla saw Mama bent over her. Springing unexpectedly, she clung to her, all the way on to her shoulder; her claws grasped her shawl and had to be removed one by one. She let them put her back as she was.]

Pizzuto heightens our sensory apprehension by isolating detail, to the point that the presence of the cat becomes obsessive, her gestures and sounds a haunting incantation reminding us of the sovereignty of what has now become a useless body:

Il babbo accendeva fiammiferi contro quel dolcissimo occhio. Sì, non so, pare che si muova, non diciamolo per ora alla mamma. E le vibrisse, mai in giù per tutta l'agonia, rimasero erte come spade di argento. La stufetta arrossata riverberava dall'alto dei cuscini calore ronzando nel gran silenzio notturno. (53–54)
·[Dad lit some matches and put them up to that cherished eye. Yes, I don't know, it looks like it's moving, let's not say anything yet to Mama. Her whiskers, never lowered in spite of all the agony, remained straight like steel swords. The small stove, reddened, reflected heat from above the pillows, droning in the imposing silence of the night.]

The episode of Camilla is emblematic of our need to survive. It addresses our being-in-the-world and thus raises fundamental ontological questions: What happens when different worlds (those of the cat and of people) confront each other? What is the world of another being? Ultimately, it testifies to Pizzuto's desire to reassert the cognitive value of a historical event. Camilla exerts on our memory a powerful stimulus; she enables us to cling to what is, fundamentally, an aesthetic experience ("Era bellissima. Si chiamava Camilla" [47] [She was gorgeous. Her name was Camilla]) in order to fend off our final annihilation. As such, it testifies at once to the reality of a history and to the need for the certainty that history, as a practical ideal, satisfies.

In *Signorina Rosina*, Pizzuto writes from a position very close to the disappearance of history. His world is a contemporary social system that has replaced historical memory with what Jurgen Habermas calls "the heroic affinity of the present."[15] Tradition has been normalized, neutralized in the name of utility for the sake of consumption. Capitalist modernization can retain its own past only as a marketable historiographic account, as one among many objects that assert the power and forces of consumer society. Pizzuto senses the beginning of this new hegemony. While his novel illustrates the need to reappropriate history as event and sensation, it transcribes the fragmentation of historical memory in the choice and selective development of discrete moments of existence, disconnected from meaning as such but nostalgic of meaning as historical certainty.

Such a compositional process may be seen from the standpoint of the distinction Pizzuto draws between storytelling and narration. In contrast to the *racconto*, which has exact limits, narration, for Pizzuto, is an indeterminate ideal with no fixed values. Technically, the narrative process presents a series of unconnected frames whose linkage is at best tenuous and can be varied in accordance with any proposed condition. In *Signorina Rosina*, the story line relies on an indefinite number of possible solutions and is in no way determined by a sequence of causes. In chapter 8, for example, Bibi takes a group of students on a tour of a town hit by an earthquake. The scene is completely detached from the preceding account of Camilla's death and the following episode, where Bibi has been sent to oversee the restoration of a penitentiary. From chapter 10 to chapter 15 Bibi is absent altogether, reference to him being made only through his letters to Compiuta. Throughout the individual parts of the book, the spatial dimension of narrative exists only as possibility. It is not objectified into sets belonging to a finite plan of representation but rather is conceived as the matter of estimation and anticipation, a relatively arbitrary locus on which particular items of reality are inscribed.

Time also has no objective dimension; it does not encompass the vital cycle of an individual's life, as in classical narrative, nor is it confined to the vertical plane of reverie, stream of consciousness, or analytical subjective commentary, as in Svevo. It is at once perception and data, which exist in an eternal movement from one point of arrival to another, without any application or effect on things prior.[16] The conditioning element in the realms of both spatiality and temporality is the subject and its relation to the world. But the Pizzutian subject has no locus of certainty. It interrogates fruitlessly, without result or force. The questioning itself is ineffectual. Bibi—we learn mostly from his letters to Compiuta—is a philosopher intent on investigating the ontological foundations of human existence. We get the impression, however, that Pizzuto, rather than representing, is mimicking his character's metaphysical aspirations, thus neutralizing them to the status of worthy but ineffectual impulses.

Bibi's position in the formal structure of *Signorina Rosina* is analogous to his thematic role. He is an itinerant, an incorrigible wanderer and amateur metaphysician, which accounts for the fact that there is no fixed point from which his actions emanate nor any objective to which they tend. He is decentered and uncommunicable; the letters he sends to Compiuta seem to be signs of madness, marked by restlessness and confusion. The difference between him and his mistress (we assume Compiuta and Bibi are lovers) is that he is a kind of bracketed abstraction, unrepresentable in her mind as a stable unit of meaning, the indeterminate ideal of his author's narration. Her experience, on the other hand, can be reformulated as a concrete reality, as factuality confirmed coherently and literally within an assured and stable, albeit repressive, context of family rituals and familiar objects. The fragmented, atomized form of *Signorina Rosina* objectifies the metaphysical detachment of its protagonist, codifying it into what will become the destiny of narration itself: repetition, a mirroring of the repetitive structure of human existence. As the novel begins with Bibi and Compiuta arguing at the train station, so it ends. They will never understand each other, they will fight, make up, and promise to see each other again:

> Venne infine la pace. Bibi palpeggiava qualche graffio nel collo, Compiuta incominciò a sentire freddo, brividi. Cibib, Bibicin, gli faceva. Non lungi da casa sua si arrestarono. A domani, ella disse avviandosi con passo stanco. Tornò indietro. Se non mi vedrai, avvertì, sii certo che sto a letto. E allora postdomani. Va bene? Così si allontanò. Nella fresca capigliatura i raggi occidui mettevano fulgori. Ogni tanto si rivolgeva levando il braccio. Dirimpetto a Bibi in attesa che ella varcasse il portone entravano pel carico nella centrale del latte i veicoli disposti là fuori a fila. Ciascuno si accostava all'alta banchina su cui erano ammassate le metalliche gabbie colme, che operaie e operai tutti in bianco vi sospingevano dentro. Le bottiglie cozzando tintinnivano come dei sonaglini. (148)
> [Finally they made peace. Bibi rubbed a scratch on his neck, Compiuta began feeling cold, shivers. Cibib, Bibicin, she said. They stopped not far from her

house. Tomorrow, she said as she began walking away, tired. She turned around. If you don't see me, she cautioned, you'll know I'm in bed. Then the day after tomorrow. Okay? She thus left. The sun's rays glistened in her shiny hair. Every so often she turned around, raising her arm. Opposite Bibi, who was waiting for her to disappear through the doorway, milk trucks, lined up outside, began entering the dairy to load up. Each of them pulled up to the high platform on which were amassed metallic cages that male and female workers dressed in white shoved into the trucks. The jostled bottles tinkled like bells.]

Here the thematic circularity of the book is reasserted. The unchangeable destiny of these two middle-class entities is to repeat the words, gestures, and actions that keep them at once together and apart. Like a recurring motif in a musical score, Bibi returns to Compiuta from a position beyond despair, a position that is the very condition of his fictional existence. Bibi's life as a character is possible only because he has repaired the split between his desire and his consciousness, built on the rubble of his existence, and left the prison house of phenomena (the chapters on the earthquake site and the penitentiary are emblematic in this regard) in order to reexhibit himself, formulaically, as a dispersed image. Like the author, the characters are resigned to alienation and fragmentation. The objective, schizophrenic state has become just another object of fetishistic enchantment. The perception of sights and sounds is intensified to exhibit an objective, hallucinatory reality.

Pizzuto's style is an attempt to reorient the perspective of the narrator, as well as the attention of the reader, to the regenerative potential of the literary image. Our attention now rests on the sensual materiality of a world abandoned by its characters, for which nothing is claimed but that they are there. Implicit in such a process of intensification and allurement is the sense that communication amid fragmented and reified existences, rather than being impossible, is actually the matter of ecstasy, a singular form of pleasure that stands in the place of the mourning and loss of a world that can no longer be ("Un lumacone lasciava sulla parete nere strisce fosforescenti di vago disegno che al mattino poi erano degli scarabocchi" [125] [A snail left on the wall black phosphorescent streaks of a vague design, which in the morning appeared as scribble]). Thus, what appears in the first part of of Pizzuto's second novel, *Si riparano bambole* (1960) to be the nostalgic journey of the protagonist's memory into the past of childhood experiences and attachments, the restoration of a dimension capable of soothing the pain and the misery of old age, is actually an attempt to stimulate the narrative eye with vigorous and powerful images of a fossilized domestic universe.

What we witness in *Signorina Rosina* (and perhaps to an even greater extent in *Si riparano bambole*) is the disappearance of a human community, of symbolic practices and ways of affirming social unity through ritual. The *Ravenna* Bibi carries around with him, in which the past is canceled altogether, where the characters relinquish all personal identity to become grammatical constructs, and where everyday things and events take on an impersonality hitherto unknown in modern fiction, is an ironic illustration of the perspective from which *Signorina Rosina* was written—ironic because the book represents a traditional humanist ideal while it also contains the total effacement of the conditions that make possible the generation and dissemination of such an ideology. *Signorina Rosina*, in this sense, is Bibi-Pizzuto's illusion of human solidarity, of a world to which tired travelers can return, a world of myths and aspirations to plenitude.

Our reading of *Signorina Rosina* now makes possible some reflection on the emergence of neocapitalism in the late 1950s, of which the novel is in many different ways a powerful expression. The time witnessed the beginning of a radical transformation in the economic and social structures of Italian society, brought on by the intensification of industrial production geared toward mass consumption and the creation of a cultural marketplace, regulated by the needs of technology. Intellectuals now belonged to a workforce. They were recruited by the culture industry, and their products (whether works of imaginative or philosophical literature) had become goods or services to be bought and sold for profit in a society where economic, political, and cultural power were one. The written word had given way to the images and sounds that convey the financial imperatives of industry and the mass media. Like Gadda, Pizzuto has his roots deeply set in the humanist culture that neocapitalism subjugated to its rationale. But in constrast to Gadda, Pizzuto's personalized sense of the turn in capitalist development comes not from Milan but from Palermo, from a subaltern social perspective in which capitalism is represented not by an extensive industrial and technological structure but rather by traditionally based individual initiatives. Here, the products of Italy's industrial boom are

alien phenomena, ushered in to destroy the myth of a superior Mediter-
ranean intellectual and emotional homeland, cultivated by the island's petite bourgeoisie to compensate for their peripheral existence.

These are the objective preconditions against which Pizzuto works out
the thematics of *Signorina Rosina*, surveyed above. What characterizes its
authorial perspective is much less the loss of values or a radical separation
from a past of humanist ideals than the feeling that from the present there
is neither defense nor retreat, that the present invests and penetrates the
entire fabric of our daily existence, that it has put an end to what once was
the intimacy of our private world. The effect is a wheeling sense of danger
that comes from overexposure to the images and sounds that, as in Anto-
nioni's *Il deserto rosso*, color our inner landscape of despair.

CHAPTER EIGHT

Giuseppe Tomasi di Lampedusa
and Luchino Visconti

Substances of Form

In light of current film and literary theory, the initial responses to Luchino Visconti's 1963 adaptation of *Il Gattopardo* appear unfounded. The issues raised at that time regarding thematic or ideological fidelity to Giuseppe Tomasi di Lampedusa's original have now been largely superseded by a deeper understanding of the differences between verbal and visual systems of narration. Alberto Moravia was no doubt justified in drawing attention to the disproportion between the vast landscape Visconti paints in the film and the restricted content of the novel,[1] as was Pio Baldelli in arguing that Visconti was not faithful to the novel's internal structure.[2] It, of course, could not have been otherwise. For although the novel and the film reproduce the same historical account of a revolution that failed, their systems of narration are entirely different.

The difficulties associated with the specificity of visual media are compounded by the way the literary text itself is interpreted. Visconti comes to Lampedusa's novel carrying his own ideological baggage, and within the political circumstances of 1963; he is also responding to the demands of the film industry. The issue of Visconti's fidelity to Lampedusa's narrative is, then, necessarily, a question of Visconti's cinematic response to his own reading of Lampedusa. This discussion is an attempt to articulate the differences between the novel and the film at the level of textual ideology, in such a way that each work retains its own structural and aesthetic peculiarities at the same time that it questions the meaning of the other.

Criticism has often argued that *Il Gattopardo* is a well-made novel in the classical sense.[3] In no way does it represent an experiment in writing against the conventions of fictional narrative, as do the works of Lampedusa's older contemporaries Gadda and Pizzuto. It would also be difficult to locate the novel within the modernist canon, however wide and flexible its boundaries might be, for it lacks the stylization and open-endedness one generally associates with modernist texts. The humor and paradox it contains, rather than distance realistic portrayal, appear to make the story all the more intelligible. Hence, early reviewers, whether admirers or detractors, had little difficulty in understanding what Lampedusa was saying. Rather, what they questioned was his interpretation of Sicilian history. Was his pessimism warranted? Did it renounce social progress and the value of committed political action? Could the novel's message be pressed into the service of right-wing politics?[4] As Manzoni's narrative omniscience established the authority of his interpretation of history, so Lampedusa's text placed definite limits on the play of critical reason.

Further comparison with Lampedusa's predecessors in historical fiction may be useful for our discussion. The active relation with social reality, displayed in Manzoni's conceit of rewriting history by transforming an illegible text into a pleasant and uplifting story, consists, as we have seen, in bringing the present into the texture of a past through compromise and accommodation. Manzoni writes from a perspective of confidence in society's capacity to move ahead by a slow, gradual evolution that entails assimilation rather than exclusion. His perspective is moderately romantic, in that, although he conceives of the historical past as a lost plenitude, his Eden is irretrievable in earthly life.

By comparison, Federico De Roberto's authority in *I Viceré* rests firmly on scientific induction. Unlike Manzoni, who opposes history to society, De Roberto equates the terms. The history he recounts of the Uzeda family is emblematic not only of the social and political history of Italy from 1850 to 1880 but of modern Italian history itself. The inaccessible, romantic ideal of wholeness becomes, in his novel, a search for scientific authenticity, for a community knowable through positive analysis. His objectivity is that of the family chronicler who stands outside events to capture, from a seemingly neutral perspective, the effects on history of a social class intent only on perpetuating its rule. From De Roberto's *I Viceré* Tomasi di Lampedusa will draw the historical thematics of *Il Gattopardo:* the landed Sicilian aristocracy, a natural enemy of the risorgimento, has succeeded in quelling the movement's revolutionary impetus by bringing it under control and exploiting it to further its own survival as a ruling class. *I Viceré*'s political message rings loud and clear:

> La storia è monotona ripetizione: gli uomini sono stati, sono e saranno sempre gli stessi. Le condizioni esteriori mutano; certo, tra la Sicilia di prima del Sessanta, ancora quasi feudale, e quella di oggi pare ci sia un abisso; ma la differenza è tutta esteriore. . . . Il prestigio della nobiltà è e non può essere spento.[5]
>
> [History is monotonous repetition. Mankind has been, is, and will be always the same. External conditions change. No doubt an abyss seems to separate today's Sicily from the still almost feudal Sicily that existed before 1870. The difference, however, is totally external. . . . The nobility's prestige is a reality that will never die.]

This objective reality, which Consalvo rehearses before Donna Ferdinanda, is the function of his class's existence. The common truth is that, although the nobility looks like it is disintegrating, it will never die. What is generally taken as the political message of *Il Gattopardo* is noticeably similar: "Se vogliamo che tutto rimanga come è, bisogna che tutto cambi."[6] [If we want things to stay as they are, things will have to change.] However, these messages are in many respects very different; and, although they are ideologically coded messages, they should not be confused with the ideologies of their respective texts.

That literary ideology is mainly an effect of form can be illustrated by dwelling a moment longer on *I Viceré*. Through Consalvo's words, De Roberto expresses his bitter irony toward a history that, at least for his social class, seemed never to change. However, this belief is less important than the textual strategy the ideological message employs. By juxtaposing the contradictory notions of history as progress and history as monotonous repetition, thus creating the paradox that progress and stasis are one and the same, De Roberto alters his narrative perspective. Like Donna Ferdinanda herself, the reader enjoys a momentary pause from the contradictory movement of historical events. History, as a result, is bracketed, while our attention is drawn to the problem of concrete existence in which the paradox is based.

De Roberto writes his historical novel from the vantage point of a petit bourgeois stationed outside the arena of contending social forces. Lampedusa, in fact, referred to it as a "romanzo sull'aristocrazia vista da un domestico"[7] [novel on the aristocracy seen from the perspective of a family domestic]. Seeing no end to the ideological dilemma, De Roberto suspends it indefinitely in the humor of paradox. Instantly, we leave the closed space of a linear narrative that has reached its dead end and move into the infinitely open-ended world of possible being. Thus, De Roberto cancels his realistic narrative, recoding secular reality in terms of its inherent creative possibilies. The ideology of the text crystallizes in the uncertainty that realism may not be the best cognitive instrument for recording the truth of social reality and the suspicion that the form in which history is written may be, in itself, a lie. The distance from here to Pirandellian modernism can be measured in inches.

The historical paradox on which *Il Gattopardo* is founded (conservation equated with change) generates notably different textual meanings in Lampedusa's novel and in Visconti's film. If in *I Viceré* analysis begets paradox, in Lampedusa's novel paradox itself is the object of analysis. It takes on the function of a discourse to be explained or, better, interpreted from the narrative perspective of a historical subject (the Sicilian aristocracy, embodied in the figure of Prince Fabrizio) in the process of being displaced to the margins of power.

The prince of Salina is helpless in opposing the tide of compromise and pragmatic accommodation that has overtaken his relatives and friends. He stands alone, like the leopard he symbolizes, in resisting the snare of paradoxical logic. Unlike those around him, Lampedusa's prince knows that the monarchy is dead and cannot be resurrected, save only rhetorically; he knows that, no matter how profitable the compromise may seem, it can never restore the substance of an idea that has been lost forever. At the same time, Fabrizio learns quickly that any genuinely democratic alternative to the old order has been thoroughly defeated. Less dignified and less charitable forms of authority have strangled to death the newborn child of liberty and good faith. From here emerges the deepseated skepticism underlying the prince's ironic perspective on Sicilian history.[8]

The narrative voice, one step removed from the immediacy of the action, constructs the prince's consciousness from the hindsight of history. The advantage of understanding the degree to which this formidable figure lives outside the historical moment justifies his silencing of history or, better, his transferal of the historical problematic onto the plane of existence. We are thus able to see the way Fabrizio and the others mystify their world, how their desire for stability generates the various defensive strategies employed to ward off the inevitable: the fetid stench of history that emanates from the decomposed body of the soldier found hidden in the thick clover under a lemon tree outside the prince's palace. The prince, indeed, remembers the stench, as the narrator visualizes for the reader the act of repair that the image of death and putrefaction undergoes:

> Era stato Russo, il soprastante, a rinvenire quella cosa spezzata, a rivoltarla, a nascondere il volto col suo fazzolettone rosso, a ricacciare con un rametto le viscere dentro lo squarcio del ventre, a coprire poi la ferita con le falde verdi del cappottone; sputando continuamente per schifo, non proprio addosso ma assai vicino alla salma. Il tutto con preoccupante perizia. (9)
> [Russo, the caretaker, discovered this broken object, turned it over, covered its face with his red kerchief, thrust the guts back into the gaping stomach with some twigs, and then covered the wound with the green flaps of the cloak; spitting continuously with disgust, meanwhile, not right on, but very near, the body. And all this with meticulous care.] (21)

Here at the novel's outset, Lampedusa provides us, perhaps unwittingly, with an important metanarrative directive. The cosmetic adjustments that Russo performs on the disemboweled corpse, the covering up of the fatal wound, are indicative of what the narrator is forced to do in recounting the memories of the prince. The work of reverie demands that history be subjected to a cleansing, that its overbearing material reality be hidden from view and that it be replaced with the romantic yearning for a lost innocence. But at the same time, Lampedusa cannot allow his narrator to escape the reality he is forced to conceal. While he must be loyal to his subject's mystifying perspective, he cannot help but reveal the disjunction, the false consciousness, the illusion. Following Althusser,[9] we might say that Lampedusa shows us the operations of ideology at work. Through his narrating voice, which establishes a distance between him and his princely alter ego, he makes visible the process of ideological coding. He gives us a story line that reflects the point of view of the Sicilian aristocracy in a state disintegration.

Thus, Lampedusa produces a story of lethargy and inertia, of mystical reflection, fatalism, and meditation on the deep mysteries of the land and of the Self. This is how the aristocracy tells its ideological tale. It thus replaces the objective economic and political causes, in much the same way that Russo replaces the violent image of death, with an imaginary form in which it represents itself to itself. The reader cannot help but see the ideology, and, since it is portrayed as an internally coherent and noncontradictory whole, it is, or seems to be, historically true. At the same time, it is revealed as myth, a myth founded on the real history it suppresses or conceals.

The ideological fault lines in the prince's perspective may also be explored from the standpoint of epistemology. On this score, Gregory Lucente has shown how throughout the text the narrative finds ways of questioning the validity of its own signifying process and, therefore, the reliability of Don Fabrizio's point of view.[10] Lucente interprets the following passage as further illustration of the form of textual cognition that disengages our mind from the attitude toward reality that the story appears to project. We are practically at the novel's end, at the point when Concetta realizes that Tancredi might have loved her after all. The narrator glosses her perceptions first with a kind of existential lacquer: "Dal fondo atemporale dell'essere un dolore nero salì a minacciarla tutta dinanzi a quella rivelazione della verità" (183). [From the timeless depth of her being, a black pain came welling to threaten her all over at that revelation of the truth] (314). Then he throws into question the very validity of her feelings:

> Ma era poi la verità questa? In nessun luogo quanto in Sicilia la verità ha vita breve: il fatto è avvenuto da cinque minuti e di già il suo nocciolo genuino è scomparso, camuffato, abbellito, sfigurato, oppresso, annientato dalla fantasia e dagli interessi. . . . tutte le passioni . . . si precipitano sul fatto e lo fanno a brani; in breve è scomparso. E l'infelice Concetta voleva trovare la verità di sentimenti non espressi ma soltanto intravisti mezzo secolo fa! La verità non

era più. La sua precarietà era stata sostituita dall'irrefutabilità della pena. (183–84)

[But was this the truth? Nowhere has the truth so short a life as in Sicily; a fact has scarcely happened five minutes before its genuine kernel has vanished, has been camouflaged, embellished, disfigured, squashed, annihilated by imagination and self-interest. . . . All the passions . . . fling themselves on the fact and tear it to pieces; in short, it has vanished altogether. And poor Concetta was hoping to find the truth of feelings that have never been expressed but only glimpsed half a century before! The truth no longer existed. The precariousness of fact had been replaced by the irrefutability of pain.] (314)

This thematization of the ironic perspective suggests that the ahistorical understanding of history attributed to the prince may be itself false, not because it is at odds with what is true, but because it is itself unstable, by virtue of its being thought. Ideology here is suspended, and an attitude emerges that is very different from what appears to be accepted uncritically by the narrator. Lampedusa's history is a mythologizing account, in that it is a report of the prince's self-interrogation, based in the opposition between matter and spirit, history and existence. Spirit and existence must naturally prevail, while material reality and historical forces are kept at a distance. In focusing on Fabrizio's solitude, inner thoughts, and secret feelings, his refined sensuality and his obsession with astronomy, which, fulfilling the demands of his unique intelligence, connects him to the eternal and incorruptible, Lampedusa alludes to his figure's loss of social and political power while reproducing the relations of power. The prince's real power comes from his spirit rather than from his ability to control the material conditions of his life and the institutions in which those conditions find their expression. The book's final passage, which has the same metanarrative poignancy as Russo's cosmetic rehabilitation of the soldier's cadaver, is Lampedusa's most ironic reflexion on this process:

Mentre la carcassa veniva trascinata via, gli occhi di vetro la fissarono [Concetta] con l'umile rimprovero delle cose che si scartano, che si vogliono annullare. Pochi minuti dopo quel che rimaneva di Bendicò venne buttato in un angolo del cortile che l'immondezzaio visitava ogni giorno: durante il volo giù dalla finestra la sua forma si ricompose un istante: si sarebbe potuto vedere danzare nell'aria un quadrupede dai lunghi baffi e l'anteriore destro alzato sembrava imprecare. Poi tutto trovò pace in un mucchietto di polvere livida. (187)

[As the carcass (the stuffed simulacrum of Bendicò) was dragged off, the glass eyes stared at (Concetta) with the humble reproach of things that are thrown away, that are being annulled. A few minutes later, what remained of Bendicò was flung into a corner of the courtyard visited every day by the dustman. During the flight down from the window, his form recomposed itself for an instant; in the air one could have seen dancing a quadruped with long whiskers, and his right foreleg seemed to be raised in imprecation. Then all found peace in a heap of livid dust.] (320)

This passage reaffirms Lampedusa's preference for the spiritual and the imaginary, restating his essentialist opposition of matter and spirit. But it does so in such a way that we are forced again, because of the narrative distancing, to confront the rhetorical strategy and thus to accept the prince's mythologized experience as truly historical and the perspective from which it is recounted as a means of establishing its genuine historicity. By having his prince suppress history, Lampedusa is, in effect, suppressing history only as it is conceived in an objectivist-positivist manner. At the same time, he foregrounds a history that, rather than mirroring what actually happened, is a way of thinking and a way of writing about the past. His history is at once his invention of Fabrizio's consciousness and the assertion of his own idea of what history is.[11]

Visconti transposes this metanarrative, or self-referential, form of the novel into ideological analysis. On the whole, Visconti translates rather literally from the novel. In many instances, the film dialogue and scenario reproduce Lampedusa's text word for word, and, with the exception of chapter 5 (Father Pirrone's return to his native village) and the final two chapters (the prince's death and its aftermath in the Salina household), the story line is accurately followed. Visconti also does not lose sight of Lampedusa's central theme, the self-questioning of an aristocrat estranged from a past whose death knell has sounded, disillusioned and forced to survive in a world of uncertain if not questionable values. But the object of Visconti analysis is not, strictly speaking, the consciousness of Prince Fabrizio but rather the political maneuvering undertaken by the house of Salina to further its survival within the process of transformation from the old order to the new. The question, put to Visconti in an interview that was published with the screenplay, is to what extent did history and ideology take the upper hand in his adaptation of the novel, and did it do so to the

detriment of the value Lampedusa placed on the interior reality of his characters.[12] Visconti repies:

> Non credo che questi momenti [quegli storico-ideologici e quei psicologici ed
> esistenziali] si possano separare. . . . I motivi storico-politici non prevalgono
> sugli altri: corrono nelle vene stesse dei personaggi, come una parte essenziale
> della loro linfa vitale. In alcuni affiorano e si manifestano apertamente, in altri
> sedimentano opachi o trascorrono rapidissimi. (24)
>
> [I do not think that [the historical, ideological, psychological, and existential]
> moments can be separated. . . . The historical-political issues do not prevail
> over the others: they run through the characters' veins as an essential part of
> their blood. In some characters, these issues come to the surface and are shown
> in open light; in others, they remain either latent and opaque or are rapidly
> confronted.]

Visconti's defense can hardly be questioned: how can we separate historical and psychological issues? His defense, of course, is not of Lampedusa's novel but of his own film and is directed against those readers and
viewers who believed that he had betrayed Lampedusa's intimacy and, in
so doing, was neither sensitive nor attentive to the inner life of his characters; specifically, that he ignored the prince's anxiety of identity.

Whether Visconti understood better than many of Lampedusa's early
critics the novel's historical and psychological complexity is not the issue
here. His problem in translating the verbal text into the medium of film was
how to reproduce visually the perspective from which Lampedusa tells his
story. The narrator in the novel is the keeper of the prince's mind and conscience, and, therefore, he is the prince, for we know no other Fabrizio
than the one he gives us; in other words, he is the prince's "historian." To
duplicate this perspective, Visconti would have had to film, not Lampedusa's story but, rather, Lampedusa himself writing it, much as Lampedusa
narrates the prince's writing of his and his class's experience. As a distinguished French reviewer succinctly put it, he would have had to do what
Fellini did with Marcello's life in 8 1/2.[13] Instead, in choosing to film the
story rather than the narrative process, Visconti had to abandon certain dimensions of the prince's existence and put himself in their place as the
maker of the narrative, thus forcing the reader of Lampedusa's text out of
the familiar pattern of perception prescribed by its author and into a different attitude, one more tendentious with regard to the historical moment.

According to Visconti, *Il Gattopardo* is essentially the story of a marriage contract, a contract with clearly stated terms, obligations, and promises:

Dietro il contratto matrimoniale di Angelica e Tancredi si aprono altre prospettive: quella dello stato piemontese, che nella persona di Chevalley viene quasi a far da notaio e a mettere il sigillo al contratto; quella della nuova borghesia terriera, che nella persona di don Calogero Sedara richiama il duplice conflitto dei sentimenti e degli interessi quale Verga lo delineò in modo memorabile in Mastro Don Gesualdo . . . quella dei contadini oscuri protagonisti subalterni e quasi senza volto, ma non per tanto meno presenti; quella della sopravivenza contaminata, anacronistica, ma cionondimeno ancora operante, delle strutture e del fasto feudali, colti a mezzo tra la stagione della loro inarrestabile decadenza e l'intromissione nel loro tessuto di corpi estranei (don Calogero, gli ufficiali piemontesi, gli stessi garibaldini) che, ieri respinti, vengono oggi sopportati e assimilati. (25)

[The marriage contract between Angelica and Tancredi involves different points of view. The State is represented by Chevalley who, almost in the person of a notary, comes to put his seal on the contract. The new bourgeois landowning class, symbolized by don Calogero Sedara, rehearses the conflict between personal feelings and interests that Verga depicted so memorably in *Mastro don Gesualdo* . . . The peasants, obscure, subaltern protagonists, unseen, but nevertheless present; feudalism, contaminated, yet still operative, is captured midway between its season of fateful decline and its absorption of such foreign bodies as don Calogero, the Piedmontese officers, and Garibaldi's followers themselves—all once shunned, but now borne patiently and incorporated.]

What in Lampedusa are important events affecting the prince's being in a world of change are thematized by Visconti into a political narrative in which Fabrizio's outlook on life is one among many perspectives presented in the text. In the film, these themes are energized, foregrounded, and highlighted by excursions outside of Lampedusa's protective inner space, literally out into the streets where the historical drama is being played out:

Abbiamo dato corpo ad alcuni motivi che nel romanzo sono presentati in accenni informativi. Prima di tutto la rivoluzione palermitana, le battaglie garibaldine, il linciaggio degli sbirri borbonici: tutto questo era importante per spiegare la potenza dirompente della congiuntura storica e il rischio reale che

Tancredi accetta di correre, per inseguire il suo deliberato disegno di essere alla testa dei fatti per dominare i fatti stessi.

In secondo luogo il rapporto tra don Calogero e i contadini (cui più volte si accenna nei dialoghi del libro), per rendere evidente una delle componenti del prezzo e della posta in gioco nel contratto di matrimonio fra Angelica e Tancredi.

In terzo luogo le consequenze della disperata impresa di Aspromonte. Come saprai, alcuni disertori dell'escercito regio che nel 1862 obbedirono all'appello di Garibaldi di seguirlo ad Aspromonte furono fucilati come disertori. Naturalmente non ci siamo presi la libertà di introdurre questo episodio nel film; ma è una realtà che echeggia nel ballo, e della quale don Fabrizio è ben consapevole. (26)

[We have given body to some motifs intimated in the novel. Above all, the revolution in Palermo, the battles fought by the Garibaldini, and the lynching of Bourbon informers. All of this was important in order to explain the explosive potential of that moment in history and the real risks Tancredi ran in order to be in the forefront of the events so that he could control them.

In the second place, we have made explicit the relationship between don Calogero and the peasant farmers (often hinted at in the novel's dialogues) in order to show what was really at stake in the marriage contract.

Third, the consequences of the last ditch battle at Aspromonte. As you know, those who left the king's army in 1862 to fight with Garibaldi were shot as deserters. Of course, we did not take the liberty of introducing this episode into the film; it is, nonetheless, a reality that echoes through the ballroom sequences, of which don Fabrizio is well aware.]

The product of such a political reading of Lampedusa is different from the verbal narration, even more different than one might realize from a comparative reading of scenario and novel; the signifying process of film not only presents us with specific referents but, in this case, goes a step further by creating new signs, revealing what has, in the literary text, been purposefully concealed.

Let us look at the first of these additions, to see what effect it has on the meaning of the story. We must note that Visconti is talking about a scene not present in the novel. In order to fit it coherently into the film narrative, he must prepare the viewer by defining (actually recreating) the context in which it will be situated. Thus, in the film's first scene, our entry into the text does not begin with "Nunc et in hora mortis nostrae. Amen," pronounced by the prince who, as we know from the novel, has again led his family in their daily recitation of the sorrowful mysteries of the holy rosary. (It therefore deletes, strictly speaking, the novel's incipit that signals the circularity of ritualistic time in the commingling of the here and now and the eternity of death.)[14] Instead, the camera pans slowly across the palace's open windows from the outside until, attracted by the chorus of cadenced voices in recital, it moves into the hall where the family is gathered. For over two minutes, the viewer hears the recitation, first clearly, then interrupted by the incoherent rumbling of voices from outside, which also invade the prince's sanctuary through the open windows. The camera immediately establishes its perspective as a consciousness from without: it comes from where the voices originate.

Visconti thus positions himself on the side of those historical events that dare not intrude into the novel, save indirectly as a grounding for the action, which the narrator would prefer to ignore. In the novel, the world outside the palace is not fully acknowledged until the second scene, when Fabrizio, amid the sweet-smelling flowers of his garden, remembers the offensive odor of human decay. And it is in the garden through other remembered experiences, that the reader confronts the noise of history, kept at both a temporal and spatial distance.

By contrast, in the film, the viewer is overwhelmed by the intrusion. As soon as the recitation is finished, the door is opened by a servant, who brings the news of a soldier's corpse found in the garden and, with it, a letter accompanying a newspaper sent from the prince's brother-in-law the duke of Malvica, announcing the beginning of the end. The prince reads aloud: "Caro Fabrizio, leggi le terribili notizie che sono sul giornale. I piemontesi sono sbarcati. Siamo tutti perduti. Questa sera stessa io con tutta la famiglia ci rifugeremo sui legni inglesi. Certo vorrai fare lo stesso. Il Signore salvi ancora il nostro amato re." [Dear Fabrizio, read the terrible news in the paper. The Piedmontese have landed. We are all lost. Tonight I will take refuge with the family on English ships. Certainly, you will want to do the same. Let God save once again our beloved king.] Fabrizio continues, reading from the paper: "L'undici maggio gente armata è sbarcata alla marina di Marsala. Posteriori rapporti hanno chiarito esser la banda distaccata di circa ottocento uomini, e comandata da Garibaldi. I filibustieri appena preso terra hanno evitato con ogni cura lo scontro colle truppe reali." [Eleven May, armed men have landed at Marsala. Later reports have confirmed them to be a platoon of about eight-hundred soldiers commanded by Garibaldi. As soon as these pirates touched land, they avoided clashing with the royal troups.]

The house is in turmoil, the ladies carry on hysterically; we hear the cries of "war" and "revolution" amid the confusion, and the film has hardly begun. This is the first of seven scenes, leading to the street fighting in Palermo, that prioritize the historical moment, thus preparing the viewer's direct entry into that space of lived conflict, which, in the novel, has been removed from the reader's purview. Scene 2 (the garden scene in the novel, representing the half-hour interval between rosary and supper, in which the reader learns of Fabrizio's reaction to the dead soldier, Malvica's apology of the monarchy as institution, and the prince's audience with King Ferdinand) is very brief, centering only on the reclining, painterly image of the soldier. Scene 3 is the carriage ride with Father Pirrone to Palermo, where we learn of Tancredi and of the political company he keeps. In scene 4 we are shown the brothel district of the city, where Fabrizio goes to visit Mariannina and where we catch glimpses of soldiers and the harsh voices of youths arguing.

In scene 5, Tancredi visits Fabrizio in his dressing room and explains to him that the moderate revolutionary forces are the aristocracy's best insurance against genuine change ("E allora vuoi la repubblica di don Peppino Mazzini? Credimi, zione. Se non ci siamo anche noi, quelli ti combinano davvero la repubblica" [42] [Do you want, then, don Peppino Mazzini's republic? Believe me, uncle. It's a good thing we are here, or else they would really contrive a republic for you]). Scene 6 ends with Fabrizio's mumbling of Tancredi's conservation=change equation, while in scene 7 Father Pirrone states his objection to the prince's new political discovery, expressing his fear that the new alliance will be destructive to both the church and the poor. At the end of this scene, while Fabrizio looks out the window at the Sicilian landscape, noting its eternal beauty to the good father, his gaze is interrupted by a bugle sounding the attack; suddenly, we have before us the spectacle of battle, operatically orchestrated to heighten the dramatic impact of the fighting.

Visconti thus infringes radically on Lampedusa's perspective, violating, so to speak, the scene of the problem: "Il problema vero, unico," Lampedusa writes, "è di poter continuare a vivere questa vita dello spirito nei suoi momenti più astratti, più simili alla morte" (30). [The one, true question is whether we can continue to live our life of the spirit in its most abstract moments, those closest to death.] The prince's sense of human frailty, of the vanity of all things, finds with Visconti its referent in history, on the barricades of revolution, in the concrete, physical deaths of those who, ironically, fought, in the last analysis, to preserve the prince's leisure.

A comparative reading of the literary and filmic texts leaves little doubt that the product of Visconti's historicization of Lampedusa's narrative is completely new, primarily because the prince ceases to be an extension of the narrator's viewpoint and takes on an independent identity as one among many historical agents. Visconti, as Nowell-Smith correctly observes, detaches himself from his character by dissociating himself from his account of the history of the Sicilian aristocracy.[15] That is to say, he detaches himself from Fabrizio's detachment because, as a Marxist, he understands that this detachment is class bound. The prince is, of course, involved in the economic survival of his family, and it is precisely this emphasis Visconti places on the economic, as opposed to the spiritual, in remaking the character of the prince that causes a general shift in textual ideology.

One clear element in the novel is Fabrizio's ironic attitude toward his class. He looks upon its ineptitude and political nearsightedness as an obstacle to any genuine evolution through which it could legitimately preserve vitality and prestige. Lampedusa's model of progress was, no doubt, Great Britain, where the transformation from the old order to the new was inspired by ideals shared by both the landed gentry and the bourgeoisie. If, on the one hand, the feudal nobility in Sicily had deteriorated to a point beyond repair, on the other, the bourgeoisie safeguarded the privileges it inherited in a low-minded and immoral way. In the novel, however, the historically fictionalized prince can only intuit the future and, because of his pessimism, predict the negative outcome of transformation. For this reason, Lampedusa presents the major representatives of the new ruling class, Sedara and Chevalley in particular, according to the logic of their historical moment and not against the wisdom of hindsight. Lampedusa creates his historical narrative by virtue of his reluctance to superimpose his historical knowledge on the protagonists of another time. Nevertheless, since their reasonings are viewed from the prince's standpoint, they are represented as flawed, though perhaps given in good faith. And, even when the political strategy is transparent, as is the case with Colonel Pallavicino's interpretation of Aspromonte, the reader cannot ignore the historically viable basis of that deception.

Faithful as Visconti is to his interpretation of the novel as a marriage contract, his purpose is not to reveal in his characters the logic of their historical moment but rather to show that logic as part of an overall political design to gain and maintain power at any cost. This may explain why the sequences of Fabrizio and Don Ciccio Tumeo's hunting discussion and Fabrizio's conversation with Chevalley take on a tone in the film somewhat different from that in the novel. Visconti believes that the importance of these scenes consists not so much in the reactionary points of view they display (Don Ciccio's on the plebiscite and Fabrizio's on the unification) but rather in the way Lampedusa, through them, exhibits the manner in which the Piedmontese and their Sicilian allies further their sense of the new order, that is,

> servendosi unicamente degli strumenti più menzogneri e deprimenti del vecchio: la malafede e la sopraffazione, l'inganno. Io ho sottolineato questi momenti e passaggi non soltanto per il loro interesse riguardo all'asse storicopolitico della vicenda, ma per il modo con cui una simile mistificazione investe dall'interno i rapporti umani e sentimentali, ribaltando sul loro destino libero e individuale i limiti di una società, di una morale e di una cultura. Ti sei mai chiesto, leggendo il *Gattopardo*, se un uomo come Tancredi avrebbe un giorno potuto dire di sì non solo alla repressione dei moti del '96, ma addirittura al fascismo? (29)

> [by adopting the old order's most deceitful and degrading means: bad faith, tryanny, deceit. I have underscored these moments and transitions not only because they are essential to the historical-political axis of the story but also for the way this kind of mystification influences human relationships internally, showing how the social, moral, and cultural limitations of a society can affect individual freedom. Reading *Il Gattopardo*, have you ever asked yourself if a man like Tancredi one day could have said yes not only to the suppression of the revolts in 1896 but also to fascism?]

This helps us better understand the transformation that some characters, if not all, undergo in Visconti's adaptation. Don Calogero, for example, in Lampedusa's novel is hardly the puppetlike, comic figure he becomes in the film; nor is Chevalley the mummified simulacrum of Cavour he is turned into by Visconti's subtle parody. Visconti is intent on portraying these characters critically, as bearers of negative meanings, not as historical entities who live out the logic of class conditioning and historical circumstance but as roleplayers in a historical drama leading to the fatal denouement of fascism.

In Visconti's film, Lampedusa's work of reverie becomes a stage on which the Sicilian aristocracy acts out its ineptitude, lethargy, and propensity for accommodation while the new ruling class parades with impunity its guile and calculations. Decay and corruption, on the one hand, philistinism and vulgarity on the other; between them the lucid consciousness of an aging prince who, unlike his predecessor in the novel, is somewhat more concerned with the real politics of this earth than the eternal motion of heavenly bodies. Yet, this highly politicized drama is, as most students of Visconti's cinema know, undermined at the level of style. Nowell-Smith, among others, has made the point that it would be reasonable to expect from Visconti's films "an elaboration of the original values of the scenario expressed in the most appropriate seeming mode, which would be realism."[16] Although this is not the place to begin a discussion of Visconti's style, it is worthwhile to note the apparently contradictory aspects of the film: on the one hand, its progressive political schema, which at once foregrounds the history that Lampedusa keeps at a distance and imprints on its protagonists the seal of a destiny fulfilled, having the jackals and the hyenas show their spots, so to speak; on the other, the aestheticizing frame, in particular, its painterly quality and melodramatic temper.

As stated above, Visconti's transformation of the narrative content is much more a reading than a representation, a deciphering of the historical signs present in the literary text. The standard is not historical accuracy (in many respects, the novel is historically more accurate than the film) but rather visual verisimilitude. Visconti constructs the narrative as a series of simulacra of nineteenth-century paintings, which, rather than creating a sense of unreality, brings the viewer into a more contemplative relation with the events and actions in question. Paolo Bosisio mentions Tobey, Winterhalter, Hayez, Monet and the entire tradition of nineteenth-century southern Italian realism (Palizzi, Gigante, Fontanesi) as definite reference points of Visconti's pictorial imagination.[17]

Visconti's political narrative recognizes and somehow confirms the viewer's stereotypical knowledge of aristocratic customs by expanding pictorially the material of Lampedusa's plot. Thus, the compositional problem is not, for Visconti, what it appears to be: it is not the fusing of Marxist progressive intent with formal extravagance, nor is it the articulation of history and aesthetics. Rather, Visconti must reconfirm our prior knowledge of the passing of an era, by incorporating into one discourse both the opulence and the deterioration of an entire way of life, and he must do so not at the expense of historical events but in consonance with them. The rich, majestic, and opulent features, what has been called Visconti's "scenographic baroque," are the events themselves and not visual gratuities designed to exhalt the decadence of the aristocratic Bourbon world nor a "veil of unreality" that separates us from the reality of the historical moment.[18] Visconti's visual imagination thus recreates the melancholy that Lampedusa expressed through his prince's reflective soliloquies.

Lampedusa and Visconti join hands in evoking a world that has been thoroughly eclipsed by the exchange value of capitalism. It is no small irony that what their detractors labeled either aristocratic substance or residue were nothing other than memories of an era translated into style as the only means left capable of repossessing cultural properties on the verge of oblivion.

CHAPTER NINE

Italo Calvino's *Le città invisibili* and Architecture

Postmodern Rhetoric

The concept of a postmodern moment in contemporary cultural history came into being in the middle 1970s across various artistic fields and individual disciplines and paralleled a new cognitive orientation in the human sciences. Jean-François Lyotard was among the first to address the problem systematically, and it is from his well-known essay, *La condition postmoderne* (1979), that many of the issues discussed in the ongoing controversy on the postmodern and postmodernism derive. Lyotard's principal argument is that the once prominent mastercodes, the *"grands récits,"* and truths deemed absolute since the middle 1950s have undergone a process of delegitimation. Contemporary society has become characterized by a multiplicity of languages, or language games, each in itself true, each a small narrative ("petite histoire"): "The principle of a universal metalanguage is replaced by the principle of a plurality of formal and axiomatic systems capable of arguing the truth of denotative statements; these systems are described by a metalanguage that is universal but not consistent. What used to pass as paradox, and even paralogism, in the knowledge of classical and modern science can, in certain of these systems, acquire a new force of conviction and win the acceptance of the community of experts."[1]

Lyotard believes this new world of "pragmatic performativity" has heightened our sensibility to difference, strengthening our capacity to tolerate viewpoints different from our own. Although empirical evidence could easily disprove such a contention, the fact remains that in recent times the traditional barriers that once separated high from popular culture have been thoroughly effaced, thus legitimitizing a whole array of positions vis-à-vis art, individual behavior, and social reality. Therefore, according to the postmodern perspective, the modern age has come to an end. Liberated from manipulative reason and from the fetishes of totality, we have been ushered into the space of heterogeneity, which is, in effect, no "place" at all, no locus where something can be fixed in meaning, but rather a position from which meaning is multiplied and disseminated.

The concrete, pluralistic realities of Western societies are living proof that the heterogeneity of which Lyotard speaks is not altogether an illusion. Charles Jencks has put it succinctly: "Like it or not, the West has become a plurality of competing subcultures where no one ideology or *episteme* dominates for long."[2] In the area of cultural production, plurality's presence asserts itself in a textual practice that incorporates a multiplicity of conflicting or competing styles, the result being the decentering of any one particular narrative discourse. One devotee of postmodernism refers to the postmodern text as a "semiotic train station without a *Zeitgeist*,"[3] a characterization that is descriptively accurate. But one problem with such an eclecticism of textual practice is that, even if its prime motivation is to interrogate, or to come to terms with, cultural and historical differences, it loses all its political efficacy in the very moment it promotes difference or otherness to the level of an aesthetic, displaying itself as the distinguishing mark or label that confirms its own originality in the marketplace of culture. For it then becomes a cultural product that meets the demands of being different, that is, of being produced for the market of diversity.

In this sense, heterogeneity, as envisaged by Lyotard and by almost all other advocates of postmodernism, is much less a concept that refers to a reality of different things (a universal, in the classical sense, that includes all the particulars of a given species) than an image of itself: an image of an image, appearance become reality, simulacra, hyperreality, and so on. Thus, it does not necessarily follow that by replacing demoted metanarratives with a plurality of small narratives, each having its own force of conviction, we have escaped the prison of universality and absolutism. For if small narratives acquire value only by virtue of their being signs of plurality, they, too, then constitute a metanarrative. Admittedly, it is a metanarrative that is notably different from traditional metanarratives, in that it does not exclude but includes and tolerates everything, even its antithesis: the absolute, the homogeneous, which it neutralizes as one among other discourses, all potentially commodifiable. In this sense, any attempt to gain critical distance from postmodern knowledge is futile. If it is true that this condition exists, then we are part of it.

The concern that postmodern culture displays toward social and individual differences and the emphasis it places on the difficulty of human communication and, generally, on the complexity of culture cannot be ignored. The principle of plurality represents an enormous gain with respect to universal metalanguages, which have tended to exclude racial, class, and sexual differences. But at the same time, it must be acknowledged that such metanarratives as Marxism and Freudianism resist the kind of unilateral characterization that postmodern thought enjoys giving them. The works of Walter Benjamin, Antonio Gramsci, and Louis Althusser demonstrate that Marxism can be as open and subtle as one wants it to be; and the notion of the unconscious has developed far beyond Freud's initial understanding of it. As David Harvey has argued, the modern consciousness that postmodernity opposes has been ideologically reconstructed to appear much more resistant and insensitive to difference than it actually was.[4] The fact of the matter is that Marx, Darwin, and Freud never enjoyed the universal preeminence that postmodern theory assigns to them. Harvey is also right in pointing out that the relation of the modern to the postmodern is one of continuity as well as diversity and that what is normally referred to as postmodern can be viewed as an overvaluation of the contingent and disruptive side of the modernist paradigm: the "sogno angoscioso" described by Pirandello in a 1893 essay as the waving of "mille bandiere, in cui le parti avversarie si sian confuse e mischiate, [lottando] ognuno . . . per la sua difesa, contro all'amico e contro al nemico[5] [thousands of banners, behind which the opposing factions mix and coalesce, each . . . fighting to defend itself against friends and foes alike]. This is the same awareness that later Yeats [quoted by Harvey] captures in the well-known verse "Things fall apart; the centre cannot hold; / Mere anarchy is loosed upon the world."[6]

What postmodernity renounces in modernism is the impulse toward unity and the recomposition of the ephemeral and fragmentary within the eternal and inalterable space of art. To call again on Pirandello, who puts his modernist stamp on the anarchy: "Sorgerà forse anche adesso il genio, che stendendo l'anima alla tempesta che appressa . . . creerà il libro unico, secolare, come in altri tempi è avvenuto"(11). [Perhaps one day a genius will arise who, confronting the impending storm, will create a unique book for our times, as has happened in other ages.] Postmodern theory refutes recomposition and thus, by refusing to give chaos meaning, deprives the chaotic of its status as a term in the ideological conflict. As a result, the chaotic is raised to the level of a metaphysics that celebrates the relativity of all things, the cacophony of voices, and the activities of dissimulation, pretense, and fetishism. So, although the postmodern moment recognizes the authenticity of the Other, of difference, and of the fragment, it prevents this authenticity from acquiring, as Harvey puts it, "a new force of conviction," from acceding to the status of "truth." The real authenticity of difference is "[ghettoized] . . . within an opaque otherness, the specificity of this or that language game. It therefore disempowers those voices (of women, ethnic and racial minorities, colonized peoples, the unemployed, youth, etc.) in a world of lop-sided power relations" (117).

From a more radical perspective, Terry Eagleton sees postmodernism's hypostatization of difference as a final stage of the Left's response to the aestheticizing of early modernism, that is, as an attack on ideology in the name of human creative power, which resists reification and commodification by the capitalist mode of production.[7] It is this development of the modernist revolt (still linked, however tenuously, to the liberal-humanist notion of individuality and subject autonomy) that politically meets defeat at the hands of the modernist Right's fascistic regrounding of the ego in tradition and in the blood and transcendent material body of the nation. The rehabilitation of free-market capitalism in the war's aftermath sets a very different kind of stage, onto which the revolutionary impetus will reemerge from the ashes of history, one capable of accommodating, integrating, and legitimizing a host of different artistic and literary directives.

In Italy, there is a whole literature that registers the cognitive effects of such a transition, which we might refer to as high modernism or, perhaps more accurately as a modernism that, although aware of the liability of any excessive valorization of the artifice, is unwilling to abandon the normative pleasure of the *grands récits*. As we have already seen, the Italy of the 1950s displays this turn most powerfully in the mature work of Carlo Emilio Gadda and in the early narratives of Antonio Pizzuto. In Gadda, parody aids a retreat in defense of the devalued norm by providing a kind of comic (albeit painful) release, while in Pizzuto, we get the impression that from the present there is neither defense nor release, that the present invests and penetrates the entire fabric of our daily existence to the degree that our by now beleaguered individuality, that concrete difference revolutionary modernism surrendered to fascism, has no space at all. On account of the economic urgency of commodity production and the expansion of advertising technique, the intimacy of our private world has become a sense of hazard (Baudrillard), mitigated by nostalgic revisiting.[8] Once the norm is forgotten or effaced and the hazard removed, we have entered into the space of the postmodern.

It is not hard to understand why what are generally viewed as the properties of the postmodern (its fetishism of style and surface, its depthlessness or two-dimensionality, its hedonistic investment in technique, its valorization of the multivalent and the hybrid, its reification of the signifier, etc.) can be, as Eagleton remarks, either defended as subversive of metaphysical truth claims and epistemological hierarchy or debunked as complicit with consumerism's philistine rationale. The ambiguity, however, as Eagleton argues, derives much less from artistic intent than from the logic of the commodity itself. What point is there in taking a stand for or against postmodernism, if postmodern cultural production can be at once "radical and conservative, iconoclastic and incorporated" (373)? Its equivocal structure and stylistic features mirror "the transgressive, promiscuous, polymorphous" nature of the commodity: "its selfexpansiveness, its leveling passion to exchange with another of its kind" (374). In other words, the commodification of art spells the ruin of its distinctive identity, "craftily conserving the difference of use value but only by dint of sublating it into that sameness-in-difference which for Walter Benjamin was fashion."

We can now see why a poetics of postmodernism may be of negligible critical usefulness. What is to be gained in rehearsing, as, for example, Linda Hutcheon does, the epistemological grounds of historiographic metafiction, when its object, the forms and contents of the past rethought as human constructs, is tacitly established as the starting point of sustained apology? The postmodern concern for the multiplicity and relativity of truths puts us at a double disadvantage with respect to the object of inquiry. Not only can we not get outside its rambling parameters, but, given the uncertain nature of its cultural physiognomy, we are at odds in determining which of its features is the crucial term of its identity.

We could, following Frederic Jameson, engage in a kind of "cognitive mapping," which, however, would allow us only, to dialectically defer the answer to a time (unimaginable) when we are in a position to understand ourselves as individual and collective subjects;[9] or we could take the political offensive, behind Said and Eagleton, and resist pluralistic hegemony by critiquing the legitimizing impulse of the kind of postmodern narratives offered by such diverse yet complimentary voices as Lyotard and Baudrillard. Who benefits from the postmodern decentering of the subject and the abandonment of truth claims? And why are small narratives better than big ones? Answers may be available, but they do not serve as solutions, for any critique of the cultural politics of pluralism, any explanation of the particular hegemonic practices of late capitalism, is grist for the mill of current intellectual, moral, and philosophical consent. As it stands now, the hegemonic strategies of liberal pluralism opt for an ever growing extension of the range of ideological commerce. How then does one approach the problematics of postmodernism?

In *A Poetics of Postmodernism*, Linda Hutcheon argues that the dominant feature of postmodern literature is the blurring of boundaries between history and fiction.[10] She acknowledges that such a crossing of boundaries has always been a general feature of literature but suggests that postmodernism's blurring is overt, because the writer truly "acknowledges the limits and powers of 'reporting' or writing of the past" (117). According to Hutcheon, postmodernism forces us to accept the "inevitable textuality" of historical knowledge, its value and limitations; in support of her argument she cites, among other works, Italo Calvino's *Le città invisibili*.

It would be hard to find a more paradigmatic text to illustrate the postmodern perspective in literature. *Le città invisibili* contains all of the ingredients essential to portraying what Lyotard calls the condition of knowledge in our time: reality as an infinity of interpretations to be found in a game of signs–self-legitimizing, seductive language games.[11] The novel takes as its immediate referent the architectural image of cities, cities with names that are differentiated according to their architecture and the social practices it facilitates. It matters less that Calvino's cities are mental constructs, and therefore invisible, than that they create and are the expression of the same fascination their discovery engenders. This is Marco's discovery of new languages containing coherent meanings about real things. Calvino's cities are no doubt a metaphor for literature: they are the inner landscapes of desire and fantasy; at the same time, they are concretized in material structures and endowed with meanings. Their meanings are striking but uncertain. For the great Khan, although capable of deciphering the signs, can never know Marco's purpose in communicating them. The only thing he can be sure of is their emblematic power, a self-generating power that, fueled by facts, adds meaning on to meaning on to meaning.

If we approach *Le città invisibili* as a metafictional game of signification played out in the text, we must inevitably equate the game's language with the novel's message and agree with Hutcheon, who sees the novel as a discourse on textuality. But what if we were to regard textuality itself as a language Calvino makes use of, a local cultural idiom that he must adopt lest his message fall on deaf ears? Then the game of signification becomes a function, rather than a telos, which at the same time conveys the postmodern condition and defines the limits of that condition, thus disputing its truth claims.

Marco forces polymorphous architectural worlds into limited gestural and verbal codes because he has no other vehicle available; he transforms the cities he has visited into verbal signs because he cannot carry them back to Kublai Khan, save in the form of traces (objects acquired, mementos). And if it is true that he throws into question the authority of his reportage, his doing so does not dispute the real, objective complexity of the objects of his knowledge. The experience he reports to Kublai Khan, the experience of the kind of imaginary worlds we find in literary texts, is not his subjective experience of another text. Rather it is that part of the thing itself that, to be communicated, has to enter into a collective mode of discourse. The discourse is not the thing, although the thing, for it to retain its status as a sign, cannot be separated from it:

Marco Polo descrive un ponte, pietra per pietra. — Ma qual è la pietra che sostiene il ponte? — chiede Kublai Kan. — Il ponte non è sostenuto da questa

o quella pietra, risponde Marco, ma dalla linea dell'arco che esse formano. Kublai Kan rimane silenzioso, riflettendo. Poi soggiunge: — Perchè mi parli delle pietre? É solo dell'arco che m'importa. Polo risponde: –Senza pietre non c'è arco. (89)
[Marco Polo describes a bridge, stone by stone. "But which stone supports the bridge?" asks Kublai Khan. "The bridge is not supported by this or that stone," Marco replies, "but by the line of the arch that they form." Kublai Khan remains silent, reflecting. Then adds, "Why do you talk to me about stones? It's only the arch that matters." Polo replies, "Without the stones there is no arch."]

Hence, the sense of history that would appear lost in the combinations and relations of the game of signification is forcefully reinstated. The universal value of the concept arch consists not in its generality but, like the concepts need, labor, and production, in its specific referentiality. Marco does not create the bridge in his mind; rather, he remembers it as a materially verifiable fact that came into being through a process having the status of an event. That Marco, historian of his own travels, cannot disengage the fact from his own experience of it and the event from the reconstruction it undergoes in his mind does not mean that the bridge has no independent existence outside of his memory. At the same time, "bridgeness" is not a metaphysical guarantee but rather a practical construct with which Marco communicates a thing of interest to his interlocutor.

Through Marco's descriptive travelogue and philosophical debate, Calvino addresses human values and problems from a postmodern perspective. His novel is about the responsibilities of imaginative literature and, by extension, about art in general. One of its essential messages involves the laws that govern experience in relation to character and environment. The space of Khan's empire, like literature itself, contains many different and mutually exclusive worlds; within it exist, side by side, incompatible ways of thinking and feeling. Each of these orders exists separately within its own linguistic dimension. Together, they form a collage of discontinuous and inconsistent entities, each possessing an exotic name and defined by a complex of surrealistic images. There appears to be no pattern connecting them, save that they are all sites of human need. To learn about these different worlds will give new meaning to Kublai Khan's life and will challenge him to understand and combat the forces of evil in his domain.

Properties of Writing

The process is one of enlightenment by means of enchantment; its purpose is to make the emperor see one city in terms of another, to confront unfamiliarity and the complexity of existence through artful construction and reportage. Each description is a tale of difference, each world a small narrative that, invariably, has to be dissected and reconstructed into a perspective or vision.

Marco's imaginary worlds are really in some way his native Venice; it is the only historically and geographically real site that is not described, for fear that, by fixing it in words, it will be lost altogether. Better to lose it little by little through the continuous foregrounding of otherness. Calvino's postmodern space of otherness, although governed by the rules of the game of signification, contains signpost warnings that its reality is much more than an exercise in immanentist thought. Through fable, Calvino has us face the inevitability of social change. These worlds have come into being because they are of human agency: they all presuppose the application of human will, hence they are all the products of political action. The fundamental thing that the emperor must understand is that there is no one explanation, no center to his empire of cities, no one fixed and accepted authority or hierarchy, though his own particular authority and hierarchies exist.

Marco's reportage generates a spiral of questioning and differential relations that lead inevitably to the infernal city, to the nihilism that is the last landing place in the mind's journey. Calvino has used the rhetoric of fable to reproduce the logic of postmodernism; he has mapped out a world of diversity, of small narratives, so complex in variation that their invisible order of meaning eludes even the most experienced traveler. This paradoxical complexity, which harbors the anarchic force of the commodity, brings us to the final question of how to escape suffering the effects of the infernal city, how to move forward. Marco answers that there are two ways:

Il primo riesce facile a molti: accettare l'inferno e diventarne parte fino al punto di non vederlo più. Il secondo è rischioso ed esige attenzione e apprendimento continui; cercare e saper riconoscere chi e cosa, in mezzo all'inferno, non è inferno, e farlo durare, e dargli spazio. (170)
[The first is what most of us find easiest: to simply accept hell and become so much a part of it that we no longer notice it is hell. The second is riskier and demands continuous attention and study; it involves searching out and know-

ing how to recognize who and what, in the midst of hell do not belong to hell, and knowing how to give them space and sustenance to endure.]

The writer's responsibility is thus connected to a rhetoric, grounded in a semiotics that communicates the meanings a culture holds dear at the same time that it chooses to experience and inhabit the space in which new and provocative meanings will find expression. This is perhaps a way of both asking and answering Jameson's final question of whether there is a way of resisting the logic of consumer capitalism. Between Calvino's alternatives, the second is obviously the most difficult to realize, because it requires an understanding of the map of human diversity. Like Marco Polo, the post-modern writer, and the postmodern architect as well, must become respon-sible for the various meanings of the people he has visited; these meanings will be expressed in his forms.[12]

Yet what appear as Calvino's ethical concerns find no adequate formal expression. The collage effect produced by the juxtapostion of descriptions or reports suggests a flattening of the narrative perspective, creating the il-lusion of two-dimensionality. The existence of a third dimension hinges on the operations of the reader; it requires a merger of the fable with history (set off, by italic type, as a discourse apart). Hence, Marco's reports appear to Kublai Khan on multiple surfaces, as manifest signs that must be reimag-ined, thus given the unity of a mental image. Like Marco's memory, which repeats signs so that the cities can begin to exist, his interlocutor must pro-vide essence and authenticity to words.

What has been broadly described as postmodernism's concern with sur-face, depthlessness, and glorification of technique has very specific conse-quences in the realm of material culture, specifically architecture. There, postmodern literature's fascination with the multiplicity of interpretation, double meanings, and puns is tested against what Hutcheon calls the "in-evitable textuality" of knowledge. Architecture's inevitable textuality is in its "thingness" and its implacable connection to place. Recent moves to-ward paper or conceptual architecture, as evidenced by, for example the 1990 *Deconstructivist Architecture* show at New York's Museum of Modern Art, are emblematic of a recent professional trend away from architec-ture's traditional interest in program and site. A brisk international market in architectural drawings suggests that architects are uncomfortable with their discipline's inbred difficulties and envy what they read as the pure free play that characterizes the celebrated contemporary production of their literary compatriots. Architecture's thingness and sense of place make it an unlikely stage for the modern spectacle of signifier and signified. Architecture, unlike literature, never is set on a bare stage.

It should, then, be no surprise that most postmodernist activity in architecture has been in elevation and rarely in plan and section (John Hejduk and Peter Eisenman are notable exceptions). For the majority, postmodern architecture has been a play at the surface (elevation), with little attention to three- dimensional form making. Major cities in Europe and America contain the record of this work: Palladian cutouts, Bramantian broken keystones, and Walt Disney ducks mark the thin facades of buildings with radically different functions (from banks to fast-food outlets). The paradox, of course, must already be apparent. While the postmodern intention is to encourage a multiplicity of meanings, in practice the flattening of surface to accommodate billboardlike signage has created a lack of distinction, a privileging of syntax over semantics, and a general blurring of distinction rather than an encouragement of diversity.

Calvino's *Le città invisibili* offers a useful intersection between the different problems of production in the essentially separate worlds of literary and material culture. By testing the absolute freedom of language games against the relatively fixed and terrestrial problems of architecture, his narrative, or antinarrative, becomes a convenient critique of the current practice of architecture in the postmodern style (although postmodernism in architecture is the obverse of Calvino's formulation for literary "architecture"). In the novelist's material world, reality is constructed from an infinity of interpretations, to be determined by an organic game of signs; Calvino uses architecture to provide the imagination, which is essentially private and closeted, a status in the material world. The postmodern architect, on the other hand, borrows the signs, from the classical orders or from cartoons, and reinscribes them through the associative meanings of his building's program.

Marco Polo is Calvino's architect; he builds not with mortar or bricks but with narrative. His architecture, which can exist only in the putative language of the clean white page, generates its own form and space. It becomes three-dimensional as the reader reimagines the words. Paradoxically, the postmodern architect does not generate form as he plasters with signifiers, like a billboard painter with paste, his waferlike facades. His work does not sustain a multiplicity of meanings (the postmodern intention) but a reduction of them, through the sputtering binary agency of punning and irony. "Isn't it ironic?" rather than "Isn't it beautiful?" separates the postmodernist from the romantic, the interpreter from the form maker, the critic from the artist.

Whereas architecture is rich in referents, postmodern literature is rich in signs. Calvino's plot in *Le città invisibili* is an attempt to have the one enrich the other. Kublai Khan relies on Marco to transform the thing into a sign. Calvino encourages the reader to play the game and complete the process, to transform the sign back into a real thing (returning the referent to the image). Kublai Khan's world, remote from the West, where he believes culture is being reimagined and, more important, remade, is rich in things and poor in new signs. Marco Polo is most interested in the newly discovered facts of architecture, Kublai Khan in its idea. Like Alberti newly discovering and translating Vitruvius, Marco, responding to the emperor's chastisement, "Why do you speak to me of the stones? It is only the arch that matters to me," answers that "without stones there is no arch."

Consumer culture has turned intellectuals into complacent Kublai Khans, more interested in the "line of the arch" than the labor process that made it possible. The purpose of this discussion is to refocus interest on the rhetorical transformations of form into idea, signified into signifier, that mark the period called postmodern. Its intention is also to offer a perspective that mediates between the discredited universalizing of modernism and the soulless dematerializing of postmodern theorizing, thus suggesting a new correspondence between language and action.

Such a correspondence may be posited in terms that are at once ethical and aesthetic. The worlds Marco presents to Kublai Khan have their own commonsense reality, but to the emperor they are merely possible worlds. The process of reporting serves to integrate these terms aesthetically. These worlds are attractive to Khan because they are new; they break the pattern of his referential schema, of his commonplace reality, thus producing wonder and temporary escape, while, at the same time, they evoke the ethos of the other. Through his ambassador, Khan journeys to strange lands, into the "ethical" heart of different communities. Confronted with the fragments of discourse Marco brings him, he cannot help but view discourse as a relative phenomenon. But relative in what sense? In relation to form? to Marco's narrative intentions? to the existence of some transcendent reality existing beyond his texts? Relative to history, or to language, or to discourse itself? None of the above satisfies the equation, for Marco's real worlds are not objects to be understood and thus dominated; rather, they are ways of understanding. They are not represented but, instead, evoked. We can apply to Marco's discourse what Stephen A. Tyler says about the ethnographic text (Marco is the ethnographer of imaginary worlds): that "it is not only an object, it is not *the* object; it is just a means, the meditative vehicle for a transcendence of time and place that is not just transcendental but a transcendental return to time and place."[13] Thus, these worlds retain their particular, specific difference (a difference of time, place, and materialized existence in architecture) while constituting a restorative vision, a therapy designed to call forth the reality of different commonplace worlds and to fuse that reality with the world of the viewer, which, by means of the aesthetic process, has been renewed.

It is not by accident that Calvino chooses architecture or city building as his postmodern paradigm. He understands that building implies a sense of optimism about the ideas of closure and unity that normally tend to be undercut by reason. There is a boneheaded aspect to achitecture—its preoccupation with measuring and the tiniest facts—that makes it a reluctant candidate for theorizing. The aspect of optimism or healing—filling holes and remaking the world—that is implicit in architectural activity makes it an ambiguous model for the postmodernist writer. But Calvino knows that there is a shadow side to the work that implies its opposite. The first function we have assigned to Emperor Khan, the second to Marco.

For Kublai Khan, there is unity: he has constructed in his mind a model city from which all possible cities can be deduced. For Marco, it is a city made of exceptions, exclusions, incongruities, contradictions. In both cases, 180 degrees opposed, architecture remains the model. For Khan, it offers a premodern certainty that truth can be known and made palpable. Khan's city is his power. Marco is equally secure in the knowledge that the world remains fragmented and incapable of wholeness.

To the novelist Calvino, with whom we travel most intimately, both interpretations of the material world are acceptable. The characteristic feature of postmodern discourse is that, while it appears to be dialectical, it can accept either term of the dialectic and has no faith in synthesis. Calvino's novel becomes a parable of parables. Marco and Khan are playing the same game, and it is also the game the attentive reader must play. Pure discourse in what passes as plot and in narrative is constantly being transformed materially. Calvino forces the reader to rehistoricize, to connect back to the world, even when he and the reader, like Marco, have no faith in the results. Readers of *Le città invisibili* are compelled to privilege the world of things over the world of words although they can find no logical reason to do so. The infinite regresses, the loops of discourse, are broken when the reader engages Khan or Marco answering Khan. Architecture as Khanian unity or Marcoian fragment provides an antidote to the arbitrariness of postmodern language. In its very thingness or builtness, architecture is incapable of perfection and is the ancient repository of loss.

NOTES

Except where otherwise indicated, all translations, in text and notes, are mine.

Preface

1. For a thorough discussion of the concept of ideology, see Terry Eagleton, *Ideology: An Introduction* (London: Verso, 1991).

2. Frederic Jameson, *The Political Unconscious: Narrative as a Socially Symbolic Act* (Ithaca: Cornell University Press, 1981), 287. Chapter 6, in particular, develops the concept of the relation between utopia and ideology.

3. Erich Auerbach, *Mimesis: The Representation of Reality in Western Literature* (Princeton: Princeton University Press, 1968), 525–53.

4. See, in particular, Frederic Jameson, *Signatures of the Visible* (New York: Routledge, 1992), 165–66.

5. Antonio Gramsci, *Quaderni del carcere*, ed. Valentino Gerratana (Turin: Einaudi, 1975), 1:311.

Chapter One. Alessandro Manzoni: The Cultural Transformation of Narrative

Parts of this chapter have appeared in an earlier form in *Forum Italicum* 2 (1985): 247–58, as "Gertrude's Story: The Irony of Self-Discovery"; and in *Perspectives on Nineteenth-Century Italian Novels*, ed. Guido Pugliese (Ottawa: Dovehouse, 1989), 55–64, under the same title as this chapter.

1. On authorial disavowal and the English novel, see Lennard J. Davis, "A Social History of Fact and Fiction: Authorial Disavowal in the Early English Novel," in *Literature and Society: Selected Papers from the English Institute*, ed. Edward W. Said (Baltimore: Johns Hopkins University Press, 1980), 120–48.

2. On the theme of conversion in *I promessi sposi*, see John Gatt-Rutter, "When the Killing Had to Stop: Manzoni's Paradigm of Christian Conversion," *The Italianist* 10 (1990), 7–40.

3. Bernard Groethuysen, *Origines de l'espirt bourgeois en France* (Paris: Gallimard, 1927), 176. Translation from *The Bourgeois: Catholicism vs. Capitalism in Eighteenth-Century France*, trans. Mary Illford (New York: Holt, Rinehart and Winston, 1968), 138–39.

4. Jameson, *Political Unconscious*, 144.

5. Alessandro Manzoni, *I promessi sposi*, in *Tutte le opere*, ed. Mario Martelli, vol. 1 (Florence: Sansoni, 1973), 1114. Translation from *The Bethrothed*, trans. Bruce Penman (Harmondsworth, England: Penquin, 1972), 369–70. Subsequent translations of *I promessi sposi* are from this source and are cited in text by page number.

6. Quoted in Groethuysen, *Origines*, 61. Translation from Illford, *Bourgeois Catholicism*, 50. See, also, Groethuysen, *Origines*, 50–57, on the prebourgeois meaning of death.

7. Cf. Northrop Frye, *The Secular Scripture* (Cambridge: Harvard University Press, 1976), 58.

8. Too often, the issue of Manzoni's theology has been couched in terms of whether or not it was orthodox Catholic, at the expense of understanding the place it occupies in the religious controversies of the period. Responsible for the promotion of this kind of inquiry among English and American readers has been the work of Rocco Montano. See, for example, his "Manzoni Today," *Italian Quarterly* 67 (1973): 25–54.

9. Jameson, *Political Unconscious*, 111, 152.

10. On this point, see my "The Seicento as Strategy: Providence and the Bourgeois in *I Promessi Sposi*," *MLN*, 91 (1976): 80–100.

11. For the basic literature on Diderot's influence, see Alessandro Luzio, *Manzoni e Diderot: la monaca di Monza e "La Religieuse"* (Milan: Dumolard, 1884); Luigi Russo, "Manzoni poeta e Diderot oratore," in *Ritratti e disegni storici*, vol. 4 (Florence: Sansoni, 1965), 21–37; Giovanni Getto, *Manzoni europeo* (Milan: Mursia, 1971), 82–90; and Enrico De Angelis, *Qualcosa su Manzoni* (Turin: Einaudi, 1975), 121–34. On Gothic narrative modes in Manzoni's work, see Getto, *Manzoni europeo*, 88; Ettore Paratore, *Studi sui "Promessi Sposi"* (Florence: Sansoni, 1973), 27–89; and Ferruccio Ulivi, *Dal Manzoni ai Decadenti* (Caltanisetta and Rome: Sciascia, 1963), 13–58.

12. Giovanni Getto, *Letture manzoniane* (Florence: La Nuova Italia, 1964), 160.

13. Alessandro Manzoni, *Fermo e Lucia* in *Tutte le Opere*, 319.

14. Giovanni Getto, *Letture manzoniane*, 167.

15. Arcangelo Leone De Castris, *L'impegno del Manzoni* (Florence: Sansoni, 1966), 196.

16. On the symbolic character of the themes of imprisonment and claustration, see Victor Brombert, *The Romantic Prison* (Princeton: Princeton University Press, 1972), 81–83.

17. Giambattista Vico, *La scienza nuova* (Turin: Unione Tipografico-Edifice Torinese, 1951), 680–81. On Vico's idea of divine Providence, see Karl Lowith, *Meaning in History* (Chicago: University of Chicago Press, 1949), 115–36; and, more recently, James C. Morrison, "How to Interpret the Idea of Divine Providence in Vico's *New Science*," *Philosophy and Rhetoric* 12, no. 4 (Fall 1979), 256–61; and Gregory Lucente, "Vico's Notion of 'Divine Providence' and the Limits of Human Knowledge," *MLN* 97 (1982): 183–91.

18. On the notion of dogmatic biography and on the problematic individual in literature, see J. M. Bernstein, *The Philosophy of the Novel: Lukàcs, Marxism, and the Dialectics of Form* (Minneapolis: University of Minnesota Press, 1984), 165–75.

19. Jameson, *Political Unconscious*, 287.

20. On Manzoni's utopia of beneficence, see Guilio Bollati, "Un carattere per gli italiani," in *Storia d'Italia* (Turin: Einaudi, 1972) 1:951–1023. Bollati regards the Manzonian

utopia as an act of rhetorical subterfuge. In his view, Manzoni's quarrel with utilitarianism is a tactic to discredit liberalism and thus prevent any possible transition to democracy and socialism. Manzoni is a "bourgeois reactionary" who to the "nightmare of a proletarian revolution opposes a culture of universal values; to a starving populace, who would benefit from the social programs inspired by utilitarian thought, the luxury of a Christian civilization" (997). Thus, Bollati shows how Manzoni has contributed to the formation of an Italian character, the *homo italicus* whose existence thrives under the protection of the Christian tradition and the Catholic Church. At best, this essay provides a historical rationale for both the Gramscian notion of a paternalistic, condescending Manzoni and for Lukàcs's sense of the absence in the novel of a "world historical atmosphere." Georg Lukàcs, *The Historical Novel*, trans. Hannah and Stanley Mitchell (Atlantic Highlands, N.J.: Humanities Press, 1978), 71.

21. Robert S. Dombroski, "Manzoni on the Italian Left," *Annali d'Italianistica* 3 (1985): 109.

22. See, in particular, Luca Toschi, *Si dia un padre a Lucia: studi sugli autografi manzoniani* (Padua: Liviana, 1983), and *La sala rossa: biografia dei "Promessi Sposi"* (Turin: Bollati Boringhieri, 1989).

Chapter Two. Giovanni Verga: Science and Allegory in I Malavoglia

1. Giovanni Verga, *I Malavoglia*, ed. Romano Luperini (Milan: Mondadori, 1985), 3. Subsequent page references in text are to this edition.

2. On ethnographic narrative, see James Clifford's introduction to *Writing Culture: The Poetics and Politics of Ethnography*, ed. James Clifford and George E. Marcus (Berkeley: University of California Press, 1986).

3. Guido Baldi, *L'artificio della regressione: tecnica narrativa e ideologia nel Verga verista* (Naples: Liguori, 1980), 77.

4. See Alberto Asor Rosa, "Il primo e l'ultimo uomo del mondo," in *Il caso Verga*, ed. Alberto Asor Rosa (Palermo: Palumbo, 1973), 11–12.

5. Quoted from Verga's letter to his friend Salvatore Paola Verdura, cited in Giulio Cattaneo, *Verga* (Turin: Unione Tipografico-Editrice Torinese, 1963), 162.

6. Cited in Marvin Harris, *Cultural Materialism* (New York: Random House, 1980), 12.

7. Angelo Marchese, "L'arte narrativa dei Malavoglia," *Otto/Novecento* 18, no. 2 (1989): 109–94.

8. Masiello, in particular, has drawn attention to the rapid process of industrialization and the problems it caused in a still fundamentally agricultural country. Industrialization, coupled with the wave of investment activity in the North, which drove an even deeper wedge between northern and southern Italy, caused large strata of intellectuals active in the unification process to see themselves estranged from the society they rightly believed they helped create. Southern intellectuals especially felt radically cut off from the progress heralded by the dominant political ideology. For those with deep ties to patriarcal, agricultural communities, the unification was seen as a threat to an entire way of life. Vitilio Masiello, *Verga fra ideologia e realtà* (Bari: De Donato), 1970.

9. Luigi Franchetti and Sydney Sonnino, *Inchiesta in Sicilia* (Florence: Vallecchi, 1974).

Verga gathered an enormous amount of information about Sicily from this work, especially about the conditions of peasant life.

10. Jameson, *Political Unconscious,* 17.

11. On the importance of the *Inchiesta* to the historical basis of *I Malavoglia,* see Romano Luperini, *Simbolo e costruzione allegorica in Verga* (Bologna: Il Mulino, 1989), 15–50.

12. See, James Clifford, "On Ethnographic Allegory," *Writing Culture: The poetics and Politics of Ethnography,* ed. James Clifford and George E. Marcus (Berkeley: University of California Press, 1986), 98–121.

13. Ibid., 112–13.

14. In contrast to Luperini, I do not use the term *allegorical* in opposition to *symbolic.* All literary description symbolizes, in that it takes the place of something imagined to be real. At the same time, it is allegory because it is a practice referring to something else; it speaks of the other. Luperini distinguishes between symbolists and allegorists. The latter, he argues, abandon organicity and totality altogether, viewing the world solely as fragment and phenomenon. The meaning they impose on their representations does not bridge the gap between authorial intention and objective meaning. Thus, he equates allegorism with modern realism. With reference to *I Malavoglia,* Luperini argues that the contiguity between naturalistic realism and modern allegorism consists in the realization that reality is fragment and chaos but that it is still necessary to attribute value to it by means of such symbolic strategies as, for example, Verga's foregrounding of the lyrical soul of his characters. It is only in *Mastro don Gesualdo* that Verga becomes, according to Luperini, a thoroughly dispassionate observer. See Romano Luperini, *Simbolo e costruzione allegorica,* 10–11.

15. Clifford, "On Ethnographic Allegory," 111.

16. Giovanni Verga, *Fantasticheria,* in *Tutte le novelle* (Milan: Mondadori, 1979), 149–54.

17. Clifford, "On Ethnographic Allegory," 115.

18. Jameson, *Political Unconscious,* 250.

19. Cattaneo, *Verga,* 185.

20. Luperini, introduction, in Verga, *I Malavoglia,* xxii–xxiii.

21. Guido Baldi is right in pointing out that Verga's free, indirect style is not of the orthodox variety. The traditional *erlebte Rede* distinguishes between the point of view of the narrative voice and that of the characters. In *I Malavoglia,* it is practically impossible to make this distinction. As author, Verga does not disappear completely but rather retains his own identity by means of mimicking or echoing, often ironically, the speech and thoughts of the community. In sum, he masquerades as his characters. See *L'artificio della regressione,* 78–79.

22. Luigi Russo, *Giovanni Verga* (Bari: Laterza, 1968), 156.

23. See Luperini's commentary, G. Verga, *I Malavoglia,* 31.

24. Cf. Frederic Jameson, *Political Unconscious,* 252.

25. Georg Lukàcs, *Theory of the Novel* (Boston, MIT University Press, 1975), 36.

26. Cf., Luperini's commentary, in Verga, *I Malavoglia,* 328.

27. See Luperini's commentary, in Verga, *I Malavoglia,* 60–66.

28. See Guido Baldi, *L'artificio della regressione,* 131.

29. Luperini, *Simbolo e costruzione allegorica,* 65.

Chapter Three. Gabriele D'Annunzio: Mythical Narratives

This chapter was originally published, in a slightly different form, in *The Italianist*, 10 (1990): 41–70. Original quotations from the following works are taken from Gabriele D'Annunzio's *Prose di romanzi*, ed. Egidio Bianchetti, 2 vols. (Milan: Mondadori, 1968): *Il piacere*, 1:3–367; *L'innocente*, 1:170–650; *Il trionfo della morte*, 1:652–1049; *Gli idolatri*, 2:161–172; *Le vergini delle rocce*, 2:397–567; *Il fuoco*, 2:571–861; *Forse che sì, forse che no*, 2:865–1180. Volume number and page number for specific references are given in text.

1. Furio Jesi, *La cultura di destra* (Milan: Feltrinelli, 1979), 6–7.

2. D'Annunzio discusses his notion of "intrasmissibile" in *Prose di romanzi*, 1:664. It is notably similar to what Lyotard has called the "unpresentable" in modernist writings, which forms, in his view, the basis for an aesthetics of the sublime. See Jean-François Lyotard, *The Postmodern Condition: A Report on Knowledge*, trans. Geoff Bennington and Brian Massuni (Minneapolis: University of Minnesota Press, 1984), 80–81.

3. Gabriele D'Annunzio, *The Maidens of the Rocks*, trans. Annetta Halliday-Antona and Giuseppe Antona (Boston: L. C. Page, 1898), 45–46. Subsequent translations from this source are cited in text by page number.

4. Cf., Mario Ricciardi, *Coscienza e struttura nella prosa di D'Annunzio* (Turin: Giappichelli, 1970), 98.

5. Gabriele D'Annunzio, *Triumph of Death*, trans. Arthur Hornblow (New York: George Richmond, 1897), 142–43. Subsequent translations from this source are cited in text by page number.

6. Vittorio Roda, *La strategia della totalità* (Bologna: Boni, 1978), 6.

7. Ibid., 141.

8. Cited in Umberto Silva, *L'ideologia e arte del fascismo* (Milan: Mazzotta, 1973), 83–84 n. 1.

9. Jameson, *Political Unconscious*, 237.

10. See Jesi, *La cultura di destra*, 150.

11. On ritual violence, see René Girard's classic study *Le violence et le sacré*, (Paris: Grasset, 1972), especially chap. 2; see, also, Barbara Spackman's perceptive essay, "Il verbo (e) sangue: Gabriele D'Annunzio and the Ritualization of Violence," *Quaderni d'Italianistica* 4, no. 2 (1983): 218–29.

12. Gabriele D'Annunzio, *The Child of Pleasure*, trans. Georgina Harding (New York: George Richmond, 1898), 62–63.

13. Vittorio Roda, *Il soggetto centrifugo* (Bologna: Patron, 1984), 243–73.

14. Niva Lorenzini, *Il segno del corpo* (Rome: Bulzoni, 1984), 8.

15. See Gregory Lucente's pertinent remarks in *Beautiful Fables: Self-Consciousness in Italian Narrative from Manzoni to Calvino* (Baltimore: Johns Hopkins University Press, 1988), 114.

16. For an interesting attempt at reading D'Annunzio in the light of Lacan, see Lucia Re, "Gabriele D'Annunzio's Novel *Le vergini delle rocce:* 'Una cosa naturale vista in un grande specchio,'" *Stanford Italian Review* 3, no. 2 (Fall 1983): 241–71.

17. Georg Wilhelm Friedrich Hegel, *The Phenomenology of Mind* (New York: Harper, 1967), 712.

18. Antonio Gramsci, *Quaderni del carcere*, 2:1201.

19. On D'Annunzio and Fiume in relation to fascism, see Emilio Gentile, *Le origini dell'ideologia fascista* (Milan: Mondadori, 1975), 166–89; and Michel Ostenc, *Intellectuels italiens et le Fascisme* (Paris: Payot, 1983), 123–58.

20. See Stephan Sharkey and Robert Dombroski, "Revolution, Myth, and Mythical Politics: The Futurist Solution," *Journal of European Studies*, 6 (1976): 231-47.

Chapter Four. Luigi Pirandello:
Epistemology and Pure Subjectivity

Parts of this chapter appeared originally in Italian in my *Le totalità del'artificio: ideologia e forma nel romanzo pirandelliano* (Padua: Liviana, 1976).

1. On the language of Pirandello's prose narratives, see Paolo Archi, *Il tempo delle parole: saggio sulla lingua delle prose pirandelliane* (Palermo: Palumbo, 1992).

2. All references are to Giovanni Macchia's critical edition of the novels, Luigi Pirandello, *Tutti i romanzi*, 2 vols. (Milan: Mondadori, 1975). The translations are mine, drawing liberally on *One, None and a Hundred-thousand*, trans. Samuel Putnam (New York: Howard Fertig, 1983).

3. Pirandello talks about the importance of *Uno, nessuno e centomila* in an interview published in *Epoca* (July 5, 1922).

4. See Macchia's Introduction to Pirandello, *Tutti i romanzi*, 1:xlix.

5. Pirandello, *Epoca* interview.

6. Gian Paolo Biasin, "Lo specchio di Moscarda," *Paragone* (June 1972): 62–63.

7. Renato Barilli, *La linea Svevo-Pirandello* (Milan: Mursia, 1972), 218–19.

8. For more recent studies of *Uno, nessuno e centomila* from this perspective, see Corrado Donati, *La solitudine allo specchio* (Rome: Lucarini, 1980); and Gregory Lucente, *Beautiful Fables*, 116–55.

9. R. D. Laing, *The Divided Self* (Harmondsworth, England: Pelican Books, 1960).

10. From Pirandello's experience of negativity numerous routes could be taken, the most important one leading directly to the theater of the absurd (Beckett, Ionesco, Adamov). Pirandello's plays are not tragedies of depersonalization or dehumanization, and his concern with the disintegration of self does not lead to the kinds of schizophrenic representation we find in the works of Beckett or Ionesco. Instead, as I try to show, existential nothingness leads Pirandello on to the terrain of ontology and to a quest for pure subjectivity that has a striking resemblance to Husserl's concept of the transcendental ego.

11. See, for example, Marziano Guglielminetti, "Le vicende e i significati di *Uno, nessuno e centomila*, *Il "Romanzo" di Pirandello* (Palermo: Palumbo, 1976), 203–04: In *Uno, nessuno, e centomila*, "si dà voce ad un'angoscia esistenziale e ad una volontà di fuga dal tempo e dallo spazio che sono, ad un tempo, operazioni distruttive e costruttive" (2-3-4) [expression is given to existential anxiety and to the desire to flee from time and space, which entails an undertaking that is both destructive and constructive].

12. See R. D. Laing, *Divided Self*, 106–9, 137.

13. Ibid., 92.

14. Martin Heidegger, *Being and Time* (New York: Harper and Row, 1962), 164.

15. Cf. Frederic Jameson, *Fables of Agression: Wyndham Lewis, the Modernist as Fascist* (Berkeley: University of California Press, 1981), 15.

Chapter Five. Italo Svevo:
Contradiction and the Borders of Modernism

1. Crucial to Svevo's intellectual orientation is his native Trieste, a city of bourgeois entrepreneurs, situated at the junction of contrasting cultures and different languages. Svevo was brought up within a Middle-European culture in a city of businessmen, which offered little if any literary tradition of its own to build on. Svevo was a businessman himself. He did not associate with any of the cultural institutions or literary trends then prevalent in Italy, nor was he an academic or professional writer, as were his Italian contemporaries. These circumstances, together with his readings of French nineteenth-century realists and German romantic humorists, explain in large part his approach to fiction as a means of inquiry and self-analysis. On Svevo's Trieste, see Enrico Ghidetti, *Italo Svevo: la coscienza di un borghese triestino* (Rome: Editori Riuniti, 1992); Charles Russell, *Italo Svevo the Writer from Trieste* (Ravenna: Longo, 1978); and John Gatt-Rutter, *Italo Svevo: A Double Life* (Oxford: Clarendon, 1988).

2. Franco Moretti's remarks on modernist irony are pertinent in this regard. In the bourgeois world,

> one has . . . to see and not to see, to accept and to disavow at the same time. It is a contradictory predicament, and in order to make us feel at home in the bourgeois metropolis—a feeling that is bound to be very near the core of what we call the "hegemonic world view"—both external stimuli and subjective perception have to possess rather peculiar attributes, which, once more, turn out to be barely distinguishable from those usually associated with literary modernism. As for the stimulus, it has to be "evocative" more than "meaningful"; it must possess as little determinacy as possible and therefore be open to, or better still produce, such a plurality of associations that everybody can "find something" in it. It must in other words, center around the key word of modernism: ambiguity. (Franco Moretti, "The Spell of Indecision," in *Marxism and the Interpretation of Culture*, ed. Cary Nelson and Lawrence Grossberg [Urbana: University of Illinois Press, 1988], 340)

3. See Mario Lavagetto, "Correzioni su Zeno," in *Italo Svevo Oggi*, ed. Marco Marchi (Florence: Vallecchi, 1980), 140.

4. See, for example, Eduardo Saccone, *Commento a "Zeno": saggio sul testo di Svevo* (Bologna: Il Mulino, 1973); and Teresa de Lauretis, *La sintassi del desiderio: struttura e forme del romanzo sveviano* (Ravenna: Longo, 1976).

5. Italo Svevo, *La coscienza di Zeno* (Milan: Dall'Oglio, 1976), 445. Translation from Italo Svevo, *Confessions of Zeno*, trans. Beryl de Zoete (Harmondsworth: Penguin Books), 1964), 384. Subsequent translations from this source are cited in text by page number.

6. Along these lines, see Terry Eagleton's *The Ideology of the Aesthetic* (London: Basil Blackwell, 1990), 366–68:

> One may risk the rather exaggerated formulation that aesthetics is born at the moment of art's effective demise as a political force, [and] flourishes on the corpse of its social rele-

vance. Though artistic production itself plays less and less of a significant role in the social order (Marx reminds us that the bourgeoisie have absolutely no time for it), what it is able to bequeath to that order, as it were, is a certain ideological model which may help it out of its mess—the mess which has marginalized pleasure and the body, reified reason, and struck morality entirely empty. The aesthetic offers to reverse this division of labour, to bring these three alienated regions back into touch with one another, but the price it demands for this generosity is high: it offers to interrelate these discourses by effectively swallowing up the other two. Everything should now become aesthetic. Truth, the cognitive, becomes that which satisfies the mind, or what helps us move around the place rather more conveniently. Morality is converted into a matter of style, pleasure and intuition. How should one live one's life properly? By turning oneself into an artefact. (368)

7. Although the distinction between Zeno and Svevo is extremely important for an understanding of how the text works, it becomes absolutely unproductive if exaggerated to the point of obliterating all connections between the author and his character. Obviously, Svevo is not Zeno, but, on the other hand, he is what Svevo could be, someone who takes the place of the author, grapples with his predicaments, and carries to a great extent the burden of meaning that the author has intended to give to his text. In a word, Zeno is the text of Svevo's inquiry.

8. Claudio Magris has summed up Svevo's importance in somewhat similar terms:

La grandezza di Svevo consiste anche nella profondità con la quale egli ha vissuto la condizione borghese quale condizione totale del trovarsi nel mondo, la vischiosa e camaleontica capacità della civiltà borghese di confondersi con la vita stessa, di identificarsi con essa arrogandosi il diritto di rappresentarla nella sua totalità. ("Italo Svevo: la vita e la rappresentazione della vita," *Italo Svevo Oggi*, 93).
[Svevo's greatness consists even in the profound way he experienced the bourgeois condition as total: the viscid and chameleon-like capacity of bourgeois civilization to confuse its way of living with life itself, to identify with life, and to pretend it has the right to represent life in all its totality.]

9. On this issue, I do not agree with Magris, for whom Svevo is a post-modern writer par excellence: "Svevo è lo scrittore post-moderno che forse più d'ogni altro ha compreso il crepuscolo del soggetto." Ibid., 74. [Svevo is the postmodern writer who perhaps more than any other understood the decline of the subject.] As for the concept of postmodernism, I am aware of the difficulty of establishing its specific difference vis-à-vis modernism. Nevertheless, I find the concept useful in distinguishing between different sensibilities and forms of artistic practice. See below, chaps. 7 and 9.

10. Frederic Jameson, *Postmodernism or the Cultural Logic of Late Capitalism* (Durham: Duke University Press, 1992), 9.

11. On the relation of "text" and historical time, see Aldo Gargani, *Il testo e il tempo* (Bari: Laterza, 1992), 7–12.

12. Eagleton, *Ideology of the Aesthetic*, 265.

13. See Ernest Mandel, *Late Capitalism* (London: Verso, 1975), 562–89.

14. On language in *La coscienza di Zeno*, Lavagetto has made some poignant observations: "Nel caso della *Coscienza di Zeno* la seconda voce, la voce dell'autore, si coglie nella coerenza con cui il narratore viene dotato di un apparente monolinguismo refrattario, grigio, fatto di sterotipi: è Zeno rappresentato come linguaggio, come parlante individuale e

irriducibile" ("Correzioni su Zeno," 140). [In the case of *La coscienza di Zeno,* the second voice, the voice of the author, is captured in the coherence with which the narrator is endowed with an apparent monolinguism, refractory, gray, composed of stereotypes: this is Zeno represented as language, as a individual and irreducible speaking voice.]

Chapter Six.
Carlo Emilio Gadda: Travesties

The first part of this chapter, devoted to *La cognizione del dolore,* was published originally in *MLN* 99 (1984). It appears here revised.

1. See Aldo Gargani, "Robert Musil: il salto nell'inverificabile," in *Lo stupore e il caso* (Bari: Laterza, 1985), 105–6.

2. Carlo Emilio Gadda, *La cognizione del dolore* (Turin: Einaudi, 1963), 120–21. The translations given are mine, based on William Weaver's *Acquainted with Grief* (New York: George Braziller, 1969).

3. Carlo Emilio Gadda, "Fatto personale . . . o quasi," in *Viaggi la morte* (Milan: Garzanti, 1958), 101–7.

4. In the essay, "I viaggi la morte," Gadda dwells on the "schizophrenizing" of the symbolist poets:

Il migrare dei simbolisti è un determinare nuove fortune spaziali, nuove conoscenze e nuove sensazioni astratte dall'impulso coordinate dell'io, è un perdersi nella causalità oceanica; il morire è un accedere a più vasta dissoluzione, a più sconfinata causalità, ove ogni impaccio sia tolto dai vincoli d'ogni teleologia. Filosoficamente questo anelito verso il caos adirezionale rappresenta un regresso alla potenza primigenia dell'inizio, ancora privo di determinazioni etiche: una ricaduta nell'infanzia dell'essere, se così è lecito dire. (Carlo Emilio Gadda, "I viaggi la morte," in *I viaggi la morte,* 196)
[The roving of the symbolists is a way of fixing new spacial fortunes, new perceptions and sensations abstracted from the coordinating impulse of the self. It is the losing of oneself in the ocean of causality. Dying is a movement toward greater dissolution, toward more boundless causality, where every obstacle is removed from the chain of every teleology. Philosophically speaking, this impulse toward adirectional chaos represents a regression to the primeval power of the beginning, still devoid of ethical proclivities; it is a withdrawal to the infancy of being, as it were.]

5. Cf. Carlo De Matteis, "Oltraggio e riscatto, interpretatazione della *Cognizione del dolore* di C. E. Gadda," *L'Approdo Letterario* 53, no. 17 (1971): 62–63.

6. Romano Luperini, *Il novecento,* vol. 2 (Turin: Loescher, 1981), 493–94.

7. We may view Gonzalo's aggressive temperament and rages as a defensive position. See Otto Kernberg, *Borderline Conditions and Pathological Narcissism* (New York: J. Aronson, 1975). The novel expresses the hero's problematical subjectivity. Beneath the grandiose self that attacks the madness and stupidity of the Other, we have the experience of a ravenous child who seeks empathy from his mother for his emerging self. Thus, Gonzalo's rage is primarily oral; it seeks to devour linguistically everything in sight.

8. Essential in this respect is Gadda's essay, "Psicanalisi e letteratura," in *I viaggi la morte,* 41–60.

9. On Gadda's support of Mussolini and fascism, see my *Introduzione allo studio di Carlo Emilio Gadda* (Florence: Vallecchi, 1974), 145–68; Lorenzo Greco, "L'autocensura di Gadda, gli scritti tecnico-autarchici," in *Censura e scrittura. Vittorini, lo pseudo Malaparte, Gadda* (Milan: Il Saggiatore, 1983), 51–98; and Carlo De Matteis, "Guerra, dopoguerra e fascismo nella narrativa giovanile di Gadda," in *Prospezioni su Gadda* (Teramo: Giunti e Lisciani, 1985), 56–89.

10. In addition to the conservative politics of Gadda's ancestors, of which he was proud, the economic *déclassément* of his immediate family no doubt influenced his support of fascism:

La mia infelicità maggiore proveniva dalla povertà della mia famiglia. Per quanto nei primi anni abbiamo avuto delle condizioni abbastanza buone, poi le cose si sono aggravate per errori economici di mio padre. Spendeva più di quanto potesse poi recuperare. Non era un bravo uomo d'affari, sia detto con rispetto. Era un maniaco della terra, della campagna, della gente brianzola . . . aver comprato una piccola proprietà nella Brianza proprio quando non avrebbe dovuto comprarla, perché era già in cattive condizioni, con tre bambini da mantenere e non era neanche giovine. . . . Di questa proprietà ho parlato nella *Cognizione del dolore.* . . . La povertà mi ha umiliato di fronte al ceto civile borghese al quale la mia famiglia apparteneva, almeno nominalmente. (Ernesto Ferrero and Dacia Maraini, "C.E. Gadda: come scrittore, come uomo," *Prisma*, 5, [1968], 15)
[My greatest unhappiness came from my family's poverty. Even though at first our financial condition was sufficiently good, later things got worse because of my father's financial mistakes. He used to spend more than he could earn in return. He was not a good businessman, let it be said with respect. He had a mania for the land, for the countryside, for the people from Brianza . . . having bought a small piece of property in Brianza when he should not have, because things were already going badly, with three children to look after and he wasn't young anymore. . . . I talked about this property in *La cognizione del dolore.* . . . Our poverty humiliated me in the eyes of the bourgeoisie to which, at least nominally, my family belonged.]

11. Piero Pucci, "The Obscure Sickness," *Italian Quarterly* 2, no. 42 (1967): 43–62.

12. Enrico Flores, *Accessioni gaddiane* (Naples: Loffredo, 1973), 59 n. 29.

13. Luperini, *Novecento*, 509.

14. See Silvio Guarnieri, "Gadda scrittore politico," *Nuova Rivista Europea* 24 (1981): 92–18:

E necessario vincere il fascismo in noi stessi, in tutti gli animi dei cittadini: con lo spregiare, condannare, diridere e avere a schifo in noi il culto della prepotenza, il prevalere iniquo dell'io, l'ambizione fisica di essere al di sopra degli altri e la 'fede', tipicamente fascista, in una presunta nostra capacità di disporre del destino comune e di condurre al 'trionfo' certe idee di potenza che inverdiscono soltanto, quasi un'erbaccia in un orto negletto, nella nostra capoccia di superuomini cretini. (106)
[It's necessary to destroy the fascism within ourselves, in the hearts of us citizens, by deriding and condemning the disgusting cult of dominance, the iniquitous force of the ego, the physical desire to subdue others, and the typically fascist faith in our capacity to dispose of the common destiny and to "triumph" with certain ideas of power that come to life, like weeds in a neglected garden, in the skulls of cretinous supermen.]

For the best overview to date of Gadda's politics, see Giuseppe Papponetti, "Gadda e il lavoro italiano," *Otto/Novecento* 13, no. 5 (1989), 5–36.

15. Carlo Emilio Gadda, "L'Egoista," in *I vaggi la morte*, 281.

16. Carlo Emilio Gadda, *Quer pasticciaccio brutto de via Merulana* (Milan: Garzanti, 1963). Translations are mine, based on William Weaver's *That Awful Mess in Merulana* (New York: George Braziler, 1965).

17. Mikhail Bakhtin, *Rabelais and His World*, trans. Hélène Iswolsky (Bloomington: Indiana University Press, 1984), 20–21.

18. D. A. Miller, *The Novel and the Police* (Berkeley: University of California Press, 1988), 34.

19. Gian Carlo Ferretti, *Ritratto di Gadda* (Bari: Laterza, 1987), 118.

20. Carlo Emilio Gadda, "Lingua letteraria e lingua d'uso," in *I viaggi la morte*, 93.

21. Carlo Emilio Gadda, "Tecnica e poesia," in *I viaggi la morte*, 72.

22. Carlo Emilio Gadda, "Psicanalisi e letteratura," in *I viaggi la morte*, 44.

23. Angelo Guglielmi, *Avanguardia e sperimentalismo* (Milan: Feltrinelli, 1974), 33–34; and "Gadda" *I contemporanei* (Milan: Marzorati, 1964), 1063–64.

Chapter Seven. Antonio Pizzuto: The Subject of Narrative

This chapter was originally published in *Italica* 67, no. 1 (1990): 1–16.

1. Antonio Pizzuto, *Signorina Rosina* (Cosenza: Lerici, 1959), 43.

2. In a published interview, Pizzuto explains how *Ravenna* got its title:

Questa è la storia del titolo. Io andavo a Parigi e sul treno, a Genova, salì un tale. Si mise di fronte a me, si mise a chiacchierare. A un certo momento, parlando, mi parlò di musica: parlare di musica a me significa che apro subito le braccia. E, allora cominciammo a parlare di musica. . . . Mi disse che lui aveva un'industria a Parigi, in Rue . . . [e] che aveva composto della musica, soprattutto sonate per pianoforte, e si faceva aiutare, aveva una pianista che gli suonava i pezzi. Mi disse: "Mi venga a trovare, e gliela faccio sentire". Così, mi fece sentire questo "Ravenna". La seconda o terza volta gli dissi: "Ma perchè l'ha chiamato Ravenna"? Mi disse: Così, mi è capitato questo nome". . . . L'idea mi è piaciuta: che cosa c'entra Ravenna con questo? Non c'entra per niente. (*Pizzuto parla di Pizzuto* ed. Paola Peretti, [Cosenza: Lerici, 1977], 117–20.]
[This is the title's history. I was on my way to Paris and in Genoa a fellow got on the train. He sat down in front of me and began chatting. At a certain point, he started talking about music. When someone talks about music I open up to him immediately. We then began talking about music. . . . He said he owned an industry in Paris, in Rue. . . [and] that he had composed some musical scores, mainly piano sonatas, and that he was helped by a pianist who would play the pieces for him. He said to me: "Come and visit me, and I'll let you hear them." So, I heard "Ravenna." The second or third time I said to him: "Why did you name it Ravenna?" He said: "I don't know, I just happened to think of this name." I liked the idea: what does Ravenna have to do with this [piece of music]? Nothing at all.]

3. Signorina Rosina as a recurring motif in the novel has been examined in detail in Felicita Audisio, "*Signorina Rosina* e la funzione del nome titolo," *Forum Italicum* 7 (1973): 415–28.

4. Luigi Baldacci, cited in Peretti, *Pizzuto parla*, 112.

5. Paolo Milano, cited in Peretti, *Pizzuto parla*, 112.

6. Ruggero Jacobbi, *Pizzuto* (Florence: La Nuova Italia, 1971), 26–27.

7. Ruggero Jacobbi, "Antonio Pizzuto," in *Novecento: gli scrittori e la cultura letteraria nella società italiana,* ed. Gianni Grana, (Milan: Marzorati, 1980), 9997.

8. I follow the usage of the term as argued by Jameson, in *Postmodernism,* and David Harvey, in *The Condition of Postmodernity* (London: Basil Blackwell, 1989). I realize that the condition termed *postmodern* could be called just as easily, as Charles Jencks suggests, "late-modern" in order to correspond to its late-capitalist economic base (*The Post-Modern Reader,* ed. Charles Jencks [New York: St. Martin's Press, 1991], 13). However, the problem with such a designation is that it emphasizes continuity, whereas both continuity and rupture are equally present in the postmodern condition. Omar Calabrese's attempt to reclassify such a sensibility and artistic practice as "neo-baroque," on the basis of the technique of repetition and serialization (*Neo-Baroque* [Princeton: Princeton University Press, 1992]), brings little new to the debate.

9. On the difference between parody and pastiche as related to modernist and postmodernist styles, see Jameson, *Postmodernism,* 17. Jameson argues that parody depends on the belief in the existence of a linguistic norm and that the pastiche appears when language becomes an exclusively private code. Pastiche is the neutral practice of parody, "speech in a dead language," i.e., in a language devoid of a linguistic norm. I have taken Jameson's point to distinguish the satiric and comic impulses of Gadda from a kind of mimicry, prevalent in Pizzuto, that appears, as Jameson might say, as caricature without affect, a cold and inherently ironic reproduction of Gadda's outrage. My reading of *Signorina Rosina* is based on Jameson's general assessment of the relation of postmodernism to consumer society. On Jameson's argument, see Terry Eagleton, *Against the Grain* (London: Verso, 1986), 131–32. For a thorough critical discussion of Jameson's position, see *Postmodernism Jameson Critique,* ed. Douglas Kellner (Washington, D.C.: Maisonneuve), 1989.

10. For a good survey and critique of the crisis of the subject, see Paul Smith, *Discerning the Subject* (Minneapolis: University of Minnesota Press, 1988).

11. Jameson, *Postmodernism,* 15.

12. Pizzuto remarks on his nominalism as follows: "Io sono nominalista, e quindi . . . non ha nessuna importanza per me che una cosa sia in un modo o sia in un altro. Non ha nessuna importanza." Peretti, *Pizzuto parla,* 110. [I am a nominalist, therefore . . . it has no importance for me whether a thing is in one mode or in another. It has no importance.]

13. Jacobbi sees in Pizzuto

> un passo più innocente dell'animo, senza le acredini, senza le cupe vendette contro il genere umano, in un materiale erudito di origine soltanto poetica e metafisica, senza sospetti scientifici, senza rapporto con la tecnica e con la prassi, semmai sostituite da un molto meridionale bagaglio di linguaggio giuridico. L'*humour* emerge al fondo di una dolcezza patetica e poi si ragela, si irrigidisce in una interrogazione assolutizzante, religiosa. Gadda non chiede mai il perchè del mondo, si arrabbia a vederlo così malconscio, lui che saprebbe così bene a quali alti parametri di afflitta dignità ricondurlo perché, in nome delle vittime, delle genti spaurite e inermi, offese e travolte malgrado la loro sottile e inutile "nobiltà d'animo". La metafisica di Gadda è l'ultima porta dischiusa nel gelido muro della scienza, in quanto unica forse a poter rendere conto della sorditezza del mondo; in Pizzuto è slancio naturale di lirico, che ne scopre l'accento di fragilità mentre nomina le ilari feste e le brutali ingiustizie, senza compiacerne e tirando via. "Antonio Pizzuto," 10003.

[a more innocent movement of spirit, without the bitterness, without [Gadda's] doleful revenge against humanity, in an erudite subject matter whose origin is uniquely poetical and metaphysical, without scientific distrust, unrelated to technique and praxis, at most replaced by a very typically southern use of juridical language. [Pizzuto's] humor issues from a source of emotive freshness, and then it congeals, hardening in consummate, religious interrogation. Gadda never asks why the world is the way it is. Seeing it so battered makes him irate, he who would know to what lofty parameters of molested dignity to lead it back to, so that it would begin to work well. Pizzuto continually asks why, in the name of the victims, terrified, defenseless people, humiliated and violated in spite of their refined and futile "spiritual nobility." Gadda's metaphysics is the last opening in the stone wall of science, in that it is perhaps the only way capable of accounting for the world's insensitivity. In Pizzuto there is the natural ardor of a lyric poet who discovers the frailness of the world at the same time that he gives name to its festive moments and brutal injustice, without gratification, and then moves on.]

14. Cesare Segre has remarked on how, in order to reduce to a bare minimum the grammatical signs of causality, Pizzuto's syntax leaves out the conjunctions between coordinate sentence elements; in *Signora Rosina*, this *asyndeton* is manifest in the parallel structuring of imperfects and rare preterits. Cesare Segre, "Hyponopaleoneomachia di Pizzuto," in *I segni e la critica* (Turin: Einaudi, 1969), 225.

15. Jurgen Habermas, "Modernity—An Incomplete Project," in *The Anti-Aesthetic: Essays on Postmodern Culture*, ed. Hal Foster (Port Townsend, Wash.: Bay Press, 1983), 5.

16. Pizzuto discusses his conceptions of space and time in Peretti, *Pizzuto parla*, 26-34.

Chapter Eight. Giuseppe Tomasi di Lampedusa and Luchino Visconti: Substances of Form

1. Alberto Moravia, "L'erede rosso del *Gattopardo*," *L'Espresso* 9, no. 14 (1963): 22.

2. Pio Baldelli, "Luchino Visconti e la resa dei conti de *Il Gattopardo*," *Paragone letteratura* 170 (1963): 22.

3. For example, see Richard H. Lansing, "The Structure of Meaning in Lampedusa's *Il Gattopardo*," *PLMA* (May 1978): 409–21.

4. The novel appeared unexpectedly in 1958, at a time when neorealism and the neo-avant-garde occupied the center of the Italian literary stage. As a result, any current writing that could not be pressed into ideological service was regarded as out of touch with contemporary realities, a nineteenth-century flower that had come to bloom too late. For some of the more thoughtful assessments of he novel, see Francesco Orlando, *Ricordo di Lampedusa* (Bresso: Cetim, 1972); Antonio Vitello, *Giuseppe Tomasi di Lampedusa* (Palermo: Sellerio, 1987); Vanni Bramanti, "Rileggendo *Il Gattopardo*," *Studi novecenteschi* 36 (1988): 323–48. On the debate over the novel's ideological merits, see Rino Caputo, "Un tema di politica culturale degli anni '60: 'Il Gattopardo,'" *Studi novecenteschi* 10 (1975): 35–55.

5. Federico De Roberto, *I Viceré* (Milan: Garzanti, 1962), 642.

6. Giuseppe Tomasi di Lampedusa, *Il Gattopardo* (Milan: Feltrinelli, 1963), 21. Translation from Giuseppe Tomasi di Lampedusa, *The Leopard*, trans. Archibald Colquhoun (New York: Pantheon, 1960), 40. Subsequent translations from this source are cited in text by page number.

7. Cited in Nunzio Zago, *Il Gattopardo e le Iene* (Palermo: Sellerio, 1983), 85n.

8. Zago views Lampedusa's fatalism as typical of certain southern Italian intellectuals incapable of recognizing and joining the real forces of political progress. Their ideological position conveys the message that either nothing really ever changes or we must attend to a kind of global revolution. Their negative criticism, Zago adds, derives nevertheless from their strong opposition to establishment politics. *Il Gattopardo*, 25.

9. Louis Althusser, *Lenin and Philosophy* (London: new Left Books, 1971), 204.

10. Gregory Lucente, *Beautiful Fables*, 196–221.

11. Early responses from the political left on the issue of historical truth in *Il Gattopardo* are reviewed in Rino Caputo, "Un tema di politica culturale." Franco Fortini's reading is a good example of a well argued interpretation flawed by a disputable notion of history in narrative:

> L'autore insomma per esprimersi in quanto Salina, ha dovuto ridurre il mondo, evitargli antagonisti veri, evitarseli. Quali che siano insomma i motivi di questa convenzionalità dei personaggi minori . . . il loro fine è apologetico nei confronti dei Salina e dell'autore, corrisponde, più che ad una inadempienza estetica, ad una inadempienza verso la verità. Che probabilmente sono una medesima cosa. (*Saggi italiani*, vol. 1 [Milan: Garzanti, 1987], 262–63)
>
> [In sum, the author, to express himself as a Salina, had to limit the dimensions of his world in order to avoid genuine antagonists. Whatever may have been the reasons behind the use of minor characters, their function is to apologize for the Salinas and the author; more than an aesthetic shortcoming, this amounts to a failure with respect to truth, which is probably the same thing.]

According to Fortini, *Il Gattopardo* loses all its potential validity as a historical account of the decline of Sicilian aristocracy because Lampedusa cannot resolve the contradiction between history and existence. He views this conflict in perspective also from the standpoint of style. The prince writes in an ironic and epigrammatic style, which Fortini sees as being at odds with the long and attenuating rhythms of reverie that attempt to convey the slow death of an entire culture. Fortini is wrong in equating the perspectives of author, narrator, and principal character; it is, in fact, at the level of style, with its disjunctions and apparent contradictions, that the novel is most interesting. The issue, however, is not whether Fortini has understood Lampedusa's art; more important is his attempt to account for what the novel represents for the dominant culture of his day. On this score, he was no doubt right. Because of its innumerable literary qualities, *Il Gattopardo* makes a forceful statement, the consequences of which Fortini underlines:

> Il libro, come si usa dire, "ben scritto" gioca su un tema eternamente caro (il rapporto nord-sud). . . . [Rappresenta] una Sicilia senza astratti furori, e senza sindacalisti. Ma, soprattutto da l'impressione del già pensato, del già saputo. Tutta la neoborghesia italiana . . . respira. (268)
>
> [This "well-written" book plays on the eternally dear theme of the relations between north and south. . . . [It represents] a Sicily devoid of abstract furies and without trade unions. But, above all, it gives the impression of something already thought, already known. All of Italy's neobourgeoisie . . . can now breathe a sigh of relief.]

Fortini's point is that the text contains a strategy; it is a strategic articulation of the desire for power disguised as knowledge.

12. Luchino Visconti, interview by Antonello Trombatore, "Dialogo con Visconti," in *Il film "Il Gattopardo" e la regia di Luchino Visconti*, ed. Suso Cecchi d'Amico (Bologna: Cappelli, 1963), 23–24–34.

13. Bernard Dort, "Super-productions a la première personne," *Les temps modernes* 19, no. 207/208 (1963): 557.

14. On this point, see Vanni Bramanti, "Rileggendo *Il Gattopardo*," 335.

15. Geoffrey Nowell-Smith, *Visconti* (New York: Doubleday, 1968),

16. Geoffrey Nowell-Smith, "Luchino Visconti," in *Cinema: A Critical Dictionary*, ed. Richard Roud, vol.2 (New York: Viking), 1050.

17. Paolo Bosisio, "Luchino Visconti," *Belfagor* 32 (1977): 54.

18. Cf. Walter F. Korte, Jr., "Marxism and Formalism in the Films of Luchino Visconti," *Cinema Journal* 11, no. 1 (1971): 2–12.

Chapter Nine. *Italo Calvino's* Le città invisibili *and Architecture: Postmodern Rhetoric*

This chapter was written originally in Italian in conjunction with Ross Miller and appeared in *Le tèorie letterarie, il dibattito metodologico e il conflitto delle poetiche* (Lecce: Franco Angeli Editore, 1991). It was published also in English, although in a somewhat different form, in *Studi d'Italianistica* 9 (1991): 230–41.

1. Lyotard, *Postmodern Condition* 43–44.

2. Charles Jencks, "The Post Modern Agenda," in *Post Modern Reader*, 11.

3. Jim Collins, "Post-modernism As Culmination: The Aesthetic Politics of Decentered Cultures," *Post-Modern Reader*, 95.

4. David Harvey, *Condition of Postmodernity*, 115.

5. Luigi Pirandello, "Arte e coscienza d'oggi," *Saggi, Poesie, Scritti Vari*, ed. Manlio Lo Vecchio-Musti (Milan: Mondadori, 1960), 906.

6. David Harvey, *Condition of Postmodernity*, 11.

7. Terry Eagleton, *Ideology of the Aesthetic*, 369–70.

8. See Jean Baudrillard, "The Ecstasy of Communication, in Foster, *Anti-Aesthetic*, 126–33.

9. Jameson, *Postmodernism*, 51.

10. Linda Hutcheon, *A Poetics of Postmodernism* (New York: Routledge, 1988), 3–21.

11. Italo Calvino, *Le città invisibili* (Turin: Einaudi, 1972). The intricacy of Calvino's *combinatoire* has been foregrounded repeatedly by criticism, but with different emphases. See, in particular, Vittorio Spinazzola, "Catologo del caos," *L'Unità* 14 (December 1972), 3; Pier Vincenzo Mengaldo, "L'arco e le pietre," in *La tradizione del Novecento* (Milan: Feltrinelli, 1980), 410; Bruno Ferrero, "Italo Calvino's *Le città invisibili* e la sfida al labirinto," *The Italianist* 8 (1988), 60–61; and Claudio Milanini, *L'Utopia discontinua: Saggio su Italo Calvino* (Milan: Garzanti, 1990), 129–33.

12. See Charles Jencks, *The Language of Post-Modern Architecture* (New York: Rizzoli, 1972), 97.

13. Stephan A. Tyler, "Post-Modern Ethnography: from Document of the Occult to Occult Document," in *Writing Culture*, ed. Clifford and Marcus, 129.

INDEX

Library of Congress Cataloging-in-Publication Data

Dombroski, Robert S.
    Properties of writing : ideological discourse in modern Italian
fiction / Robert S. Dombroski.
        p.   cm.
    Includes bibliographical references and index.
    ISBN 0-8018-4919-5
    1. Italian fiction—20th century—Political aspects.   2. Italian
fiction—20th century—Social aspects.   3. Ideology and fiction.
I. Title.
    PQ4174.D65 1994
    853'.9109—dc20   94-16037